Communications
in Computer and Information Science   **1029**

Commenced Publication in 2007
Founding and Former Series Editors:
Phoebe Chen, Alfredo Cuzzocrea, Xiaoyong Du, Orhun Kara, Ting Liu,
Krishna M. Sivalingam, Dominik Ślęzak, Takashi Washio, and Xiaokang Yang

Editorial Board Members

More information about this series at http://www.springer.com/series/7899

Boris Villazón-Terrazas ·
Yusniel Hidalgo-Delgado (Eds.)

Knowledge Graphs and Semantic Web

First Iberoamerican Conference, KGSWC 2019
Villa Clara, Cuba, June 23–30, 2019
Proceedings

 Springer

Editors
Boris Villazón-Terrazas (iD)
Arvato Bertelsmann
Madrid, Spain

Yusniel Hidalgo-Delgado (iD)
Universidad de las Ciencias Informáticas
Havana, Cuba

ISSN 1865-0929 ISSN 1865-0937 (electronic)
Communications in Computer and Information Science
ISBN 978-3-030-21394-7 ISBN 978-3-030-21395-4 (eBook)
https://doi.org/10.1007/978-3-030-21395-4

This Springer imprint is published by the registered company Springer Nature Switzerland AG
The registered company address is: Gewerbestrasse 11, 6330 Cham, Switzerland

Preface

Artificial intelligence (AI) makes it possible for machines to learn from experience, adjust to new inputs, and perform human-like tasks. Most AI examples – from chess-playing computers to self-driving cars – rely heavily on deep learning and natural language processing. Using these technologies, computers can be trained to accomplish specific tasks by processing large amounts of data and recognizing patterns in the data. AI includes several fields, such as knowledge representation and reasoning, natural language processing/text mining, machine/deep learning, among others.

The Iberoamerican Knowledge Graphs and Semantic Web Conference is an international scientific conference series devoted to knowledge representation, natural language processing/text mining, machine/deep learning research. The goals of the conference are (a) to provide a forum for the AI community, bringing together researchers and practitioners in industry to share ideas about R&D projects and (b) to increase the adoption of the AI technologies in the region.

This volume contains the main proceedings of the first Iberoamerican Knowledge Graphs and Semantic Web Conference (KGSWC 2019), which was held in Villa Clara, Cuba, in June 2019. Even though this was the first edition, we received tremendous response to our calls for papers from a truly international community of both researchers and practitioners. Every paper was thoroughly evaluated following practices appropriate for this conference and its evaluation measure. The breadth and scope of the papers finally selected for inclusion in this volume speak to the quality of the conference and to the contributions made by researchers whose work is presented in these proceedings. As such, we were all honored and proud that we were invited to serve the community in the stewardship of this first edition of KGSWC.

We would like to thank warmly all the people who contributed toward making this first edition possible, workshop/tutorial/poster/demo chairs, local organizers, researchers and industry participants, and sponsors. Special thanks to the summer school organizers and tutors.

June 2019

Boris Villazón-Terrazas
Yusniel Hidalgo-Delgado

Organization

General Chair

Boris Villazón Terrazas   Majorel, Spain

Local Chairs

Yusniel Hidalgo Delgado   Universidad de las Ciencias Informáticas, Cuba
Amed Leiva Mederos   Universidad Central de Las Villas, Cuba

Workshops and Tutorials

Pedro Szekely   University of Southern California, USA
José Emilio Labra Gayo   Universidad de Oviedo, Spain

Posters and Demos

Victor Saquicela   Universidad de Cuenca, Ecuador
Mauricio Espinosa   Universidad de Cuenca, Ecuador

Program Committee

Alberto Fernandez	University Rey Juan Carlos, Spain
Alejandro Rodríguez-González	Universidad Politécnica de Madrid, Spain
Alfredo Simón-Cuevas	Universidad Tecnológica de La Habana, Cuba
Amed Leiva-Mederos	Universidad Central de Las Villas, Cuba
Amelie Gyrard	Wright State University, USA
Bin Xu	Tsinghua University, China
Boris Villazón Terrazas	Majorel, Spain
Carlos Buil Aranda	Universidad Técnica Federico Santa María, Chile
Carlos García-Alvarado	Ernst & Young, Spain
C. Maria Keet	University of Cape Town, South Africa
Daniel Garijo	Information Sciences Institute, USA
Daniel Schwabe	PUC-Rio, Brazil
Diego Collarana	Fraunhofer IAIS and University of Bonn, Germany
Edelweis Rohrer	Universidad de la República, Uruguay
Emanuele Della Valle	Politecnico di Milano, Italy
Erick Antezana	Norwegian University of Science and Technology, Norway
Erik Mannens	iMinds – Ghent University – Multimedia Lab, Belgium
Ernesto Jimenez-Ruiz	The Alan Turing Institute, UK

Contents

A Model for Language Annotations
on the Web

Frances Gillis-Webber[1](✉)(iD), Sabine Tittel[2](✉)(iD), and C. Maria Keet[3](✉)(iD)

[1] Department of Knowledge and Information Stewardship, University of Cape Town,
Cape Town, South Africa
fran@fynbosch.com
[2] Heidelberg Academy of Sciences and Humanities, Heidelberg, Germany
sabine.tittel@urz.uni-heidelberg.de
[3] Computer Science Department, University of Cape Town, Cape Town, South Africa
mkeet@cs.uct.ac.za

Abstract. Several annotation models have been proposed to enable a
multilingual Semantic Web. Such models hone in on the word and its
morphology and assume the language tag and URI comes from external
resources. These resources, such as ISO 639 and Glottolog, have limited
coverage of the world's languages and have a very limited thesaurus-like
structure at best, which hampers language annotation, hence constrain-
ing research in Digital Humanities and other fields. To resolve this 'outsourced' task of the current models, we developed a model for representing information about languages, the **Mo**del for **L**anguage **A**nnotation
(MoLA), such that basic language information can be recorded consistently and therewith queried and analyzed as well. This includes the various types of languages, families, and the relations among them. MoLA
is formalized in OWL so that it can integrate with Linguistic Linked
Data resources. Sufficient coverage of MoLA is demonstrated with the
use case of French.

Keywords: Multilingual semantic web · Annotation · Language model

1 Introduction

Recent years have seen an appreciation of multilingualism in the global society,
reflecting the increase of internet users, be it in spite of or thanks to the increase
of English as *lingua franca* in global communication. This is on par with the trend
toward the *both-and* attitude for cultural heritage, rather than an *either-or* of
dominance and extinction. For example, it is European consensus that territorial
varieties of languages need to be valorized and promoted, particularly online.
International organizations emphasize the need for (culturally and) linguistically
diverse local content to be published online; for a vitalization of multilingualism
on the internet, see [30, 13–21]. Consequently, a fast-growing number of language
resources have to be annotated, managed, and retrieved, not just for the few
globally spoken languages, but also for the many local and regional languages.

© Springer Nature Switzerland AG 2019
B. Villazón-Terrazas and Y. Hidalgo-Delgado (Eds.): KGSWC 2019, CCIS 1029, pp. 1–16, 2019.
https://doi.org/10.1007/978-3-030-21395-4_1

For the Web, and the Semantic Web in particular, several proposals have been made to make it a *multilingual* Semantic Web, with solutions especially for OWL ontologies and Linked Data in RDF; for a recent state of the art, see [8]. Language data expressed in RDF should be described in a principled way, and OntoLex-Lemon [8] by the W3C Ontology Lexicon Community Group is the *de facto* standard for representing the semantic, morphologic, and syntactic properties of lexical entries in linguistic resources. When modeling linguistic data using OntoLex-Lemon, the model requires the language to be defined using a URI. A lexical entry modeled[1] using OntoLex-Lemon is, e.g.:

```
1  :mola_mola  a    ontolex:LexicalEntry ;
2     dct:language <http://id.loc.gov/vocabulary/iso639-2/eng> ,
3                  <http://lexvo.org/id/iso639-1/en> ;
4     rdfs:label   "mola mola"@en ;
5     ontolex:denotes dbr:Ocean_sunfish .
```

where the dct:language part is the focus of the paper. Recall that for RDF to be Linked Data, it should adhere to principles, among others: (1) "Use URIs as names for things", (2) "Use HTTP URIs so that people can look up those names", and (3) "When someone looks up a URI, provide useful information" (called a dereferenceable URI), using the RDF standard [2]. For the URI http://id.loc.gov/vocabulary/iso639-2/eng, although it is a persistent identifier for the language code *eng* from ISO 639 Part 2[2], information is not returned in RDF when navigating to this URI. Lexvo.org provides dereferenceable URIs for languages and mappings from Lexvo identifiers to only the ISO 639 language codes (Parts 1, 2, 3 and 5) [24]. Although ISO 639 is adequate for describing the world's main languages, when needing to assign a persistent identifier with a dereferenceable URI to a lesser-known language or dialect not included in ISO 639, an alternative catalogue has to be used. There are 7,865 language entries in ISO 639-3 [1], yet an estimated 3,000 to 10,000 languages are spoken in the world today, with some 150,000 extinct languages [10, 294–295]. Examples of alternative catalogues include Glottolog, Ethnologue, and MultiTree[3]. Glottolog is a comprehensive catalogue that provides reference information for language families, lesser-known languages, and dialects. Both Glottolog and MultiTree have persistent identifiers [17,18], but they do not have dereferenceable URIs. Ethnologue does not provide persistent identifiers to lesser-known languages and dialects, nor are there dereferenceable URIs.

Glottolog uses semantically underspecified 'broader/narrower than'-hierarchies, which is typical of Knowledge Organization Systems (KOSs). In order to account for languages and dialects, pseudo sub-groupings and names have been created that are, as the Glottolog developers also note, artificial. These shortcomings concern both under-resourced and well-resourced languages. For example, 'Loreto-Ucayali-Spanish' (Peru) is categorized under 'South Castilic', which is

---

[1] For the sake of brevity, namespaces are assumed defined the usual way.

[2] ISO 639 is the International Standard for language codes [1].

[3] https://glottolog.org, www.ethnologue.com, http://multitree.org [05-03-2019].

a sibling of 'Spanish' which, in turn, has a sub-language 'American Spanish'[4]: not only is 'South Castilic' not a sibling class of 'Spanish', its language grouping is also questionable. Furthermore, it is not identifiable as being a pseudo-classification, hence it likely would—erroneously—be perceived as a legitimate classification by a non-expert. Another example is the subfamily 'Zulu-Xhosa' under Nguni, although no such classification exists. In fact, the Nguni group contains four languages on par with each other: isiZulu, isiXhosa, isiNdebele, and siSwati (all spoken in Southern Africa). Other language hierarchies and resources do not fare better; e.g., the alternate names given for isiXhosa in MultiTree[5] are archaic and hugely problematic, yet they have been propagated into Linked Data elsewhere, such as the US Library of Congress[6].

A KOS does not—and cannot—capture the intricacies of how 'languoids' (language family, sub-family, language, lect, or variant [17]) relate meaningfully: e.g., isiXhosa and isiZulu may be *sibling* languages where a language is *member of* a sub-family, Spanish and French *evolved from* Vulgar Latin and are *influenced by* Medieval Latin[7], and Afrikaans *evolved from* the Cape Dutch dialect that was a *dialect of* (old) Dutch. Not only is this an obstacle in the efforts to realize a multilingual Semantic Web but the underspecification of the subject domain and the lack of dereferenceable URIs for language tags also negatively impacts Humanities research pertaining to accurate language identification (cp. [29]). In addition, it hampers internationalization and localization.

In order to address these problems, we propose a model for representing information about languages: the '**Mo**del for **L**anguage **A**nnotation' (MoLA). MoLA provides a structured way for language annotation of objects on the Semantic Web. A modeler may include additional features of a languoid, such as its time period and geographic location for the period, as well as relate it to the language(s) it has evolved from, influences and has been influenced by. This enables more comprehensive RDF data about the languages of the world to be represented and, therewith, queried and analyzed. The model is formalized in OWL so as to achieve seamless integration with extant Linguistic Linked Data resources, and evaluated with competency questions and French as use case.

The remainder of the paper is structured as follows: Sect. 2 discusses related work, Sect. 3 describes MoLA, Sect. 4 revisits French and shows how MoLA is sufficiently expressive. We close with a discussion (Sect. 5) and conclusions (Sect. 6).

---

[4] https://glottolog.org/resource/languoid/id/sout3200 [22-02-2019].

[5] http://multitree.org/codes/xho [03-03-2019].

[6] http://id.loc.gov/authorities/subjects/sh85148822.rdf [03-03-2019].

[7] Language is constantly evolving. Influences by other languages due to cultural contact can result in lexical, phonetic and morphologic changes. The question when to characterize a language 'a' as 'being influenced' by a language 'b' depends on the granularity level of the analysis and is subject to discussion of linguists.

2   Related Work

The most comprehensive resource for languages, particularly for under-resourced languages, is Glottolog, which we describe first. We discuss related works on KOSs and language models afterward.

2.1   Glottolog as a KOS

Glottolog is a controlled vocabulary that provides a "comprehensive list of languoids" [17]. Each languoid is a concept as defined in SKOS [18, 195–196], where a SKOS concept "can be viewed as an idea or notion; a unit of thought" [25].

Each languoid as an (instance of a) concept is placed only once in the hierarchy (i.e., it does not have multiple inheritance) to represent genealogical relationships [11, 3]. The only SKOS relations Glottolog uses is skos:broader and skos:narrower [18, 195], i.e., there are no 'related term', 'use', or user-defined relations [25]. Glottolog also permits 'orphans', which are languoids that do not relate to another language [17], because too little information is known to reliably put it in the hierarchy.

Representing Glottolog's Information. Based on the information provided by Glottolog about its system [17, 18] and the data in the hierarchy, we have constructed a conceptual model of the information of its system. This is shown in Fig. 1 in Object-Role Modeling (ORM) notation [16], where the rounded rectangles are entity types, the smaller rectangles with a divider are the fact types (relationships), and dots and small lines on the relations are the constraints (mandatory and unique, respectively).

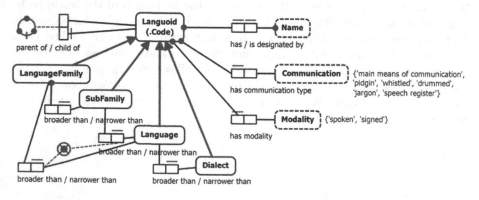

Fig. 1. Approximation of the conceptual model of Glottolog's system.

Use Case: Shortcomings of Glottolog's French. In its present state, Glottolog reveals major shortcomings with respect to the needs of linguists modeling data from the Romance languages, particularly regarding regional varieties and old language stages. For example, the categorization of varieties of French conflates diachronic and diatopic criteria within its hierarchies: Old French, the French spoken in the Middle Ages, is classified as a sibling of modern 'Central Oïl', Francoprovençalic, and Walloon (a French dialect).[8] Middle French however, the period following Old French, is classified four levels down into the branches and sub-branches of 'Central Oïl', together with 14 modern French varieties (including some of those spoken in the Americas) and, also, historical Anglo-Norman, spoken in England in medieval times. Other modern dialects are classified within other branches of 'Oïl'.[9] A selection of the 'broader/narrower than'-hierarchy of French varieties in Glottolog is shown in Fig. 2, which will serve as a means of comparison when we return to this case study in Sect. 4.

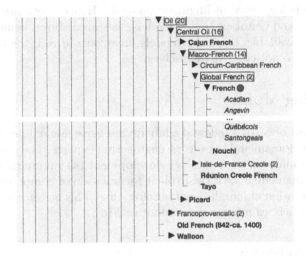

Fig. 2. Section of the 'broader/narrower than'-hierarchy of French (stan1290) in context in Glottolog.

2.2 Limitations of KOSs and Other Ontologies and Models

Shortcomings with thesauri and KOSs are well-documented. For instance, the semantic underspecification of 'related term' RT (rather than a meaningful relation) means that one cannot query the system on, e.g., "what are the dialects of isiXhosa?" or "what are the languages between Vulgar Latin and modern-day French spoken in France?". Over the past twenty years, several proposals have been put forward to 'convert' a KOS to an ontology and add meaning in the process. Early works are, notably, the "rules as you go" proposal by Soergel et al.

---

[8] As sub-languoids of 'Oïl' (varieties that use an adaptation of the Vulgar Latin term *hoc ille* "this (is) it" as 'Yes'); note that Francoprovençalic is a non-Oïl language.

[9] Independent from diachronic issues, the hierarchy of modern French varieties also needs a revision (in line with "Most of the information on dialects in Glottolog [...] contains numerous errors and inconsistencies which we are aware of" [17]).

[28], who defines rules once a pattern is discovered during the manual stage of the conversion process. More recently, Kless et al. [22] proposed a method for converting thesauri and vocabularies more generally, but this is still a manual process and it was not evaluated beyond using illustrations from the popular AGROVOC[10]. There are some attempts at automation, e.g. [5], but in the case of Glottolog, it would mean transferring the semantic errors into OWL, which does not help with querying and annotation needs.

There are several domain ontologies and models in the subject domain of languages. The OLiA ontologies [7] are domain ontologies for linguistic annotation at the word level and word fragment level of information, rather than the languages themselves that is needed for language tags and the management thereof. The NCS for linguistic task ontologies [6] are at the same level of detailed word level and morphology level of linguistic analysis. Hence, both are not applicable. The *Lemon* and OntoLex-Lemon models, as stated above, assume a suitable language tag is available, i.e., these models have 'outsourced' the language tags issue, and thus do not cover it themselves.

3   Designing MoLA

The development of MoLA followed a labour-intensive manual iterative bottom-up process with domain and knowledge engineering experts. The process adhered to the common main tasks of ontology development (as summarized and generalized in [27]) augmented with the explicit formulation of competency questions and the consideration of foundational ontology use. This is described in the next section, after which we present the content of MoLA.

3.1   Design Approach

In order to demarcate the scope of the first version of the model that will improve sufficiently over the prevalent 'broader/narrower than'-hierarchies, we specify the following set of competency questions (CQs) for the model or (lightweight) ontology, as the case may be. The text in '[]' denotes a variable, meaning that it could take any subclass or individual classified into that class, as applicable.

1. Which languoids are dialects of [language]?
2. How many [languoids] does [language family] have?
3. Is a dialect a language?
4. Which types of languages have been classified?
5. Is a [languoid/language] divided into different time periods?
6. Does [language] have a region defined?
7. Which languages are spoken in [region]?
8. Is [language] the standard variety?
9. Is [language] in ISO 639?

---

[10] http://aims.fao.org/vest-registry/vocabularies/agrovoc [22-02-2019].

When evaluating MoLA, these CQs must be answerable. We will revisit them further below, to test the efficacy of the proposed model.

We considered various principal approaches, methodologies, and methods for the development of the model (for a recent overview, see [19]):

1. reverse engineer the KOS (*in casu*, Glottolog) using a script;
2. use a foundational ontology as the basis from which to start structuring the knowledge of the subject domain;
3. start from scratch with a 'clean slate', availing mainly of non-ontological resources for informal suggestions of names of classes, relations, and attributes.

We considered the first option unsuitable, because it would retain the under-specification and mis-classifications of the languages in the KOSs. For the second option, the generic, or at least top-domain, ontologies in the area of languages available are GOLD [12] and, to some extent regarding the design inspirations, DOLCE [23]. Due to the expected small size of the artifact, taking a top-down approach would unnecessarily clutter the ontology with classes and properties that would not be required, as only a very small fragment of a foundational ontology (FO) would be used. As such, we deemed more appropriate to indicate which elements of the model would bear a semantics as in one of those extant ontologies. A future, larger version of MoLA may include a module of a FO that will be aligned with equivalence and subsumption axioms. In addition, the competency questions are directed at ABox-level queries, rather than predominantly TBox-level, which suggests that the scope is more that of a knowledge base, ontology-based data access, and/or guidance for Linked Data. In that case, the artifact will not resemble an ontology in the principled sense, but rather a conceptual data model formalized in OWL for which the inclusion of a FO is atypical (see [15,19] for definitions and discussions thereof).

The third option amounts to creating the artifact from scratch. For this development process, we followed the process of scoping and then an iterative process cycling through the conceptualization, formalization, and evaluation stages. Besides consulting aforementioned resources, a domain expert also created content that has to be able to handle queries useful from that perspective (i.e., for digital humanities research). This domain input use case is depicted in Fig. 4. Subsequently, in a joint activity of the same domain expert (ST) and information and knowledge experts (FGW, CMK), we constructed a conceptual model using ORM notation which we formalized manually in OWL. Collaborative software used were mainly WebProtégé and GitHub, as well as the standalone tools Norma (for VS2017) and the Protégé v5.x desktop version.

3.2 Content

The core idea of Glottolog's languoid is reused in MoLA, although the conceptual model in Fig. 3 and the subsequent OWL file of MoLA is more comprehensive. Importantly, several relations between languages have now been included, effectively adding the semantics that is typically underrepresented in KOSs, as well as the addition of basic time and space properties.

There are different definitions of 'language' in the literature but the consensus can be described as follows: Language is a complex and heterogeneous but structured system of communication used within a community of speakers. Within this system, a number of varieties—also called lects—reflect diatopic aspects referring to geographic areas (regional varieties, dialects, patois), diaphasic aspects referring to the communicative context (formal or informal style, technical language), and diastratic aspects referring to the social classes (sociolect, idiolect, youth language) [9]; cp. [4, 14]. These thus resulted in the most relevant classes in MoLA. The ABox axioms are primarily class membership assertions, e.g., `Language(vulgar_latin).Lect` and its sub-classes are added, for it would be expected by a sociolinguist. Instead of broader/narrower, languages may now be member of a language family, or dialects may be member of a dialect cluster. RBox axioms were mostly domain and range axioms and inverses. To permit inclusion of languoids for which only partial information is known, few hard constraints have been enforced.

Some entities seem to operate at different levels of granularity, such as that a language may refer to a collection of dialects at the finer-grained level of analysis. This distinction is reflected in MoLA with the collections.

Because the model needs to be used in praxis and record data about individual languoids, the other salient feature of the model is that there are data properties and data types, such as the link to ISO codes, for compatibility with other language resources.

Notable distinctions with Glottolog (recall Fig. 1) and other sources are:

- Instead of the broader/narrower relation, there is the proper subsumption relation and separate meaningful relations, such as *influenced by*;
- a language can be in more than one language family;
- the uniqueness of both languoid code and language name is no longer required, therewith more easily permitting one languoid to have multiple names and labels;
- a language family or a lect can be associated with ≥ 0 regions and periods;
- relations to/with other languages can also be represented explicitly and relatively meaningfully, including the influence on another language, and the evolution of a language;
- a languoid can be associated with language codes from ISO 639;
- a language can be associated with one or more custom language tags, as defined by IETF's BCP47, accounting for both varying regions and periods.

The translation from the ORM diagram to OWL faced only one real obstacle: time periods ought to be represented with data type `gYear`, but this XML datatype is not supported by the OWL standard. Therefore, it was encoded as an xml:string. Acyclicity on `evolvedFrom` and `influences` also cannot be represented in OWL.

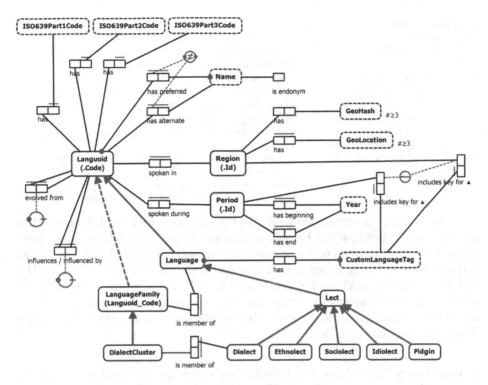

Fig. 3. The model for language annotation, MoLA.

Considering the conceptual model and the CQs, the result is a model formalized in OWL, with the characteristics of what may be called an "application ontology", which is available at https://ontology.londisizwe.org/mola.

3.3   Validation

As first pass of validation, we describe an example of MoLA's use and the CQs; the use case with French is deferred to the next section.

Illustration of MoLA Usage. To demonstrate that MoLA works for a modern language stage, we use Spanish as spoken in Cuba (refer to [3, 23–25; 102–106] for an overview of South American Spanish): it is 'Caribbean Spanish' spoken in Cuba since the first half of the 16th century, it is influenced by Spanish of the Canary Islands, French, the indigenous language Taíno, and West African languages of the slaves (Niger-Congo languages?), it evolved from Spanish and influences South-American Spanish, and it is the official language. Using MoLA, a fragment of the encoding is as follows:

```
1  : cuban_spanish
2      a                      mola : Dialect  ;
3      rdfs : label           "Cuban Spanish"@en ,
4                             "Español Cubano"@es –CU  ;
5      dct : language         : cuban_spanish ;
6      mola : inFamily        : spanish  ;
7      mola : isMemberOf      : caribbean_spanish  ;
8      mola : inPeriod        : cuban_period  ;
9      mola : inRegion        : cuba_region  ;
10     mola : evolvedFrom     : spanish  ;
11     mola : influencedBy    : canary_island_spanish  ,  : spanish ,
12                             : french  ,  : taino  ,
13                             : westafrican_languages  ;
14     mola : influences      : spanish  ,  : southamerican_spanish  .
```

Representing the current knowledge of the languoids with MoLA may suffice for some users, but it would be only a prerequisite for Digital Humanities end-users. For instance, when text documents are annotated with MoLA, one could retrieve all `caribbean_spanish` text documents for some NLP task, search the web for websites in isiXhosa dialects, or search for Medieval English texts without having to specify the exact start or end year. As such, it could assist semantic search by providing additional parameters in the query, hence better narrowing down the information request.

Competency Questions Revisited. Revisiting the CQs, all questions are answerable, with the exception of CQ 8 (which is planned for a next version, see also the discussion in Sect. 5). CQ 3, 5 and 7 are shown here, with the remaining CQs answered in the online supplementary material at [13]. For **CQ 3**, this can be answered with the following query (in SPARQL-OWL shorthand notation) $\alpha \leftarrow$ SubClassOf(Dialect Language) where α is the answer, being 'yes'. For **CQ 7**, this can be answered with the query $\alpha \leftarrow$ Type(Languoid ObjectSomeValuesFrom(inRegion cuba_region)), which will retrieve, at least, `cuban_spanish`. For **CQ 5**, this can be answered with the SPARQL query ASK { :cuban_spanish mola:inPeriod ?any } where the result will return 'True'.

Note that the ontology-as-knowledgebase is not fully populated with language data, so an answer may be empty. Most CQs are knowledge base queries, in fact, not TBox queries. While this may seem disappointing from an ontology development viewpoint, it merely highlights the prospective aims where the language annotations are needed.

4   Use Case: Structuring French Languoids

As briefly mentioned in Sect. 2, there are various shortcomings of how French has been represented with respect to the state of affairs scientifically. Therefore, we deem a remodeling of French with its historical language stages and dialects necessary to meet the needs of linguists. To put the remodeling on solid historico-linguistic ground, we consider the formation of the French language and the

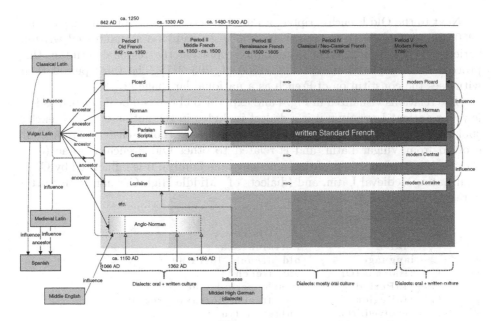

Fig. 4. Diachronic diagram of French.

development of its spoken and written varieties, as visualized in Fig. 4 and briefly explained in the following. We identified five language periods of French.

period I   Old French: 842 AD (*Serments de Strasbourg*: 'formation deed' of France [4, 183–189]) – ca. 1350 (major grammatical changes),
period II   Middle French: ca. 1350 – ca. 1500,
period III French of the Renaissance: ca. 1500 – 1605 (influences of the Reformation, the Humanists, and the Renaissance [21, 89]),
period IV   Classical and neo-classical French: 1605 (F. de Malherbe was called to the court of Henri IV [21, 116]) – 1789 (French Revolution),
period V   1789 – today.

Primary Dialects and the Emergence of French as a Standard. During the Old French period, the diagram shows the emergence of the primary dialects, Old French scriptae respectively[11], that were the result of the Romanization process and derived from Vulgar Latin, the (almost exclusively) spoken form of Latin. The dialects and the standard French have been influenced by written Classical Latin and also Medieval Latin from the beginning of the Romanization until today [26, 91–93; 118f.; 142]. Examples of Old French dialects are ancient Picard, ancient Norman, ancient Lorraine or Anglo-Norman. Anglo-Norman was used in England from mid 12th century until mid 15th century [20, 5–19; 57f.; 92].

---

[11] The term for the written representation of the spoken dialects of Old French [4, 206].

Next to the Old French scriptae, a Parisian scripta started to emerge around 1250 and around 80 years later it started to spread as a standardized written variety of Old-/Middle French, gradually replacing the regional scriptae; this process was completed around 1480–1500 [4, 203–211]. The third period then witnesses the constitution of French as a national language [21, 89].

The relations visualized in Fig. 4 and explained above can be described as follows for ancient **Lorraine**: it is a dialect included in the notion of 'Old French', spoken in time period I in the region of Lorraine (north-eastern France), it evolved from Vulgar Latin, and is related to other Old French scriptae (e.g., Picard, Norman, members of the same language family), it is influenced by Classical Latin, Medieval Latin, and (dialects of) Middle High German.[12] In Turtle notation with MoLA, one obtains:

```
1  : old_french_lorraine
2       a                      mola: Dialect  ;
3       rdfs: label            "Lorraine"@en  ;
4       dct: language          : old_french_lorraine  ;
5       mola: isMemberOf       : old_french  ;
6       mola: inPeriod         : french_period_one  ;
7       mola: inRegion         : old_french_lorraine_region  ;
8       mola: evolvedFrom      : vulgar_latin  ;
9       mola: influencedBy     : classical_latin ,  : medieval_latin ,
10                              : middle_high_german  .
11
12 : french_period_one
13      a                      mola: Period  ;
14      rdfs: label            "Old French Period"@en  ;
15      mola: hasBeginning     "842"^^xsd: string  ;
16      mola: hasEnd           "1350"^^xsd: string  ;
17      mola: duration         "508"^^xsd: int  .
18
19 : old_french_lorraine_region
20      a                      mola: Region  ;
21      mola: hasCoordinate    : old_french_lorraine_region_coord1  ,
22                             : old_french_lorraine_region_coord2  ,
23                             : old_french_lorraine_region_coord3  ,
24                             : old_french_lorraine_region_coord4  ;
25      rdf: _1                : old_french_lorraine_region_coord1  ;
26      rdf: _2                : old_french_lorraine_region_coord2  ;
27      rdf: _3                : old_french_lorraine_region_coord3  ;
28      rdf: _4                : old_french_lorraine_region_coord4  .
29
30 : old_french_lorraine_region_coord1
31      a                      mola: GeographicCoordinate  ;
32      geo: lat               "4.91473"^^xsd: decimal  ;
33      geo: long              "49.62686"^^xsd: decimal  .
34
35 # Due to space constraints , other coordinates are not shown.
36
```

---

[12] I.e., Moselle and Rhine Franconian for which a thorough revision on Glottolog is advised as well, see https://glottolog.org/resource/languoid/id/fran1268 [24-02-2019].

```
37  :old_french            a     mola:LanguageFamily  .
38  :vulgar_latin          a     mola:Language  .
39  :classical_latin       a     mola:Language  .
40  :medieval_latin        a     mola:Language  .
41  :middle_high_german  a     mola:Language  .
```

5   Discussion

Designing MoLA exhibited several main challenges that had to be resolved, one of which was principally a knowledge engineering issue, the other that of languages. Regarding the former, this first issue concerned LanguageFamily and Language, which surfaced for Old French, and induced related questions on dialect clusters and language: it is not the case that something is ontologically two different kinds of things *at the same time*, but it depends on (1) what a term denotes, in particular whether it is monosemous or polysemous, and (2) the level of granularity of analysis of the entity. The modeling issue exhibited both, which was due to mixing levels of granularity. For instance, the term 'Old French' has several meanings: (i) it is used to refer to the *language* spoken by the people in the northern part of what is now France, (ii) it is the umbrella term for a collection of dialects, (iii) it is used to precisely designate the intersection of (lexemes, phonemes, syntactic structures of) the distinct varieties that are part of the collection. Old French is a language and a member of the family of the Romance languages. At the same time, however, Old French is a language family consisting of the distinct dialects such as Picard and Norman. And then, also Picard can be seen as a language system with a number of varieties such as the ones spoken in Artois and Santerre which makes it a language family. Regarding the latter, the question "how to define 'language' and 'language family'?" is inescapable, and the consensus approach was taken. For the notion of the 'ancestor' relation between languages, there was no consensus, however the pseudo-synonymity of the verbs *to evolve* and *to derive* used in the literature led to the decision to only introduce one property, i.e., evolvedFrom to MoLA.

MoLA enables a modeler or annotator to define both periods and regions for a languoid, reflecting its diachronicity. A custom language tag, encoded using a pattern [14], can then be associated with languoid and period or region or both, which is more comprehensive than the standard ISO 639 language codes. Not only does MoLA provide dereferenceable URIs with persistent identifiers, it can also be queried, returning useful information about that languoid. This thus means that it is, by design, amenable to accommodate new languages and the identification and recording of extinct languages. In this respect, MoLA is apolitical. It is envisioned for a version 2 to accommodate also what Glottolog calls "orphans" (i.e., linguists do not know where to classify it yet), and the societal or political status of a language, with notions such as official, standard, minority, and dominant languages, a country's *lingua franca*, and contested languoids.

Note that MoLA does facilitate diachronic naming of languoids by availing of the period property, for when there are alternate names of languages over different periods. For instance, the official Dutch used to be called *Algemeen Beschaafd Nederlands* 'General Civilised Dutch' until the 1970s, which is now called *Standaardnederlands* 'Standard Dutch'. This may also resolve the afore-mentioned problem with isiXhosa in MultiTree (see footnote 5), as one of the older names of isiXhosa listed there would have one disciplined, at the very least, if used in present-day South Africa. Alternate *current* names can be specified as well, but, in version 1, only as preferred and alternate. Model extensions in this direction are possible and planned.

6   Conclusions

The paper presented a proposal for relatively comprehensive and semantically meaningful language annotation tags, well beyond the extant lists and structured resources of basic Knowledge Organisation Systems. This Model for Language Annotation, MoLA, whilst backward-compatible with these systems, allows a user to specify more languages, lects, and language and dialect families ('languoids'), as well as some of their properties, such as the region and time period they are or were spoken in, and relations among the languoids, such as which language is evolved from or is influenced by which other language. In conjunction with the *de facto* standard word-level annotation models, or on its own, it enables more detailed querying of language information and MoLA-annotated documents and objects on the Web that can be useful for Digital Humanities.

MoLA has been demonstrated to sufficiently represent the complexity of Old French. Future work includes populating it with more languoids and their properties as well, extending the model with further possible information about languages. Given the Linked Data direction of applicability of language tags, MoLA is intended to be published in the Linguistic Linked Open Data cloud.

References

1. Language codes - ISO 639. https://www.iso.org/iso-639-language-codes.html
2. Berners-Lee, T.: Linked Data (2009). https://www.w3.org/DesignIssues/LinkedData.html
3. Berschin, H., Fernández-Sevilla, J., Felixberger, J.: Die spanische Sprache. Georg Olms Verlag, Hildesheim (2012)
4. Berschin, H., Goebl, H.: Französische Sprachgeschichte. Georg Olms Verlag, Hildesheim (2008)
5. Cardillo, E., Folino, A., Trunfio, R., Guarasci, R.: Towards the reuse of standardized thesauri into ontologies. In: Proceedings of WOP 2014. CEUR-WS, vol. 1302, pp. 26–37 (2014)
6. Chavula, C., Maria Keet, C.: An orchestration framework for linguistic task ontologies. In: Garoufallou, E., Hartley, R.J., Gaitanou, P. (eds.) MTSR 2015. CCIS, vol. 544, pp. 3–14. Springer, Cham (2015). https://doi.org/10.1007/978-3-319-24129-6_1
7. Chiarcos, C., Sukhareva, M.: OLiA - ontologies of linguistic annotation. Semant. Web J. **6**(4), 379–386 (2015)

8. Cimiano, P., McCrae, J.P., Buitelaar, P.: Lexicon model for ontologies: community report. Final community group report, 10 May 2016, W3C (2016). https://www. w3.org/2016/05/ontolex/
9. Coseriu, E.: 'Historische Sprache' und 'Dialekt'. In: Göschel, J. (ed.) Dialekt und Dialektologie. Ergebnisse des Internationalen Symposions "Zur Theorie des Dialekts". Marburg/Lahn, 5–10 September 1977, pp. 106–122. Franz Steiner Verlag (1980)
10. Crystal, D.: The Cambridge Encyclopedia of Language. Cambridge University Press, Cambridge (2010)
11. Dimitrova, V., Fäth, C., Chiarcos, C., Renner-Westermann, H., Abromeit, F.: Interoperability of language-related information: mapping the BLL Thesaurus to Lexvo and Glottolog. In: Proceedings of LREC 2018, pp. 4555–4561. ELRA, Miyazaki, 7–12 May 2018
12. Farrar, S., Langendoen, D.T.: A linguistic ontology for the semantic web. In: GLOT International, vol. 7, no. 3, pp. 97–100 (2003)
13. Gillis-Webber, F., Keet, C.M., Tittel, S.: A model for language annotations on the web: supplementary material (2019). https://ontology.londisizwe.org/mola/ article/2019-kgswc-supplementary-material
14. Gillis-Webber, F., Tittel, S.: The shortcomings of language tags for linked data when modelling lesser-known languages. In: Proceedings of LDK 2019, Leipzig, 20–23 May 2019 (2019)
15. Guarino, N., Oberle, D., Staab, S.: What is an ontology? In: Staab, S., Studer, R. (eds.) Handbook on Ontologies, pp. 1–17. Springer, Heidelberg (2009)
16. Halpin, T., Morgan, T.: Information Modeling and Relational Databases, 2nd edn. Morgan Kaufmann, Burlington (2008)
17. Hammarström, H., Haspelmath, M., Forkel, R.: Glottolog 3.3. About languoids (2018). https://glottolog.org/glottolog/glottologinformation. Accessed 17 Feb 2019
18. Hellmann, S., Stadler, C., Lehmann, J.: Linked data for linguistic diversity research: Glottolog/Langdoc and ASJP online. In: Chiarcos, C., Nordhoff, S., Hellmann, S. (eds.) Linked Data in Linguistics, pp. 191–200. Springer, Heidelberg (2012). https://doi.org/10.1007/978-3-642-28249-2_18
19. Keet, C.M.: An introduction to ontology engineering, Computing, vol. 20, p. 334. College Publications (2018)
20. Kibbee, D.: For to Speke Frenche Trewely. John Benjamins Publishing Company, Amsterdam (1991)
21. Klare, J.: Französische Sprachgeschichte. Klett, Stuttgart (1998)
22. Kless, D., Jansen, L., Lindenthal, J., Wiebensohn, J.: A method for re-engineering a thesaurus into an ontology. In: Proceedings of FOIS 2012, pp. 133–146. IOS Press (2012)
23. Masolo, C., Borgo, S., Gangemi, A., Guarino, N., Oltramari, A.: Ontology library. WonderWeb Deliverable D18 (version 1.0, 31–12-2003) (2003). http://wonderweb. semanticweb.org
24. de Melo, G.: Lexvo.org: language-related information for the linguistic linked data cloud. Semant. Web **6**(4), 393–400 (2015)
25. Miles, A., Bechhofer, S.: SKOS simple knowledge organization system reference: W3C recommendation, 18 August 2009 (2009). https://www.w3.org/TR/2009/ REC-skos-reference-20090818/. Accessed 17 Feb 2019
26. Rickard, P.: A History of the French language. Hutchinson University Library, London (1974)
27. Simperl, E., Mochol, M., Bürger, T.: Achieving maturity: the state of practice in ontology engineering in 2009. Int. J. Comput. Sci. Appl. **7**(1), 45–65 (2010)

28. Soergel, D., Lauser, B., Liang, A., Fisseha, F., Keizer, J., Katz, S.: Reengineering thesauri for new applications: the AGROVOC example. J. Digit. Inf. 4(4) (2004). http://journals.tdl.org/jodi/article/view/jodi-126/111
29. Tittel, S., Chiarcos, C.: Historical lexicography of old french and linked open data: transforming the resources of the Dictionnaire étymologique de l'ancien français with OntoLex-Lemon. In: Proceedings of LREC 2018. GLOBALEX Workshop 2018, Miyazaki, Japan, pp. 58–66. (ELRA), Paris (2018)
30. Vannini, L., Le Crosnier, H.: Net.lang. Towards the multilingual cyberspace. C & F Éditions (2012)

A Description Logic for Unifying
Different Points of View

Paula Severi[1], Edelweis Rohrer[2(✉)], and Regina Motz[2]

[1] Department of Computer Science, University of Leicester, Leicester, England
[2] Instituto de Computación, Facultad de Ingeniería, UdelaR, Montevideo, Uruguay
erohrer@gmail.com

Abstract. Multilevel modelling is the conceptual modelling problem of having concepts that could be instances of another concepts. It is a relevant problem for many areas and in particular for ontology design. We motivate our work by a realworld case study on the accounting domain in which the points of view of expert and operator users are conceptualized as two knowledge levels. In this paper we address theoretical aspects of extending the tableau algorithm for a description logic that enables unifying different user perspectives in a multilevel knowledge modelling, following a Henkin semantics.

1 Introduction

There are real scenarios from diverse domains which have in common the need of representing different user perspectives as two or more knowledge levels. Such scenarios naturally lead to model the higher level (e.g. the view of the expert user) as relations between instances, and the lower level (e.g. the view of the operator user) as relations between concepts. For users at higher levels, who visualize the whole organization landscape, work procedures are naturally represented as instances. Hence, defining work procedures by creating instances and associating values on their properties is a flexible mechanism for defining business rules. However, for users at lower levels, a work procedure is better represented as a set of instances (a concept), since they execute the same procedure many times.

In the past few years, we have investigated extensions of description logics to provide ontology engineers with a unifying framework for modelling knowledge at many different levels of abstraction [13,14,16]. We first introduced the description logic $\mathcal{SHIQM}$ as an extension of $\mathcal{SHIQ}$ with meta-modelling axioms of the form $a =_m A$ that equate individuals to concepts and also defined a tableau algorithm for checking consistency of knowledge bases in $\mathcal{SHIQM}$ [14]. Here we have adopted a direct Henkin semantics, which gives exactly the same interpretation to the individual a and concept A. Recently we introduced a new role characteristic to transfer pairs of individuals related by a role in the higher level, into subsumption axioms involving the corresponding concepts in the lower level [16]. We showed the usefulness of having such role characteristics for a real case study on the accounting domain since experts can dynamically introduce rules

© Springer Nature Switzerland AG 2019
B. Villazón-Terrazas and Y. Hidalgo-Delgado (Eds.): KGSWC 2019, CCIS 1029, pp. 17–32, 2019.
https://doi.org/10.1007/978-3-030-21395-4_2

as assertions in the Abox which are restrictions on the accounting entries registered by operators. No research has been done on consistency algorithms for this new extension and the current paper intends to fill that gap.

This paper defines the description logic $\mathcal{SHIQM}^*$ as an extension of $\mathcal{SHIQM}$ with the new role characteristic introduced for the accounting domain in [16], and builds a new tableau algorithm for $\mathcal{SHIQM}^*$ by extending the tableau algorithm for $\mathcal{SHIQM}$ [14].

The remainder of this paper is organized as follows. Section 2 gives an overview of the motivating accounting domain. Then, Sect. 3 defines the description logic $\mathcal{SHIQM}^*$, and gives an intuition of the difference between Henkin and Hilog semantics. Section 4 describes the tableau algorithm. Sections 5 and 6 prove its correctness. Section 7 presents the related work and finally some conclusions and future work are given in Sect. 8.

2 Motivation

The motivation for the description logic $\mathcal{SHIQM}^*$ is given by those scenarios that require to model different user perspectives. In the present work, we address a particular scenario of the accounting domain, by recalling a real case study already presented in much more detail in [16]. This case study is about the accounting module of the information system called "Integrated Rental Guarantee Management System" (SIGGA) at the General Accounting Agency of the Ministry of Economy and Finance in Uruguay[1]. The Uruguayan government acts as a guarantor for employees who want to rent a property. The application helps manage renter payments, as salary discounts or direct cash payments, and the payments to landlords. The accounting module is in charge of recording the accounting entries for the business rules of SIGGA.

Figure 1 shows two knowledge levels of the SIGGA ontology: (i) the *definitional level* (upper part), that represents the view of expert users on accounting, who define what kind of accounting entry (with debit and credit accounts) must be done for each financial movement, and (ii) the *operational level* (lower part) that represents the view of users that operate the application, and register concrete accounting entries, according to definitions of experts.

In the *definitional level*, different kinds of accounting entries are identified, called *entry definitions* (concept *EntryDef*). They are specified by a set of valid details at debit and credit, called *detail definitions* (concept *DetDef*), which have associated an *account* (concept *Account*). Roles *detailDefD* (for debit) and *detailDefC* (for credit) connect entry definitions to detail definitions. For example, the "Renter payment" entry definition (individual *renterPay* of *EntryDef*) is defined by the expert user as having two valid details at debit represented by individuals *payBankDet* and *payCashDet* in *DetDef*, and two valid details at credit represented by individuals *payDebtDet* and *payDamageDet* in *DetDef*. Detail definitions at debit are respectively connected to accounts *bank* and *cash*

---

[1] Sistema Integrado de Gestión de Garantía de Alquileres, Contaduría General de la Nación, www.cgn.gub.uy.

(for payments in cash or by a bank deposit) and detail definitions at credit are connected to accounts *renterDebt* and *damageExp* (for the rent debt and the home damage expenses of the renter) by the functional role *account*.

In the *operational level*, concrete accounting entries are represented by disjoint subclasses of the concept *Entry*, as *RenterPayEnt* which contains concrete "Renter payment" accounting entries, and corresponds to the definition represented by the individual *renterPay* in *EntryDef* at the definitional level. Concrete details are represented by disjoint subclasses of the concept *Det* such as *PayBankDet* and *PayCashDet*, which correspond to detail definitions given by individuals *payBankDet* and *payCashDet* in *DetDef* at definitional level. For example, the "Juan Perez payment" for $10,000 at operational level has a debit detail for the account "Cash" and two credit details for accounts "Renter Debt" and "Damage Expenses", what means that he pays $10,000 in cash which corresponds to $7,500 of his renter debt and $2,500 of damages expenses.

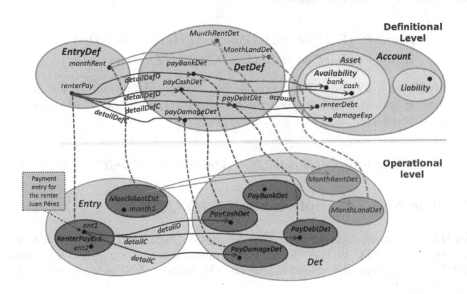

Fig. 1. Fragment of the SIGGA ontology

The new description logic $\mathcal{SHIQM}^*$ allows to explicitly represent the relations that hold between definitional and operational levels. It extends $\mathcal{SHIQ}$ with Mboxes where an Mbox contains (i) *equalities between individuals and concepts* and (ii) *role characteristics* of the form MetaRule(R, S).

Equalities between individuals and concepts allow us to express the correspondence between individuals in the definitional level and concepts in the operational level. These are represented by dotted lines in Fig. 1. For example, the individual *renterPay* should be equal to the concept *RenterPayEnt* because they are semantically equal even though they are represented differently in the definitional and operational levels. To solve this problem, we add the equality

$renterPay =_m RenterPayEnt$ to the Mbox. Similarly, we would add the equality statement $payCashDet =_m PayCashDet$.

The intuition behind the new role characteristic MetaRule(R, S) for roles R and S, is that pairs (a, b) in R in the higher level are translated as TBox axioms with S in the lower level. In the example, Abox axioms such as

$$detailDefD(renterPay, payCashDet) \quad detailDefD(renterPay, payBankDet)$$
$$detailDefC(renterPay, payDebtDet) \quad detailDefC(renterPay, payDamageDet) \tag{1}$$

represent dynamic rules given by experts (definitional level) that restrict relations between accounting entries and details in the operational level. In the example, individuals of the class $RenterPayEnt$ can only be related to individuals of classes $PayCashDet$ and $PayBankDet$ by $detailD$, and to individuals of classes $PayDebtDet$ and $PayDamageDet$ by $detailC$. These restrictions can be expressed by the Tbox axioms:

$$RenterPayEnt \sqsubseteq \forall detailD.(PayCashDet \sqcup PayBankDet)$$
$$RenterPayEnt \sqsubseteq \forall detailC.(PayDebtDet \sqcup PayDamageDet) \tag{2}$$

To avoid declaring these Tbox axioms for all entry definitions (a lot for an accounting system), we introduce the MetaRule axioms below which infer the Tbox axioms Eq. 2.

$$\text{MetaRule}(detailDefD, detailD) \quad \text{MetaRule}(detailDefC, detailC) \tag{3}$$

3 The New Description Logic $\mathcal{SHIQM}^*$

In this section we introduce the new description logic $\mathcal{SHIQM}^*$ which is an extension of $\mathcal{SHIQM}$ [14]. Equality statements $a =_m A$ extends $\mathcal{SHIQ}$ into $\mathcal{SHIQM}$, whereas the role characteristic $MetaRule(R, S)$ extends $\mathcal{SHIQM}$ into $\mathcal{SHIQM}^*$.

We assume three pairwise disjoint sets of individuals $a, b, \ldots$, atomic concepts $A, B, \ldots$ and atomic roles $R, S, \ldots$. The set of atomic roles contains all role names R and all inverse of role names R^-. To avoid roles such as R^{--}, the function $Inv(R)$ is defined such that $Inv(R) = R^-$ for R a role name, and $Inv(R) = S$ for $R = S^-$. A role is *transitive* if it has a declaration of the form $Trans(R)$.

Let $\sqsubseteq^*$ be the transitive-reflexive closure of $\sqsubseteq$ over $\mathcal{R} \cup \{Inv(R) \sqsubseteq Inv(S) \mid R \sqsubseteq S \in \mathcal{R}\}$. A role R is a *subrole* of S if $R \sqsubseteq^* S$. A role is *simple* if it is neither transitive nor has any transitive subroles. Concepts are defined by the grammar:
$C, D ::= A \mid \top \mid \bot \mid (\neg C) \mid (C \sqcap D) \mid (C \sqcup D) \mid (\forall R.C) \mid (\exists R.C) \mid (\geqslant n\ S.C) \mid (\leqslant n\ S.C)$
where n is a non-negative integer and S is a simple role.

An *ontology* $\mathcal{O} = (\mathcal{T}, \mathcal{R}, \mathcal{A}, \mathcal{M})$ *in* $\mathcal{SHIQM}^*$ consists of a Tbox $\mathcal{T}$, an Rbox $\mathcal{R}$, an Abox $\mathcal{A}$, and an Mbox $\mathcal{M}$ where $(\mathcal{T}, \mathcal{R}, \mathcal{A})$ is an ontology in $\mathcal{SHIQ}$ and $\mathcal{M}$ is a set of two different *meta-modelling statements*: (1) *equality statements* of the form $a =_m A$ that equate an individual a to a concept A, and (2) *role characteristics* of the form $MetaRule(R, S)$ for roles R and S.

The intuition behind $MetaRule(R, S)$ is that for each $a =_m A$ the Tbox is enriched with $A \sqsubseteq \forall S.(\sqcup X)$ where X is the set of all concepts B with (a, b) in R and $b =_m B$. The example in Sect. 2 shows the usefulness of this new role characteristic.

We denote by $\mathsf{dom}(\mathcal{M})$ the set of individuals in equality statements and we assume the roles in $MetaRule(R, S)$ are simple. We denote $\mathbf{R}_{\mathcal{O}}$ the set of roles occurring in $\mathcal{T}$, $\mathcal{R}$, $\mathcal{A}$ and $\mathcal{M}$ together with their inverses, and $\mathbf{I}_{\mathcal{O}}$ the set of individuals ocurring in $\mathcal{A}$ and $\mathcal{M}$.

As in [14], an *interpretation* $\mathcal{I}$ of a $\mathcal{SHIQM}^*$ ontology $\mathcal{O} = (\mathcal{T}, \mathcal{R}, \mathcal{A}, \mathcal{M})$ has a domain of interpretation Δ that can contain sets, sets of sets, and so on, since with equality statements, an individual (equated to a concept) is interpreted as a set. To express this, the set S_n is defined recursively from a set S_0 of atomic objects as $S_{n+1} = S_n \cup \mathcal{P}(S_n)$.

Definition 1 (Model of an ontology in $\mathcal{SHIQM}^*$).

An interpretation $\mathcal{I}$ is a model of an ontology $\mathcal{O} = (\mathcal{T}, \mathcal{R}, \mathcal{A}, \mathcal{M})$ in $\mathcal{SHIQM}^*$ (denoted as $\mathcal{I} \models \mathcal{O}$) if the following holds:

1. *the domain Δ of the interpretation is a subset of some S_n for some $n \in \mathbb{N}$.*
2. *$\mathcal{I}$ is a model of the ontology $(\mathcal{T}, \mathcal{R}, \mathcal{A})$ in $\mathcal{SHIQ}$.*
3. *$a^{\mathcal{I}} = A^{\mathcal{I}}$ holds for each equality statement $a =_m A$.*
4. *$A^{\mathcal{I}} \subseteq (\forall S.(\sqcup X))^{\mathcal{I}}$ holds for each role characteristic $\mathsf{MetaRule}(R, S)$ and each equality statement $a =_m A$, where $X = \{B \mid (a^{\mathcal{I}}, b^{\mathcal{I}}) \in R^{\mathcal{I}} \text{ and } b =_m B \in \mathcal{M}\}$.*

The third part of Definition 1 says that a and A have the same interpretation if $a =_m A$ is in the Mbox. The fourth part says that for each $a =_m A$ and $\mathsf{MetaRule}(R, S) \in \mathcal{M}$ if $x \in A^{\mathcal{I}}$ and $(x, y) \in S^{\mathcal{I}}$ then $y \in B^{\mathcal{I}}$ for some $b =_m B \in \mathcal{M}$ and $(a^{\mathcal{I}}, b^{\mathcal{I}}) \in R^{\mathcal{I}}$.

We adopt a Henkin semantics that gives the same interpretation to the individual and the corresponding concept name. The Hilog semantics would give (possible different) interpretations to the individual and the concept: an *intension*, which acts as an *identifier* of the individual name, and an *extension* to the concept name, which is the set of intensions of its instances [8,9]. The Henkin approach satisfies *intensional regularity* and *extensionality*, i.e. for all $\mathcal{O}$, $a =_m A$ and $b =_m B$, we have that

1. If $\mathcal{O} \models a = b$ then $\mathcal{O} \models A \equiv B$ (*intensional regularity*).
2. If $\mathcal{O} \models A \equiv B$ then $\mathcal{O} \models a = b$ (*extensionality*).

However, the Hilog semantics satisfies *intensional regularity* but does not satisfy *extensionality*, since the interpretation of the individual and the concept names may not be the same [2,9,12]. A Henkin style semantics is best suited for scenarios that need to represent the same real object from different perspectives, e.g. the expert's and the operator's perspectives in the motivating accounting domain, since it ensures the coherence between both views. While a Hilog style semantics is best suited for scenarios that need to make use of description logic as a meta-language, for describing facts about the names (not the objects they represent), e.g. "the word "vista" is defined in the Real Academia Española and consists of 5 letters".

4 A Tableau Algorithm for Checking Consistency in $\mathcal{SHIQM}^*$

In this section we define a tableau algorithm for checking consistency of an ontology in $\mathcal{SHIQM}^*$ by extending the tableau algorithm for $\mathcal{SHIQM}$, by adding rules that handle the *MetaRule* role characteristic [14]. As usual the tableau algorithm builds a special graph called *completion forest*.

A *completion forest* $\mathcal{F}$ for a $\mathcal{SHIQM}^*$ ontology $\mathcal{O} = (\mathcal{T}, \mathcal{R}, \mathcal{A}, \mathcal{M})$ consists of

1. a set of nodes, labelled with individual names or variable names,
2. directed edges between some pairs of nodes,
3. for each node labelled x, a set $\mathcal{F}(x)$ of concept expressions,
4. for each pair of nodes x and y, a set $\mathcal{F}(x, y)$ containing role names, and inverses of role names in $\mathbf{R}_\mathcal{O}$, or labels $\sim R$ in $\mathbf{R}_\sim$, where the set $\mathbf{R}_\sim$ is used in the algorithm to keep record of pairs of nodes in $\mathsf{dom}(\mathcal{M})$ not connected by an arc labelled with a role R in $\mathbf{R}_\mathcal{O}$ which is in some role characteristic $MetaRule(R, S)$, and
5. two relations between nodes, denoted by $\approx$ and $\not\approx$. These relations keep record of the equalities and inequalities of nodes. The relation $\approx$ is reflexive, symmetric and transitive whereas $\not\approx$ is symmetric. The relation $\not\approx$ is *compatible with* $\approx$, i.e. if $x' \approx x$ and $x \not\approx y$ then $x' \not\approx y$ for all x, x', y. Every time we add a pair in $\approx$, we close $\approx$ under reflexivity, symmetry and transitivity. Moreover, every time we add a pair in either $\not\approx$ or $\approx$, we close $\not\approx$ under compatibility with $\approx$.

Note that $\mathbf{R}_\sim \cap \mathbf{R}_\mathcal{O} = \emptyset$. Nodes labelled with individual names in the ABox and the Mbox, and those generated by the $\not\approx$-rule (see Fig. 2) are named *root nodes*. Notions of *successor*, *predecessor*, *neighbour* and *blocking* are exactly as in [14].

The initialization builds an initial forest following exactly the same procedure as in [14]. The nodes of the initial tableau graph are created from individuals that occur in the Abox as well as in the Mbox. After initialization, the tableau algorithm proceeds by non-deterministically applying the expansion rules of Fig. 2 and also the ones for $\mathcal{SHIQ}$ [6].

The rules $\approx$, $\not\approx$ and *close* deal with the equality statements of the form $a =_{\mathsf{m}} A$ [14]. The $\approx$-rule transfers the equality $a \approx b$ to the level of concepts by adding two statements to the Tbox which are equivalent to $A \equiv B$. The $\not\approx$-rule is similar to the $\approx$-rule. However, in the case that $a \not\approx b$, we cannot add $A \not\equiv B$ because the negation of $\equiv$ is not directly available in the language, we add an

≈-rule:

Let $a =_m A$ and $b =_m B$ in $\mathcal{M}$. If $a \approx b$ and $A \sqcup \neg B, B \sqcup \neg A$ does not belong to $\mathcal{T}$ then add $A \sqcup \neg B, B \sqcup \neg A$ to $\mathcal{T}$.

≉-rule:

Let $a =_m A$ and $b =_m B$ in $\mathcal{M}$. If $a \not\approx b$ and there is no root node z such that $A \sqcap \neg B \sqcup B \sqcap \neg A \in \mathcal{F}(z)$ then create a new root node z with $\mathcal{F}(z) = \{A \sqcap \neg B \sqcup B \sqcap \neg A\}$

close-rule:

Let $a =_m A$ and $b =_m B$ in $\mathcal{M}$ where $a \approx x$, $b \approx y$, x and y are their respective representatives of the equivalence classes. If neither $x \approx y$ nor $x \not\approx y$ then we add either $x \approx y$ or $x \not\approx y$. In the case $x \approx y$, we also do the following:
1. add $\mathcal{F}(y)$ to $\mathcal{F}(x)$,
2. for all directed edges from y to some w, create an edge from x to w if it does not exist with $\mathcal{F}(x, w) = \emptyset$,
3. add $\mathcal{F}(y, w)$ to $\mathcal{F}(x, w)$,
4. for all directed edges from some w to y, create an edge from w to x if it does not exist with $\mathcal{F}(w, x) = \emptyset$,
5. add $\mathcal{F}(w, y)$ to $\mathcal{F}(w, x)$,
6. set $\mathcal{F}(y) = \emptyset$ and remove all edges from/to y.

Close-Meta-rule:

Let $a =_m A$, $b =_m B$ and MetaRule(R, S) in $\mathcal{M}$, $a \approx x$, $b \approx y$ with x, y representatives of equivalence classes for a, b. If neither $R \in \mathcal{F}(x, y)$ nor $\sim R \in \mathcal{F}(x, y)$, then add either R to $\mathcal{F}(x, y)$ or $\sim R$ to $\mathcal{F}(x, y)$.

MetaRule(R, S)-rule:

Let $a =_m A$ and MetaRule(R, S) be in $\mathcal{M}$, and suppose that the Close-Meta-rule cannot be applied. If $\neg A \sqcup \forall S.(\sqcup X)$ does not belong to $\mathcal{T}$, then add $\neg A \sqcup \forall S.(\sqcup X)$ to $\mathcal{T}$ for $X = \text{Image}_{\mathcal{F}}(R, a)$ where $\text{Image}_{\mathcal{F}}(R, a) = \{B \mid P \in \mathcal{F}(x, y), b =_m B, P \sqsubseteq^* R, a \approx x, b \approx y$ with x, y representatives of equivalence classes for $a, b\}$.

Fig. 2. $\mathcal{SHIQM}^*$ expansion rules for meta-modelling statements

element z that witnesses this difference. The close-rule adds either $a \approx b$ or $a \not\approx b$ and it is needed for completeness.

The rules Close-Meta and MetaRule(R, S) deal with the role characteristics of the form MetaRule(R, S). The MetaRule(R, S)-rule changes the Tbox by adding inclusion axioms of the form $A \sqsubseteq \forall S.C$. The filler C is a disjunction of concept names with meta-modelling obtained from the individuals related to a via R. For example, suppose MetaRule$(R, S) \in \mathcal{M}$ and R only belongs to $\mathcal{F}(a, b_1)$ and $\mathcal{F}(a, b_2)$, with $a =_m A$, $b_1 =_m B_1$, $b_2 =_m B_2$ then, the Tbox axiom added by the MetaRule(R, S)-rule is $A \sqsubseteq \forall S.(B_1 \sqcup B_2)$. The Close-Meta-rule creates arcs non-deterministically with either R or $\sim R$ and it is also needed for completeness. The MetaRule(R, S)-rule is only applied when the Close-Meta-rule cannot be applied any more. This guarantees that $\text{Image}_{\mathcal{F}}(R, a)$ is always the same, i.e. if $\mathcal{F}'$ is obtained by expanding $\mathcal{F}$ then, $\text{Image}_{\mathcal{F}}(R, a) = \text{Image}_{\mathcal{F}'}(R, a)$.

The completion forest $\mathcal{F}$ has a *contradiction* if either

- A and $\neg A$ belongs to $\mathcal{F}(x)$ for some atomic concept A and node x or
- there are nodes x and y such that $x \not\approx y$ and $x \approx y$.
- there is a node x such that $\leqslant n S.C \in \mathcal{F}(x)$, and x has $n+1$ S-neighbours $y_1, \ldots y_{n+1}$ with $C \in \mathcal{F}(y_i)$, $y_i \not\approx y_j$ for all $i, j \in \{1, \ldots n+1\}$ with $i \neq j$.
- R and $\sim S$ belong to $\mathcal{F}(x, y)$, for nodes x, y, roles R, S in $\mathbf{R}_{\mathcal{O}}$, $\sim S \in \mathbf{R}_\sim$ and $R \sqsubseteq^* S$.

To ensure the well-foundness of the interpretation domain, we require that the forest has no cycles [14]. A completion forest $\mathcal{F}$ *has a cycle with respect to* $\mathcal{M}$ if there is a sequence $A_0 =_m a_0, A_1 =_m a_1, \ldots A_n =_m a_n$ in $\mathcal{M}$ such that

$$
\begin{aligned}
A_1 &\in \mathcal{F}(x_0) & x_0 &\approx a_0 \\
A_2 &\in \mathcal{F}(x_1) & x_1 &\approx a_1 \\
&\;\;\vdots & &\;\;\vdots \\
A_n &\in \mathcal{F}(x_{n-1}) & x_{n-1} &\approx a_{n-1} \\
A_0 &\in \mathcal{F}(x_n) & x_n &\approx a_n
\end{aligned}
$$

We say that $(\mathcal{T}, \mathcal{F})$ is $\mathcal{SHIQM}^*$-complete if none of the expansion rules for $\mathcal{SHIQM}^*$ is applicable.

The algorithm says that the ontology $(\mathcal{T}, \mathcal{R}, \mathcal{A}, \mathcal{M})$ is consistent iff the expansion rules can be applied in such a way they yield a $\mathcal{SHIQM}^*$-complete $(\mathcal{T}, \mathcal{F})$ without contradictions nor cycles. Otherwise the algorithm says that it is inconsistent. Due to the non-determinism of the algorithm, implementations have to guess the choices and have to backtrack if a choice already made has led to a contradiction. The algorithm stops when reachs *some* $\mathcal{SHIQM}^*$-complete $(\mathcal{T}, \mathcal{F})$ that has neither contradictions nor cycles or when all the choices have yield $(\mathcal{T}, \mathcal{F})$ that has either contradictions or cycles.

The $\approx$ and $\mathsf{MetaRule}(R, S)$ rules change the Tbox $\mathcal{T}$ while all the rest change the completion forest $\mathcal{F}$. Though both increase in size, they are bounded since the new axioms added to the Tbox are finite combinations of roles and concept names of $\mathcal{M}$ and the number of nodes as well as the lengths of paths in the forest are finite. This gives an intuitive justification of termination (the formal proof is omitted for lack of space).

Theorem 1 (Termination). *The tableau algorithm for* $\mathcal{SHIQM}^*$ *always terminates.*

5   Soundness of the Tableau Algorithm for $\mathcal{SHIQM}^*$

This section proves soundness of the tableau algorithm described in the previous section. We first define *tableau for a* $\mathcal{SHIQM}^*$ *ontology* which extends the tableau for $\mathcal{SHIQM}$ by adding (P20) and (P21), while a tableau for $\mathcal{SHIQM}$ extends a tableau for $\mathcal{SHIQ}$ by adding (P17), (P18) and (P19) [6,14].

Definition 2 (Tableau for $\mathcal{SHIQM}^*$**).** *Let* $\mathcal{O} = (\mathcal{T}, \mathcal{R}, \mathcal{A}, \mathcal{M})$ *be a* $\mathcal{SHIQM}^*$ *ontology, with* $\mathbf{I}_{\mathcal{O}}$ *and* $\mathbf{R}_{\mathcal{O}}$ *the set of individuals and roles in* $\mathcal{O}$.

We say that $\mathbb{T} = (\mathbf{S}, \mathcal{L}, \mathcal{E}, \mathcal{J})$ is a tableau for $\mathcal{O}$ if $\mathbf{S} \subseteq S_n$ for some S_n, $\mathcal{L}$ maps each element in $\mathbf{S}$ to a set of concepts, $\mathcal{E} : \mathbf{R}_\mathcal{O} \cup \mathbf{R}_\sim \to 2^{\mathbf{S} \times \mathbf{S}}$, $\mathcal{J} : \mathbf{I} \to \mathbf{S}$ maps individuals to elements in $\mathbf{S}$ and for all $s, t \in \mathbf{S}$, $a, b \in \mathbf{I}_\mathcal{O}$, $R, S \in \mathbf{R}_\mathcal{O}$, $\sim R \in \mathbf{R}_\sim$ and concepts C, C_1, C_2 the following properties hold:

(P1) if $C \in \mathcal{L}(s)$, then $\neg C \notin \mathcal{L}(s)$.

(P2) if $C_1 \sqcap C_2 \in \mathcal{L}(s)$, then $C_1 \in \mathcal{L}(s)$ and $C_2 \in \mathcal{L}(s)$.

(P3) if $C_1 \sqcup C_2 \in \mathcal{L}(s)$, then $C_1 \in \mathcal{L}(s)$ or $C_2 \in \mathcal{L}(s)$.

(P4) if $\forall S.C \in \mathcal{L}(s)$ and $(s, t) \in \mathcal{E}(S)$, then $C \in \mathcal{L}(t)$.

(P5) if $\exists S.C \in \mathcal{L}(s)$, then there is some $t \in \mathbf{S}$ such that $(s, t) \in \mathcal{E}(S)$ and $C \in \mathcal{L}(t)$.

(P6) if $\forall S.C \in \mathcal{L}(s)$ and $(s, t) \in \mathcal{E}(R)$ for some $R \sqsubseteq^* S$ with $Trans(R)$, then $\forall R.C \in \mathcal{L}(t)$.

(P7) $(x, y) \in \mathcal{E}(R)$ iff $(y, x) \in \mathcal{E}(Inv(R))$.

(P8) if $(s, t) \in \mathcal{E}(R)$ and $R \sqsubseteq^* S$, then $(s, t) \in \mathcal{E}(S)$.

(P9) if $\leqslant n\ S.C \in \mathcal{L}(s)$, then $\sharp\{t \mid (s, t) \in \mathcal{E}(S) \text{ and } C \in \mathcal{L}(t)\} \leq n$.

(P10) if $\geqslant n\ S.C \in \mathcal{L}(s)$, then $\sharp\{t \mid (s, t) \in \mathcal{E}(S) \text{ and } C \in \mathcal{L}(t)\} \geq n$.

(P11) if $\leqslant n\ S.C \in \mathcal{L}(s)$ or $\geqslant n\ S.C \in \mathcal{L}(s)$, and $(s, t) \in \mathcal{E}(S)$, then $C \in \mathcal{L}(t)$ or $\sim C \in \mathcal{L}(t)$.

(P12) if $C \in \mathcal{T}$ then $C \in \mathcal{L}(s)$ for all $s \in \mathbf{S}$.

(P13) if $C(a) \in \mathcal{A}$, then $C \in \mathcal{L}(\mathcal{J}(a))$.

(P14) if $R(a, b) \in \mathcal{A}$, then $(\mathcal{J}(a), \mathcal{J}(b)) \in \mathcal{E}(R)$.

(P15) if $a \neq b \in \mathcal{A}$, then $\mathcal{J}(a) \neq \mathcal{J}(b)$.

(P16) if $a = b \in \mathcal{A}$, then $\mathcal{J}(a) = \mathcal{J}(b)$.

(P17) if $a =_m A \in \mathcal{M}$, then $\mathcal{J}(a) = \{s \in \mathbf{S} \mid A \in \mathcal{L}(s)\}$.

(P18) if $\mathcal{J}(a) = \mathcal{J}(b)$, $a =_m A \in \mathcal{M}$ and $b =_m B \in \mathcal{M}$, then $A \sqcup \neg B \in \mathcal{L}(s)$ and $B \sqcup \neg A \in \mathcal{L}(s)$ for all $s \in \mathbf{S}$.

(P19) if $\mathcal{J}(a) \neq \mathcal{J}(b)$, $a =_m A \in \mathcal{M}$ and $b =_m B \in \mathcal{M}$, then there is some $t \in \mathbf{S}$ such that $A \sqcap \neg B \sqcup B \sqcap \neg A \in \mathcal{L}(t)$.

(P20) If $\mathsf{MetaRule}(R, S)$, $a =_m A$, $b =_m B$ in $\mathcal{M}$ then $(\mathcal{J}(a), \mathcal{J}(b)) \in \mathcal{E}(R)$ iff $(\mathcal{J}(a), \mathcal{J}(b)) \notin \mathcal{E}(\sim R)$.

(P21) If $\mathsf{MetaRule}(R, S)$, $a =_m A$ in $\mathcal{M}$ then $\neg A \sqcup \forall S.(\sqcup X) \in \mathcal{L}(s)$ where $X = \{B \mid (\mathcal{J}(a), \mathcal{J}(b)) \in \mathcal{E}(P), b =_m B \in \mathcal{M}, P \sqsubseteq^* R\}$.

The following lemma will be used to prove Theorems 2 and 3.

Lemma 1. *Let* $\mathcal{O} = (\mathcal{T}, \mathcal{R}, \mathcal{A}, \mathcal{M})$ *be a* $\mathcal{SHIQM}^*$ *ontology.* $\mathcal{O}$ *is consistent iff there exists a* $\mathcal{SHIQM}^*$-*tableau for* $\mathcal{O}$.

Proof. We first prove the direction from right to left. $\Leftarrow$. Let $\mathbb{T} = (\mathbf{S}, \mathcal{L}, \mathcal{E}, \mathcal{J})$ be a tableau for a $\mathcal{SHIQM}^*$ ontology $\mathcal{O}$. We consider the interpretation $\mathcal{I} = (\Delta, \cdot^\mathcal{I})$ where $\Delta := \mathbf{S}$ and

$$
\begin{aligned}
A^\mathcal{I} &:= \{s \in \mathbf{S} \mid A \in \mathcal{L}(s)\} \\
a^\mathcal{I} &:= \mathcal{J}(a) \\
R^\mathcal{I} &:= \begin{cases} \mathcal{E}(R)^+ & \text{if } Trans(R) \\ \mathcal{E}(R) \cup \bigcup_{P \sqsubseteq^* R, P \neq R} P^\mathcal{I} & \text{otherwise} \end{cases}
\end{aligned}
\tag{4}
$$

where $R \in \mathbf{R}_\mathcal{O}$ and $\mathcal{E}(R)^+$ is the transitive closure of $\mathcal{E}(R)$. Similar to Lemma 2 of [6], one can prove that $C \in \mathcal{L}(s)$ iff $s \in C^\mathcal{I}$ for all concepts C. We prove that $\mathcal{I}$ is a model of $\mathcal{O}$. We only prove item 4 of Definition 1 since the remaining items are similar to Lemma 14 in [14]. Suppose MetaRule(R,S) and $a =_m A$ in $\mathcal{M}$. By the definition of $\mathcal{I}$ above, $X = \{B \mid (\mathcal{J}(a), \mathcal{J}(b)) \in \mathcal{E}(P), b =_m B \in \mathcal{M}, P \sqsubseteq^* R\} = \{(a^{\mathcal{I}}, b^{\mathcal{I}}) \in R^{\mathcal{I}}, b =_m B\}$ since R is simple. It follows from (P21) of Definition 2 that $\neg A \sqcup \forall S.(\sqcup X) \in \mathcal{L}(s)$ for all $s \in \mathbf{S}$. Hence, $s \in (\neg A \sqcup \forall S.(\sqcup X))^{\mathcal{I}}$ for all $s \in \Delta^{\mathcal{I}}$ which implies that $A^{\mathcal{I}} \subseteq (\forall S.(\sqcup X)^{\mathcal{I}}$.

We now prove the converse. Given $\mathcal{I} = (\Delta, \cdot^{\mathcal{I}})$ a model of $\mathcal{O}$. We define a tableau $\mathbb{T} = (\mathbf{S}, \mathcal{L}, \mathcal{E}, \mathcal{J})$ for $\mathcal{O}$ as follows.

$$
\begin{aligned}
\mathbf{S} &:= \Delta \\
\mathcal{L}(s) &:= \{C \in \mathsf{clos}(\mathcal{O}) \mid s \in C^{\mathcal{I}}\} \\
\mathcal{E}(R) &:= R^{\mathcal{I}} \text{ for } R \in \mathbf{R}_{\mathcal{O}} \\
\mathcal{E}(\sim R) &:= \{(a^{\mathcal{I}}, b^{\mathcal{I}}) \mid (a^{\mathcal{I}}, b^{\mathcal{I}}) \notin R^{\mathcal{I}}, a =_m A, b =_m B, \\
&\qquad \mathsf{MetaRule}(R,S) \text{ in } \mathcal{M}, R \in \mathbf{R}_{\mathcal{O}}, \sim R \in \mathbf{R}_{\sim}\} \\
\mathcal{J}(a) &:= a^{\mathcal{I}}
\end{aligned}
\tag{5}
$$

where clos is defined as follows:

$$
\begin{aligned}
\mathsf{concepts}(\mathcal{M}) =\ &\{A \sqcap \neg B \sqcup B \sqcap \neg A, A \sqcup \neg B, B \sqcup \neg A \mid a =_m A, b =_m B \in \mathcal{M}\} \cup \\
&\{\neg A \sqcup \forall S.(\sqcup X) \mid a =_m A \in \mathcal{M}, X \subseteq \{B \mid b =_m B \in \mathcal{M}\}\} \\
\mathsf{clos}(\mathcal{O}) =\ &\bigcup\nolimits_{C(a) \in \mathcal{A} \text{ or } C \in \mathcal{T} \cup \mathsf{concepts}(\mathcal{M})} \mathsf{clos}(C)
\end{aligned}
$$

To show that $\mathbb{T}$ is a tableau for $\mathcal{O}$, we only prove (P21) of Definition 2 since (P1) to (P19) are proved similarly to Lemma 14 in [14] and (P20) is easy to prove. Assume $a =_m A$, MetaRule(R,S) in $\mathcal{M}$. Since $\mathcal{I}$ is a model of $\mathcal{O}$, we have that: $A^{\mathcal{I}} \subseteq (\forall S.(\sqcup X)^{\mathcal{I}}$ with $X = \{B \mid (a^{\mathcal{I}}, b^{\mathcal{I}}) \in R^{\mathcal{I}}, b =_m B\}$. It is easy to prove from Eq. 5 that $X = \{B \mid (\mathcal{J}(a), \mathcal{J}(b)) \in \mathcal{E}(P), b =_m B, P \sqsubseteq^* R\}$. Hence, $\neg A \sqcup \forall S.(\sqcup X) \in \mathcal{L}(s)$ for all $s \in \mathbf{S}$.

Now we recall the definition of path in a forest [6]. A *path* is a sequence of pairs of nodes of $\mathcal{F}$ of the form $p = \left[\frac{x_0}{x_0'}, \ldots, \frac{x_n}{x_n'}\right]$, with $\mathsf{Tail}(p) = x_n$ and $\mathsf{Tail}'(p) = x_n'$. We denote $\left[p \mid \frac{x_{n+1}}{x_{n+1}'}\right]$ the path $\left[\frac{x_0}{x_0'}, \ldots, \frac{x_n}{x_n'}, \frac{x_{n+1}}{x_{n+1}'}\right]$.

The set $\mathsf{Paths}(\mathcal{F})$ is defined inductively as follows: for a root node a in $\mathcal{F}$ which is a representative, $\left[\frac{a}{a}\right] \in \mathsf{Paths}(\mathcal{F})$, and for a path $p \in \mathsf{Paths}(\mathcal{F})$ and a node z in $\mathcal{F}$ representative of some equivalence class: (i) if z is a successor of $\mathsf{Tail}(p)$ and z is neither blocked nor a root node , then $\left[p \mid \frac{z}{z}\right] \in \mathsf{Paths}(\mathcal{F})$, or (ii) if, for some node y in $\mathcal{F}$, y is a successor of $\mathsf{Tail}(p)$ and z blocks y, then $\left[p \mid \frac{z}{y}\right] \in \mathsf{Paths}(\mathcal{F})$.

We recall the definition of the bijective function set which transforms paths of the form $p = \left[\frac{c}{c}\right]$ such that c is an individual with meta-modelling into sets [14].

Definition 3 (From basic paths to sets). *Let $\mathcal{O} = (\mathcal{T}, \mathcal{R}, \mathcal{A}, \mathcal{M})$ and let $\mathcal{F}$ be a complete completion forest without contradictions nor cycles w.r.t. $\mathcal{M}$. For $p \in \mathsf{Paths}(\mathcal{F})$ we define $\mathsf{set}(p)$ recursively as follows.*

$$
\begin{aligned}
\mathsf{set}(p) &= \{\mathsf{set}(q) \mid A \in \mathcal{F}(\mathsf{Tail}(q))\} && \text{if } p = \left[\tfrac{c}{c}\right] \text{ for some } c \approx a =_m A \in \mathcal{M} \\
\mathsf{set}(p) &= p && \text{otherwise}
\end{aligned}
$$

Next we define the tableau structure $\mathbb{T}' = (\mathbf{S}', \mathcal{L}', \mathcal{E}', \mathcal{J}')$ for $\mathcal{SHIQM}^*$ from the tableau structure $\mathbb{T} = (\mathbf{S}, \mathcal{L}, \mathcal{E}, \mathcal{J})$ for $\mathcal{SHIQ}$. While $\mathbf{S}$ of the tableau $\mathbb{T}$ for $\mathcal{SHIQ}$ is the set of paths [6], the domain $\mathbf{S}'$ of the tableau $\mathbb{T}'$ for $\mathcal{SHIQM}^*$ consists of paths, sets of paths, sets of sets of paths, and so on. The function $\mathcal{J}'$ is built as the composition of the functions $\mathcal{J}$ and set.

$$\mathcal{O} \xrightarrow{\ \mathcal{J}\ } \mathbf{S} = \mathsf{Paths}(\mathcal{F}) \xrightarrow{\ \mathsf{set}\ } \mathbf{S}' = \mathsf{set}(\mathsf{Paths}(\mathcal{F}))$$

$$\mathcal{J}'$$

Definition 4 ($\mathcal{SHIQM}^*$ canonical tableau structure). *Let $\mathcal{F}$ be a completion forest for a $\mathcal{SHIQM}^*$ ontology $\mathcal{O} = (\mathcal{T}, \mathcal{R}, \mathcal{A}, \mathcal{M})$. We define the canonical tableau structure $\mathbb{T}' = (\mathbf{S}', \mathcal{L}', \mathcal{E}', \mathcal{J}')$ built from $\mathcal{F}$ as follows:*

$$
\begin{aligned}
\mathbf{S}' =\ & \{\mathsf{set}(p) \mid p \in \mathbf{S}\} \\
\mathcal{L}'(s) =\ & \mathcal{L}(p) \ \text{with } s = \mathsf{set}(p) \\
\mathcal{E}'(R) =\ & \{(\mathsf{set}(p), \mathsf{set}(q)) \in \mathbf{S}' \times \mathbf{S}' \mid (p, q) \in \mathcal{E}(R)\} \ \text{for } R \in \mathbf{R}_{\mathcal{O}} \\
\mathcal{E}'(\sim R) =\ & \{(\mathsf{set}(p), \mathsf{set}(q)) \in \mathbf{S}' \times \mathbf{S}' \mid (p, q) \notin \mathcal{E}(R)\} \ \text{for } \sim R \in \mathbf{R}_{\sim}. \\
\mathcal{J}'(a) =\ & \mathsf{set}(\mathcal{J}(a))
\end{aligned}
$$

where $\mathbb{T} = (\mathbf{S}, \mathcal{L}, \mathcal{E}, \mathcal{J})$ is defined below:

$$
\begin{aligned}
\mathbf{S} =\ & \mathsf{Paths}(\mathcal{F}) \\
\mathcal{L}(p) =\ & \mathcal{F}(\mathsf{Tail}(p)) \\
\mathcal{E}(R) =\ & \{(p, [p \mid \tfrac{x}{x'}]) \in \mathbf{S} \times \mathbf{S} \mid x' \text{ is an } R\text{-succesor of } \mathsf{Tail}(p)\} \ \cup \\
& \{([q \mid \tfrac{x}{x'}], q) \in \mathbf{S} \times \mathbf{S} \mid x' \text{ is an } Inv(R)\text{-succesor of } \mathsf{Tail}(q) \ \cup \\
& \{([\tfrac{a}{a}], [\tfrac{b}{b}]) \in \mathbf{S} \times \mathbf{S} \mid a, b \text{ are representative root nodes and} \\
& \quad b \text{ is an } R\text{-neighbour of } a\} \\
\mathcal{J}(a) =\ & \begin{cases} [\tfrac{a}{a}] & \text{if } a \text{ is itself a representative} \\ [\tfrac{b}{b}] & \text{if } b \text{ is the representative of } a \approx b \end{cases}
\end{aligned}
$$

Note that since $\mathbb{T}$ is built from the forest $\mathcal{F}$, the domains of $\mathcal{J}$ and $\mathcal{J}'$ are the set of individuals in the ontology $(\mathcal{T}, \mathcal{R}, \mathcal{A}, \mathcal{M})$ which includes the individuals occurring in the MBox.

Theorem 2 (Soundness). *Let $\mathcal{O} = (\mathcal{T}, \mathcal{R}, \mathcal{A}, \mathcal{M})$. If the expansion rules for $\mathcal{SHIQM}^*$ can be applied to $\mathcal{O}$ in such a way that they yield a complete $(\mathcal{T}, \mathcal{F})$ that has no contradictions and has no cycles w.r.t. $\mathcal{M}$ then $\mathcal{O}$ is consistent.*

Proof. From Lemma 1, it is enough to prove that there exists a tableau for $\mathcal{O}$. To this aim, we prove that the canonical tableau structure given in Definition 4 is a tableau for the $\mathcal{SHIQM}^*$ ontology $\mathcal{O}$. Properties (P1) to (P19) follow from Theorem 3 of [14]. (P20) can easily be proved using Definition 4.

To prove (P21) suppose $\mathsf{MetaRule}(R, S)$, $a =_{\mathsf{m}} A$ in $\mathcal{M}$. Since set is a bijection, it is enough to show that $\neg A \sqcup \forall S.(\sqcup Y) \in \mathcal{F}(\mathsf{Tail}(p))$ for all $p \in \mathsf{Paths}(\mathcal{F})$

with $Y = \{B \mid (\mathcal{J}'(a), \mathcal{J}'(b)) \in \mathcal{E}'(P), b =_m B, P \sqsubseteq^* R\}$. Since $\mathcal{F}$ is complete, the Close-Meta-rule and MetaRule(R, S)-rule cannot be applied, so we have that $\neg A \sqcup \forall S.(\sqcup X)$ belongs to the Tbox where $X = \text{Image}_{\mathcal{F}'}(R, a)$ for some forest $\mathcal{F}'$ previous to $\mathcal{F}$ in the algorithm. But $\text{Image}_{\mathcal{F}'}(R, a) = \text{Image}_{\mathcal{F}}(R, a)$ because the MetaRule(R, S)-rule can be applied, only when the Close-Meta-rule cannot be applied. We have that $X = Y$ because by Definition 4, $P \in \mathcal{F}(x, y)$ iff $(\mathcal{J}'(a), \mathcal{J}'(b)) \in \mathcal{E}'(P)$ for $b =_m B$, $P \sqsubseteq^* R$, $a \approx x$ and $b \approx y$ since $\mathcal{J}(a) = \left[\frac{x}{x}\right] \in \text{Paths}(\mathcal{F})$ with x the representative of a and $\mathcal{J}'(a) = \text{set}(\mathcal{J}(a))$ and $\mathcal{J}(b) = \left[\frac{y}{y}\right] \in \text{Paths}(\mathcal{F})$ with y the representative of b and $\mathcal{J}'(b) = \text{set}(\mathcal{J}(b))$. Since $\neg A \sqcup \forall S.(\sqcup Y)$ belongs to the Tbox and the Tbox-rule cannot be applied either, $\neg A \sqcup \forall S.(\sqcup X) \in \mathcal{F}(x)$ for all nodes x that are not indirectly blocked. Hence, $\neg A \sqcup \forall S.(\sqcup Y) \in \mathcal{F}(\text{Tail}(p))$ for all $p \in \text{Paths}(\mathcal{F})$.

6   Completeness of the Tableau Algorithm $\mathcal{SHIQM}^*$

This section proves completeness of the tableau algorithm described in Sect. 4 using Lemma 1. Given a $\mathcal{SHIQM}^*$ ontology that has a tableau $\mathbb{T}$, we need to show that the application of the expansion rules for $\mathcal{SHIQM}^*$ leads to a complete $(\mathcal{T}, \mathcal{F})$ without contradictions nor cycles. To this aim, we define the notion of structure preserving map [14].

Definition 5. *Let* $\mathbb{T} = (\mathbf{S}, \mathcal{L}, \mathcal{E}, \mathcal{J})$ *be a* $\mathcal{SHIQM}^*$-*tableau for a* $\mathcal{SHIQM}^*$-*ontology* $\mathcal{O}$ *and* $\mathcal{F}$ *a completion forest. We define a structure preserving map* $\pi : \mathcal{F} \to \mathbb{T}$ *as a function* π *from the set of nodes of* $\mathcal{F}$ *to* $\mathbf{S}$ *that satisfies the following conditions:*

1. $\mathcal{F}(x) \subseteq \mathcal{L}(\pi(x))$.
2. *If* y *is an* S-*neighbour of* x, *then* $(\pi(x), \pi(y)) \in \mathcal{E}(S)$.
3. $x \not\approx y$ *implies* $\pi(x) \neq \pi(y)$.
4. $x \approx y$ *implies* $\pi(x) = \pi(y)$.

for all nodes x, y *in* $\mathcal{F}$, $S \in \mathbf{R}_{\mathcal{O}} \cup \mathbf{R}_{\sim}$.

The lemma below says that given a tableau $\mathbb{T}$, if the applicaction of a rule to $(\mathcal{T}_1, \mathcal{F}_1)$ leads to $(\mathcal{T}_2, \mathcal{F}_2)$, there is a structure preserving map from $\mathcal{F}_2$ to $\mathbb{T}$ that extends the structure preserving map from $\mathcal{F}_1$ to $\mathbb{T}$.

Lemma 2. *Let* $(\mathcal{T}_1, \mathcal{F}_1)$ *be a Tbox and a completion forest generated by the tableau algorithm for* $\mathcal{O} = (\mathcal{T}, \mathcal{R}, \mathcal{A}, \mathcal{M})$ *and let* $\pi_1 : \mathcal{F}_1 \to \mathbb{T}$ *be a structure preserving map such that* $\pi_1(a) = \mathcal{J}(a)$ *for all* a *in* $\mathcal{O}$. *If an expansion rule is applicable to* $(\mathcal{T}_1, \mathcal{F}_1)$, *then it yields a forest* $\mathcal{F}_2$ *and a structure preserving map* $\pi_2 : \mathcal{F}_2 \to \mathbb{T}$ *extending* π_1.

Proof. We only do the proof for some interesting cases.

- Suppose the Tbox-rule is applicable to $(\mathcal{T}_1, \mathcal{F}_1)$. Then, we obtain $(\mathcal{T}_2, \mathcal{F}_2)$ where $\mathcal{T}_1 = \mathcal{T}_2$ and $\mathcal{F}_2(x) = \mathcal{F}_1(x) \cup \{C\}$ and $C \in \mathcal{T}_1$ for all nodes x. In this case the map π_2 is exactly the same as π_1. We have to prove that $\pi_2 : \mathcal{F}_2 \to \mathbb{T}$ is a structure preserving map. The second, third and fourth conditions of Definition 5 are trivial. For the first condition, we have to prove that $\mathcal{F}_2(x) = \mathcal{F}_1(x) \cup \{C\} \subseteq \mathcal{L}(\pi_2(x))$. Since $\mathcal{F}_1(x) \subseteq \mathcal{L}(\pi_1(x)) = \mathcal{L}(\pi_2(x))$ because π_1 is a structure presering map, it is enough to prove that $C \in \mathcal{L}(\pi_1(x)) = \mathcal{L}(\pi_2(x))$. We have three cases:

  1. $C \in \mathcal{T} \subseteq \mathcal{T}_1$. Then $C \in \mathcal{L}(\pi_1(x)) = \mathcal{L}(\pi_2(x))$ by (P12).
  2. $C \in \mathcal{T}_1 \backslash \mathcal{T}$ and C is either $A \sqcup \neg B$ or $\neg A \sqcup B$ for $a =_m A$, $b =_m B$ and $a \approx b$.
  $$\begin{aligned} \mathcal{J}(a) &= \pi_1(a) \text{ by hypothesis} \\ &= \pi_1(b) \text{ by Definition 5(4)} \\ &= \mathcal{J}(b) \text{ by hypothesis} \end{aligned}$$
  Using (P18), we conclude that both $A \sqcup \neg B$ and $\neg A \sqcup B$ belong to $\mathcal{L}(\pi_1(x)) = \mathcal{L}(\pi_2(x))$.
  3. $C \in \mathcal{T}_1 \backslash \mathcal{T}$ and C is $\neg A \sqcup \forall S.(\sqcup X)$ for MetaRule(R, S), $a =_m A$ and $X = \mathsf{Image}_{\mathcal{F}'}(R, a)$ for a forest $\mathcal{F}'$ previous to $\mathcal{F}_1$. Since MetaRule(R, S)-rule is applied only when the Close-Meta-rule cannot be applied, we have that
  $$X = \mathsf{Image}_{\mathcal{F}'}(R, a) = \mathsf{Image}_{\mathcal{F}_1}(R, a) = \mathsf{Image}_{\mathcal{F}_2}(R, a)$$
  Using (P8), (P20) and the second condition of Definition 5, one can show that
  $$X = \{B \mid (\mathcal{J}(a), \mathcal{J}(b)) \in \mathcal{E}(P), b =_m B, P \sqsubseteq^* R\}$$
  It follows from (P21) that $C = \neg A \sqcup \forall S.(\sqcup Y)$ belongs to $\mathcal{L}(\pi_1(x)) = \mathcal{L}(\pi_2(x))$.

- Suppose the Close-Meta-rule is applicable to $(\mathcal{T}_1, \mathcal{F}_1)$ for $a =_m A$, $b =_m B$ and MetaRule(R, S) with $a \approx x$, $b \approx y$, x, y representatives for a, b. By (P20), either $(\mathcal{J}(a), \mathcal{J}(b)) \in \mathcal{E}(R)$ or $(\mathcal{J}(a), \mathcal{J}(b)) \in \mathcal{E}(\sim R)$ in $\mathbb{T}$.

  1. If $(\mathcal{J}(a), \mathcal{J}(b)) \in \mathcal{E}(R)$ then we add R to $\mathcal{F}_2(x, y)$. Then we obtain $(\mathcal{T}_2, \mathcal{F}_2)$, where $\mathcal{T}_1 = \mathcal{T}_2$ and $\mathcal{F}_2$ is exactly the same as $\mathcal{F}_1$ except for nodes x, y where $\mathcal{F}_2(x, y) = \mathcal{F}_1(x, y) \cup \{R\}$. Moreover, the map π_2 is the same as π_1. We have to prove that $\pi_2 : \mathcal{F}_2 \to \mathbb{T}$ is a structure preserving map. The first, third and fourth conditions of Definition 5 are trivial. For the second condition, we have to prove that as y is an R-neighbour of x, it must hold that $(\pi_2(x), \pi_2(y)) \in \mathcal{E}(R)$. As a, b are root nodes, $a \approx x$, $b \approx y$, and π_1 is structure preserving map: $(\pi_1(a), \pi_1(b)) = (\mathcal{J}(a), \mathcal{J}(b)) = (\mathcal{J}(x), \mathcal{J}(y)) = (\pi_1(x), \pi_1(y)) = (\pi_2(x), \pi_2(y)) \in \mathcal{E}(R)$.
  2. If $(\mathcal{J}(a), \mathcal{J}(b)) \in \mathcal{E}(\sim R)$ then we add $\sim R$ to $\mathcal{F}_2(x, y)$. The rest of the proof is the same as the case above replacing R by $\sim R$.

- Suppose the MetaRule(R, S)-rule is applicable to $(\mathcal{T}_1, \mathcal{F}_1)$ and we have $a =_m A$ and MetaRule(R, S) in $\mathcal{M}$. Then we obtain $(\mathcal{T}_2, \mathcal{F}_2)$, where $\mathcal{F}_1 = \mathcal{F}_2$ and $\mathcal{T}_2 = \mathcal{T}_1 \cup \{\neg A \sqcup \forall S.(\sqcup X)\}$ for $X = \text{Image}_{\mathcal{F}_1}(R, a)$. Moreover, the map π_2 is the same as π_1. The fact that $\pi_2 : \mathcal{F}_2 \rightarrow \mathbb{T}$ is a structure preserving map is direct since $\mathcal{F}_1 = \mathcal{F}_2$ and π_2 is the same as π_1.

Theorem 3 (Completeness). *Let* $\mathcal{O} = (\mathcal{T}, \mathcal{R}, \mathcal{A}, \mathcal{M})$ *be a* $\mathcal{SHIQM}^*$-*ontology. If* $\mathcal{O}$ *is consistent, then the expansion rules for* $\mathcal{SHIQM}^*$ *can be applied to* $\mathcal{O}$ *such that they yield a complete completion forest with no contradictions and no cycles w.r.t.* $\mathcal{M}$.

Proof. By Lemma 1, $\mathcal{O}$ has a tableau. The proof, then, proceeds very similarly to Theorem 4 in [14]. Basically, we start by defining an initial structure preserving map for the forest after the initialization and then show that it satisfies the conditions of Definition 5. After that, it uses Lemma 2 and Theorem 1 to obtain a completion forest that has not contradictions nor cycles.

7   Related Work

Table 1 compares the most important meta-modelling approaches, by some relevant characteristics. The first column refers to the number of meta-modelling levels that the logic allows. The second one is about the flexibility in which it is possible to change the meta-modelling level of a concept. The third one is about role assertions between individuals/concepts at different levels. The fourth and fifth ones were defined at the end of Sect. 3. The sixth one refers to the well foundness of the interpretation domain. The last one is the capability of transferring rules between different knowledge levels.

The meta-modelling approach called *Punning* provided by OWL2 allows to use the same name as an individual and as a concept but the reasoner treats them as if they were actually different [5].

The description logic of *Pan et al.* adopts a Henkin style semantics. However, the well-foundness of the interpretation domain is ensured by adding natural numbers to concept names which represent the meta-modelling level. This logic has the disadvantage of forcing the ontology engineer to know beforehand the layer of each concept. Besides, it does not allow to define role assertions between individuals/concepts at different levels [7, 15].

The meta-modelling approaches from rows three to six of Table 1 adopt a Hilog style semantics and do not require the domain of the interpretation be well-founded [1, 2, 4, 8–10, 12]. The one on the third row is the approach of Motik which does not impose the sets of concept names and individuals to be disjoint so the same name can be used as a concept and a name [12]. His approach has been extended to more expressive logics and query languages [4]. *Lenzerini et al.* and Cima et al. present a Hilog approach for OWL2 QL, which is the OWL2 profile targeted to scenarios where large amount of data are to be accessed through conjunctive queries, approaching to a practical issue of information management [1, 10]. *Homola et al.* introduce a higher order description logic which does

Table 1. Comparison of meta-modelling approaches

Approach	Base DL	Unlim. levels	Flexible struct.	Inter-layer roles	Intensional regularity	Extensionality	Well-foundness	Rule transf. between levels
Punning	$\mathcal{SROIQ}$	Y	Y	Y	N	N	N	N
Pan et al.	$\mathcal{SROIQ}$	Y	N	N	Y	Y	Y	N
Motik (v-sem.)	$\mathcal{ALCHIQ}$	Y	Y	Y	Y	N	N	N
De Giacomo et al.	$\mathcal{SHIQ}$	Y	Y	Y	Y	N	N	N
Lenzerini et al.	OWL2 $\mathcal{QL}$	Y	Y	Y	Y	N	N	N
Homola et al.	$\mathcal{SROIQ}$	Y	Y	Y	Y	N	N	N
Glimm et al.	$\mathcal{SROIQ}$	N	N	Y(1-2)	Y	N	Y	N
$\mathcal{SHIQM}^*$	$\mathcal{SHIQ}$	Y	Y	Y	Y	Y	Y	Y

not ensure the well-foundness of the domain either. Even though they does not impose fixed layers, they define a typed variant to fix the layer of each syntactic element [8,9].

Glimm et al. introduce a quite different not set-theoretical approach, which encodes meta-modelling into OWL DL for only two levels of meta-modelling [3].

The description logic $\mathcal{SHIQM}^*$ studied in this paper combines a flexible syntax (without fixed layers) with a strong semantics that ensures the well-foundness of the interpretation domain. It includes the MetaRule role characteristic, to transfer business rules expressed in the Abox at a higher level, to the Tbox in the lower level [16].

There are other forms of meta-modelling studied in the literature such as meta-modelling for roles, instantiation and subsumption which are not addressed by our approach [2,7–9,12,15].

8   Conclusions and Future Work

This paper establishes a theoretical foundation for a framework with the capability of unifying different abstraction levels of a domain conceptualization. This framework is based on description logics with a Henkin style semantics and well-founded sets. It allows ontology engineers to represent real objects and relations between those objects from different perspectives, at different levels. This helps in the conceptualization of a hierarchical user view in business organizations.

The main technical contribution of this paper with respect to our previous work in [14] is to add the role characteristic MetaRule and define a tableau algorithm for the new description logic $\mathcal{SHIQM}^*$. The role characteristic MetaRule provides the capability of transferring rules from higher to lower knowledge levels.

In a previous work we show that the problem of checking consistency of a knowledge base in $\mathcal{ALC}$ extended with equality statements is ExpTime-complete, which does not change when moving from $\mathcal{ALC}$ to $\mathcal{ALCM}$ [11]. We think that the meta-modelling extension presented here should not change the complexity of the consistency in most description logics. We leave this as future research together with the extension of some reasoner following the ideas of the algorithm presented in this paper.

References

1. Cima, G., De Giacomo, G., Lenzerini, M., Poggi, A.: On the SPARQL metamodeling semantics entailment regime for OWL 2 QL ontologies. In Proceedings of the 7th International Conference on Web Intelligence, Mining and Semantics (2017)
2. Giacomo, G.D., Lenzerini, M., Rosati, R.: Higher-order description logics for domain metamodeling. In Proceedings of the Twenty-Fifth AAAI Conference on Artificial Intelligence, AAAI 2011. AAAI Press (2011)
3. Glimm, B., Rudolph, S., Völker, J.: Integrated metamodeling and diagnosis in OWL 2. In: International Semantic Web Conference (2010)
4. Gu, Z., Zhang, S.: The more irresistible Hi(SRIQ) for meta-modeling and meta-query answering. Front. Comput. Sci. **12**(5), 1029–1031 (2018)
5. Hitzler, P., Krötzsch, M., Rudolph, S.: Foundations of Semantic Web Technologies. Chapman & Hall/CRC, Boca Raton (2009)
6. Horrocks, I., Sattler, U., Tobies, S.: Reasoning with individuals for the description logic SHIQ. In: CADE (2000)
7. Jekjantuk, N., Gröner, G., Pan, J.: Modelling and reasoning in metamodelling enabled ontologies. Int. J. Softw. Inform. **4**(3), 277–290 (2010)
8. Kubincová, P.: Higher-order description logics for metamodelling. Master's Thesis (2016)
9. Kubincová, P., Kluka, J., Homola, M.: Expressive description logic with instantiation metamodelling. In: Proceedings of KR 2016 (2016)
10. Lenzerini, M., Lepore, L., Poggi, A.: Answering metaqueries over hi (OWL 2 QL) ontologies. In: IJCAI (2016)
11. Martinez, M., Rohrer, E., Severi, P.: Complexity of the description logic ALCM. In: Fifteenth International Conference on Principles of Knowledge Representation and Reasoning, KR (2016)
12. Motik, B.: On the properties of metamodeling in OWL. J Log. Comput. **17**(4), 617–637 (2007)
13. Motz, R., Rohrer, E., Severi, P.: Reasoning for $\mathcal{ALCQ}$ extended with a flexible meta-modelling hierarchy. In: Supnithi, T., Yamaguchi, T., Pan, J.Z., Wuwongse, V., Buranarach, M. (eds.) JIST 2014. LNCS, vol. 8943, pp. 47–62. Springer, Cham (2015). https://doi.org/10.1007/978-3-319-15615-6_4
14. Motz, R., Rohrer, E., Severi, P.: The description logic SHIQ with a flexible meta-modelling hierarchy. J. Web Sem. **35**(4), 214–234 (2015)
15. Pan, J.Z., Horrocks, I., Schreiber, G.: OWL FA: a metamodeling extension of OWL DL. In: OWLED (2005)
16. Rohrer, E., Severi, P., Motz, R.: Applying meta-modelling to an accounting application. In: ONTOBRAS (2018)

OceanGraph: Some Initial Steps Toward a Oceanographic Knowledge Graph

Marcos Zárate[1,2]($\boxtimes$) (iD), Pablo Rosales[2,3], Germán Braun[4], Mirtha Lewis[1,3],
Pablo Rubén Fillottrani[5,6], and Claudio Delrieux[7]

[1] Centre for the Study of Marine Systems, Patagonian National Research Centre
(CENPAT-CONICET), Puerto Madryn, Argentina
{zarate,mirtha}@cenpat-conicet.gob.ar

[2] Facultad de Ingeniería, Universidad Nacional de la Patagonia San Juan Bosco
(UNPSJB), Comodoro Rivadavia, Argentina
prosales@unpata.edu.ar

[3] Centro de Investigaciones y Transferencia Golfo San Jorge, (CIT-GSJ CONICET),
Comodoro Rivadavia, Argentina

[4] Grupo de Investigación en Lenguajes e Inteligencia Artificial, (GILIA-UNCOMA),
Neuquen, Argentina
german.braun@fi.uncoma.edu.ar

[5] Computer Science and Engineering Department, Universidad Nacional del Sur,
(DCIC-UNS), Bahía Blanca, Argentina
prf@cs.uns.edu.ar

[6] Comisión de Investigaciones Científicas, Provincia de Buenos Aires (CICPBA),
Buenos Aires, Argentina

[7] Electric and Computer Engineering Department, Universidad Nacional del Sur
(UNS-CONICET), Bahía Blanca, Argentina
cad@uns.edu.ar

Abstract. Increasing ocean temperatures severely affects marine species and ecosystems. Among other things, rising temperatures cause coral bleaching and loss of breeding grounds for marine fish and mammals. Motivated by the need to understand better these global problems, researchers from all over the world generated huge amounts of oceanographic data during the last years. However, most of this data remain isolated in their own silos. One approach to provide safe accessibility to these silos is to map local, often database-specific identifiers, to shared global identifiers. This mapping can then be used to build interoperable knowledge graphs (KGs), where entities such as publications, people, places, specimens, environmental variables and institutions are all part of a single, shared knowledge space. This short paper describes one such effort, the *OceanGraph* KG, including the modeling and publication processes, and the current and prospective uses of the dataset.

Keywords: Knowledge graph · Oceanography · RDF · SPARQL · GeoSPARQL

© Springer Nature Switzerland AG 2019
B. Villazón-Terrazas and Y. Hidalgo-Delgado (Eds.): KGSWC 2019, CCIS 1029, pp. 33–40, 2019.
https://doi.org/10.1007/978-3-030-21395-4_3

1 Introduction and Motivation

We are transitioning from the era of Big Data to Big Knowledge, and semantic knowledge bases such as KGs play an important role in this transition. This is evident from the expanding investments in KG research and development by major corporate players, resulting in widely used systems such as IBM Watson, Google entity search, Apple Siri, and Amazon product graph. KGs are an increasingly critical component of the Semantic Web (SW) [1] and serve as information hubs for general use as well as for domain-specific applications. There is no common definition about what a KG is and what is not [2], since KG have emerged as a unifying technology in several areas of artificial intelligence, including Natural Language Processing and Semantic Web, and the scope of what constitutes a KG has continued to broaden [3]. Most KGs seek to aggregate knowledge from third party sources, either from external databases, from data aggregated through crawling the Web, or through the application of entity and relationship extraction methods [4]. KGs are not simply aggregations of Resource Description Frameworks (RDFs)[1] or Linked Data (LD) [5]. Instead they provide critical time-invariant information about entities of general interest. Their structures tend to be focused on a limited set of relations adhering to a coherent knowledge model, setting them apart from the LD cloud in general, which usually has relied on the open framework of the SW to accommodate a completely free-form use of vocabularies and ontologies.

The ocean and life sciences, in general, yielded an amount of data that is not only huge in volume, but also highly heterogeneous both in types and formats, and scattered across distributed data repositories [6]. For individual researchers, this situation presents a difficult challenge regarding discovery, access and integration of the data required to conduct scientific inquiries. This also introduces difficult knowledge management issues that must be overcome by the whole research community [7]. We can mention a couple related works which partially address these issues through KGs. The first is a proof-of-concept of a KG for the Australian fauna, combining taxonomic classifications and scientific publications. The latter is a dataset[2] including information from oceanographic cruises, physical samples, and technical reports from the geoscience metadata repositories in the United States. In both cases, data has been published according to best practices for linked data and are publicly available via a SPARQL endpoint. None of them integrate biodiversity and biogeography data as proposed here [8] and *GeoLink* [9].

In this short contribution we present the initial efforts to develop *OceanGraph* KG. *OceanGraph* has leveraged linked data principles to create a KG that allows users to seamlessly query and reason over some of the largest oceanographic data repositories such as the *National Marine Data System (NMDS)*[3], *Global Biodiversity Information Facility* (GBIF)[4] and *Ocean Biogeographic Information*

---

[1] https://www.w3.org/RDF/.
[2] http://hdl.handle.net/1912/9524.
[3] http://www.datosdelmar.mincyt.gob.ar/index.php.
[4] https://www.gbif.org/.

System (OBIS)[5]. As an illustration, we present a use case that shows how *Ocean-Graph* allows to relate species occurrences from GBIF to environmental variables from OBIS, a fundamental requirement of macroecological analyses [10], particularly those considering environmental drivers of species distributions, and how distributions are expected to shift as the climate changes [11].

2   OceanGraph Data Providers

The datasets that make up *OceanGraph* originate from areas of ocean science, Biodiversity/Biogeography, scientific publications, locations, and environmental data. Most of the datasets have information funded by the Argentine government, although there are others that belong to third parties. The datasets that currently comprise *OceanGraph* are the following:

- **Marine Biodiversity/Biogeography.** As mentioned earlier, part of the information comes from GBIF and OBIS, two of the most important international databases. Both databases use Darwin Core standard (DwC) [12] to represent species information. For additional information see [13] where is described how this information was converted and published as Linked Open Data.
- **Oceanographic campaigns.** *National Marine Data System* is a web platform that allows publishing datasets of oceanographic campaigns that was sampled in Argentine sea. These datasets are composed of (i) metadata of the oceanographic campaigns (name of the campaign, vessel, dates, people and institutions involved, geographical coverage among others), and (ii) data recorded by the vessel in its trajectory, which contains the information of the measured variables (pressure, salinity, temperature, depth, positions where the variable was sampled among others). In [14] the complete process of conversion and publication of these data sets is described.
- **Publications.** Springer Nature SciGraph [15] a Linked Open Data platform for the scholarly domain which aggregates data sources from Springer Nature and key partners from the scholarly domain. The Linked Open Data platform collates information from across the research landscape, for example funders, research projects, conferences, affiliations and publications. Data in Springer Nature SciGraph is projected to contain 1.5 to 2 billion triples (as of January 2019).
- **Environmental variables.** Data generated by fixed stations belonging to *Comodoro conocimiento agency*[6] created by the City Government of Comodoro Rivadavia (Argentina) has maritime buoys for environmental monitoring. The aim is to monitor the mariculture zones in the San Jorge Gulf and validate data from oceanographic campaigns in the area. These buoys measure radiation, wind speed, temperature, humidity, oxygen, conductivity, salinity and fluorescence, among others.

---

[5] http://www.iobis.org/.
[6] http://www.conocimiento.gov.ar/.

– **Locations.** GeoNames[7] is a free and open source geographical database. Primarily for developers wanting to integrate the project into web services and applications, it combines world-wide geographical data including names of places in various languages, elevation, population, and all latitude/longitude coordinates. Data is accessible through a number of web services and a daily database export.

3   OceanGraph Development

The general structure of *OceanGraph* is based on the relationships established among datasets of Fig. 1. The core entities are campaigns, species, publications, people, environmental variables and locations. For instance, if the knowledge graph is queried for a particular scientist, results might include the oceanographic campaigns they participated in (from NMDS), datasets they collected (from OBIS/GBIF), and papers they has written (from SciGraph). Similarly, if a particular species is queried for, the user can determine who collected it, when, where, and under which oceanographic campaign.

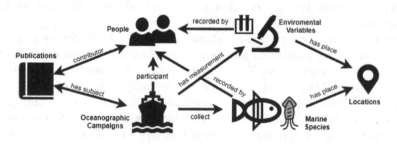

Fig. 1. *OceanGraph* KG general schema.

OceanGraph can be accessed through GraphDB[8], which is a highly efficient and robust graph database. It allows users to explore the hierarchy of RDF classes (`Class hierarchy`), where each class can be browsed to explore its instances. Similarly, relationships among these classes also can be explored giving an overview about how many links exist between instances of the two classes (`Class relationship`). The user can visually explore the dataset, accessing the URL http://web.cenpat-conicet.gob.ar:7200/login using the credentials (user: **oceangraph** password: **ocean.user**). After successful authentication, select the repository **OceanGraph**.

---

[7] http://www.geonames.org/ontology/documentation.html.
[8] http://graphdb.ontotext.com/.

3.1 Underlying Vocabularies and Ontologies

The description and management of information resources have to obey well-known standards to ensure that they will be made available for various communities of users. In this section, we will describe the main resources related to geospatial data, Biodiversity/Biogeography, oceanography and environmental data. In addition to information resources management, we selected existing standards to manage information about agents and domain entities. Several data providers use their own ontologies and existing vocabularies such as FOAF[9], Dublin Core[10] and Prov-O[11].

- **NERC Vocabulary Server** [16] Natural Environment Research Council (NERC) Vocabulary Server provides access to lists of standardized terms that cover a broad spectrum of disciplines of relevance to the oceanographic and wider community. Using standardized sets of terms in metadata and to label data solves the problem of ambiguities associated with data markup, for example, sometimes data-level errors may occur, which are caused by differences that occur in data domains due to multiple possible representations, similar data interpretations, or even spelling errors *e.g. Oxygen, O2, Oxgen.*
- **GeoSPARQL** [17] is a standard for representing and querying of geospatial linked data for the Semantic Web from the Open Geospatial Consortium (OGC[12]). The definition of a small ontology based on well-understood OGC standards is intended to provide a standardized exchange basis for geospatial RDF data which can support both qualitative and quantitative spatial reasoning and querying with the SPARQL[13] database query language.
- **Darwin Core Standard** [12] includes a glossary of terms intended for sharing information about biological diversity by providing reference definitions, examples, and commentaries. In *OceanGraph*, we use it to describe properties, elements, fields, columns, attributes and concepts.
- **Geolink** [18] describes an ontological design pattern (ODP) for oceanographic cruises using Web Ontology Language (OWL). This pattern was specified as a combination and reuse of the existing patterns: trajectory, event and information object. We consider that this ODP is sufficiently generic and adapts well to our requirements, and for this reason will be adopted to define the relationships and classes that we will designate in our data set.
- **SSN and SOSA ontologies** [19] to describe sensors and their observations we use the Semantic Sensor Network (SSN), specially the self-contained ontology SOSA (Sensor, Observation, Sample and Actuator) that describes elementary classes and properties. Both ontologies can be used for a wide range of applications and use cases for example, satellite imagery, large-scale scientific monitoring and the Web of Things among others. We use SOSA to describe the process of gathering information from fixed stations.

---

[9] http://xmlns.com/foaf/spec/.
[10] http://www.dublincore.org/specifications/.
[11] https://www.w3.org/TR/prov-o/.
[12] http://www.opengeospatial.org/.
[13] https://www.w3.org/TR/rdf-sparql-query/.

3.2   Cross-Linking

Cross-linking the *OceanGraph* datasets in a semi-automated way is crucial aiming at facilitating data integration by linking overlapping contents existing in many of the *OceanGraph* repositories. For example, people involved in an oceanographic campaign can also be authors of scientific publications or, for example, marine species observed during a campaign are published in OBIS or GBIF. Linking the same people or species in different repositories is the key feature that enables integrated querying and makes *OceanGraph* so useful. To do this, we use SILK framework[14] to express heuristics for deciding whether a semantic relationship exists between two entities. For instance, to relate people involved in an oceanographic campaign with their contributions in OBIS or GBIF, the *Levenshtein distance* is used to disambiguate two inputs through computing the similarity between them. This operator receives inputs such as `dwc:recordedBy`[15] (property used in OBIS/GBIF) and `foaf:name` and returns the links between them by using the `owl:sameAs` axioms. Figure 2 shows the relationships used to integrate *OceanGraph* datasets.

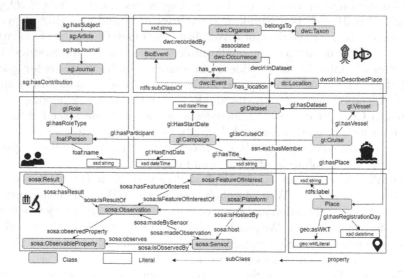

Fig. 2. Conceptual diagram of *OceanGraph*. For simplicity, only the main object properties are shown, which allow relationships between the classes of each data set to be established.

4   Use Case

As mentioned earlier, relating species occurrences with environmental variables is a very common requirement of macroecological analyses [10]. This use case

---

[14] http://silkframework.org/.
[15] https://terms.tdwg.org/wiki/dwc:recordedBy.

describes how this problem can be addressed in a simplified way. To do this we define a SPARQL query that associates the occurrences of a marine species (a fish for example) with water body temperature in a specific marine region. Firstly, we define the marine region called *San Matias Gulf*, type (`geo:Polygon`), secondly we retrieve the observations of the defined species as points using (`geo:point`). Since GeoSPARQL allows performing spatial operations, we can query if a point is contained within a polygon using the function (`geof:sfWithin`). Finally we retrieve the measured environmental variable (also georeferenced by a point). NERC provides URIs for each of the variables, so we only need to retrieve the URI for the variable temperature of the water body http://vocab.nerc.ac.uk/collection/P02/current/TEMP/. After authenticating, the query can be executed in GraphDB using the following link[16]. Figure 3 shows the results after executing the query.

	occ	⇕	measurement	⇕	PointWKT	⇕
1	http://www.cenpat-conicet.gob.ar/resource/occurrence/urncatalogcenp at-conicetcnp-pecescnp-p-2296		http://vocab.nerc.ac.uk/collection/P 02/current/TEMP/		"POINT(-63.833332 -41.650002)" http://www.opengis. net/ont/geosparql#wktLiteral>	
2	http://www.cenpat-conicet.gob.ar/resource/occurrence/urncatalogcenp at-conicetcnp-pecescnp-p-2297		http://vocab.nerc.ac.uk/collection/P 02/current/TEMP/		"POINT(-64.433334 -41.400002)" <http://www.opengis. net/ont/geosparql#wktLiteral>	

Fig. 3. Result of the query, occurrences (`occ`) associated with temperature (`measurement`) and its corresponding location (`PointWKT`) within the polygon are observed.

Although this is a simple example, it is important to highlight that KGs used as tools to integrate information, allow us to answer questions that require an integrated management of heterogeneous information sources. As *OceanGraph* begins to be disseminated in the oceanographic research community, we hope that the use of data by third parties will continue to grow and generate new answers.

5   Conclusions and Future Work

Currently the publication of KGs grew substantially in diverse areas, however, there is still much work to be done in the domain of ocean science. In this paper, we presented an overview of our initial effort to create an oceanographic KG called *OceanGraph*, reusing specific vocabularies and ontologies of this domain. This initiative will allow to model a public and freely available source of ocean science data composed of largest data repositories in this domain, and thus building applications on data reconciliation, data augmentation, and meta-analyses in these fields. Particularly, as future work we need to work on a user-friendly interface together with searching engines and visualizations that allows non-expert users to explore the data. In this same direction, we plan to link our dataset to other ones from diverse domains, f.e., fisheries [20].

---

[16] http://web.cenpat-conicet.gob.ar:7200/sparql?savedQueryName=OG-Q001.

References

1. Berners-Lee, T., Hendler, J., Lassila, O., et al.: The Semantic Web. Scientific American (2001)
2. Paulheim, H.: Knowledge graph refinement: a survey of approaches and evaluation methods. Semant. Web J. **8**, 489–508 (2016)
3. Sequeda, J.F., Kejriwal, M., Lopez, V.: Construction, management and querying. Semant. Web J. (2018). Special Issue on Knowledge Graphs
4. Wöß, W., Ehrlinger, L.: Towards a definition of knowledge graphs. In: 12th International Conference on Semantic Systems - SEMANTiCS 2016 (2016)
5. Bizer, C., Heath, T., Berners-Lee, T.: Linked data-the story so far. In: Semantic Services, Interoperability and Web Applications: Emerging Concepts (2009)
6. Malik, T., Foster, I.: Addressing data access needs of the long-tail distribution of geoscientists. In: 2012 IEEE International Geoscience and Remote Sensing Symposium (IGARSS), pp. 5348–5351. IEEE (2012)
7. Campbell, P.: Data's shameful neglect. Nature **461**(7261), 145 (2009)
8. Page, R.D.M.: Ozymandias: a biodiversity knowledge graph. bioRxiv (2018)
9. Cheatham, M., et al.: The GeoLink knowledge graph. Big Earth Data (2018)
10. Muller-Karger, F.E., et al.: Advancing marine biological observations and data requirements of the complementary essential ocean variables (EOVS) and essential biodiversity variables (EBVS) frameworks. Front. Mar. Sci. **5**, 211 (2018)
11. Pearson, R.G., Dawson, T.P.: Predicting the impacts of climate change on the distribution of species: are bioclimate envelope models useful? Glob. Ecol. Biogeogr. **12**(5), 361–371 (2003)
12. Wieczorek, J., et al.: Darwin core: an evolving community-developed biodiversity data standard. PLoS ONE **7**, 1–8 (2012)
13. Zárate, M., Braun, G., Fillottrani, P.: Adding biodiversity datasets from argentinian patagonia to the web of data (2017)
14. Zárate, M., Rosales, P., Fillottrani, P., Delrieux, C., Lewis, M.: Oceanographic data management: towards the publishing of Pampa Azul oceanographic campaigns as linked data (2018)
15. Springer Nature SciGraph. http://www.springernature.com/gp/researchers/scigraph. Accessed 24 Jan 2019
16. Leadbetter, A., Lowry, R., Clements, D.O.: The NERC vocabulary server: version 2.0. In: Geophysical Research Abstracts, vol. 14 (2012)
17. Battle, R., Kolas, D.: Enabling the geospatial semantic web with parliament and GeoSPARQL. Semant. Web **3**(4), 355–370 (2012)
18. Krisnadhi, A., et al.: An ontology pattern for oceanographic cruises: towards an oceanographer's dream of integrated knowledge discovery (2014)
19. W3C. Semantic Sensor Network Ontology (SSN) W3C recommendation (2017)
20. Froese, R., Pauly, D., et al.: Fishbase (2010)

Digital Repositories and Linked Data: Lessons Learned and Challenges

Santiago Gonzalez-Toral(✉)📓, Mauricio Espinoza-Mejia, and Victor Saquicela

Computer Science Department, University of Cuenca, Cuenca, Ecuador
{hernan.gonzalezt,mauricio.espinoza,victor.saquicela}@ucuenca.edu.ec

Abstract. Digital repositories have been used by Universities and Libraries to store their bibliographic, scientific, and/or institutional contents, and then make their corresponding metadata publicly available to the web and through the OAI-PMH protocol. However, such metadata is not descriptive enough for a document to be easily discoverable. Even though the emergence of Semantic Web technologies have produced the interest of Digital Repository providers to publish and enrich their content using Linked Data (LD) technologies, those institutions have used different generation approaches, and in certain cases ad-hoc solutions to solve particular use cases, but none of them has performed a comparison between existing approaches in order to demonstrate which one is the best solution prior to its application. In order to address this question, we have performed a benchmark study that compares two commonly used generation approaches, and also describes our experience, lessons learned and challenges found during the process of publishing a DSpace digital repository as LD. Results show that the straightforward method for extracting data from a digital repository is through the standard OAI-PMH protocol, whose performance in terms of execution time is much shorter than the database approach, while additional data cleaning tasks are minimal.

Keywords: Linked Data · Digital repositories · DSpace · OAI-PMH

1 Introduction

Today, digital repository providers of scholarly and research documents use diverse methods, standards and tools for publishing their contents. For example, DSpace[1] digital repository has become the standard platform that universities and libraries in general use to store institutional documents (such as thesis, journal articles, newsletters, etc.), mainly due to it provides a harvesting service that uses the OAI-PMH protocol that allows the metadata consumption of and interoperability between repositories.

However, the metadata that is consumed through this protocol uses a standard Dublin Core[2] (DC) schema which is not descriptive enough to be neither

---

[1] http://www.dspace.org/.
[2] http://dublincore.org/.

© Springer Nature Switzerland AG 2019
B. Villazón-Terrazas and Y. Hidalgo-Delgado (Eds.): KGSWC 2019, CCIS 1029, pp. 41–55, 2019.
https://doi.org/10.1007/978-3-030-21395-4_4

easily queried by both people and (third-party) software nor be enriched with other external content. The emergence of Semantic Web technologies and specifically Linked Data initiatives such as the one introduced by Villazon et al. in [1], have produced the interest of institutions like University of Patras [2–5], University of Vienna [6], and Institutions member of the *Ecuadorian Consortium for the Development of Advanced Internet* (CEDIA)[3] [7,8] to publish and enrich their digital repositories using LD technologies.

In order to extract the metadata content from a digital repository and generate a semantically enriched LD dataset, those institutions used different approaches and tools that in certain cases consisted of ad-hoc solutions to solve particular use cases. These use cases were developed by the authors either by directly querying the DSpace database schema or by harvesting metadata through the OAI protocol, but no comparison between both approaches have been performed in the literature in order to demonstrate which is the best solution for publishing LD from a digital repository.

In this article we present our experience, lessons learned and challenges found during the process of publishing the University of Cuenca DSpace digital repository as Linked Data, and based on a benchmark study we demonstrate which generation approach is the best. After describing some background and related work in the field in Sect. 2, Sect. 3 describes the process for publishing digital content as Linked Data using two data generation approaches. Section 4 describes the results obtained in the benchmark study, and finally, Sects. 5 and 6 outline the lessons learned and challenges encountered during the process and propose directions for future work in the field.

2   Background and Related Work

According to the last statistics report published by the Directory of Open Access Repositories (OpenDOAR)[4], DSpace is the most widely used open source digital repository by institutions worldwide. It preserves and enables an easy and open access to all types of digital content including text, images, media, etc. Digital content metadata is stored in a relational database with a flexible data model that can be customised to fit the organisational structure needs of an institute.

DSpace architecture maintains three types of metadata content to describe digital resources:

- **Administrative Metadata**: contains policy and provenance metadata information. Provenance and file size/type are stored using Dublin Core properties.
- **Structural Metadata**: contains information about how to present an item or file to the end user (i.e. XSLT files for metadata format output).
- **Descriptive Medatada**: by default, each item has a Dublin Core Metadata Registry useful for the interoperability and discovery of items in the system. Additionally, DSpace uses the DC-library Application Profile schema that

---

[3] http://www.cedia.org.ec/.
[4] http://www.opendoar.org/.

contains particular elements to define bibliographic properties that cannot be found in the Dublin Core terms vocabulary, however it is allowed to configure any other vocabulary schema or to customise the metadata fields to describe a digital resource.

To allow the interoperability between repositories, DSpace supports the OAI-PMH protocol[5] that facilitates the harvesting of metadata in XML representation and 12 different formats[6] such as *XOAI, OAI_DC, DIM*, etc. The protocol exposes specific repository metadata through a REST API with 6 verbs or request types: repository information (*identify*), repository metadata formats (*ListMetadataFormats*), repository collections structure (*ListSets*), harvesting of records (*ListIdentifiiers* and *ListRecords*), and record metadata description (*GetRecord*).

Some Institutions around the world have already performed some research and worked on approaches for the extraction and publication of library digital collections as Linked Data. For instance, Vila-Suero et al. presented in [9] an approach to automate the transformation (and linkage with external sources) of the *datos.bne.es* MARC21 library dataset to RDF using a developed tool called *MARiMbA*, that allows domain experts to map library metadata into highly specialised IFLA library models using spreadsheets. Lampert and Southwick from University of Nevada presented in [10,11] their findings during the development of the UNLV Linked Data Project, demonstrating that the transformation of digital collections metadata into linked data is feasible and a very promising investment to increase the discoverability of materials of current systems that provide limited metadata schema choices and the inability to create explicit connections between related contents from different digital collections. Authors also provided a road map, challenges found and helpful tools such as OpenRefine[7] to help guide digital collections managers along the processes of data transforming, reconciliation, and LD generation.

Haslhofer et al. [6] developed *OAI2LOD*, a tool based on the D2RQ[8] architecture and the OAI-PMH protocol for republishing the University of Vienna DSpace repository according to the Linked Data 5 stars deployment scheme [12]. Latif et al. in [13] demonstrate how an open access repository is extracted and published as Linked Data by directly mapping metadata from the database schema into Resource Description Framework format (RDF) using D2RQ and a mapping file based on the R2RML [14] recommendation published by the W3C. In [15], Hidalgo et al. outline a use case that implements a custom middleware to harvest data from open access Cuban journals with support for OAI-PMH protocol, and subsequently store the extracted metadata into a PostgreSQL database.

---

[5] http://www.openarchives.org/pmh/.
[6] https://github.com/DSpace/DSpace/tree/master/dspace/config/crosswalks/oai/metadataFormats.
[7] http://openrefine.org/.
[8] http://d2rq.org/.

Transformation is then performed using D2RQ, while linkages with others related RDF graphs were generated using Silk framework.[9]

On the other hand, Anibaldi et al. presented in [16] an ad-hoc process consisting of continuous and automatic steps for RDFizing the AGRIS repository records, which starts by loading the AGRIS XML records into a relational database model. Then, database records are consumed by a filter program that transforms and enrich them. Finally, data is converted to RDF, loaded in an AllegroGraph triple store and disseminated to the web.

Konstantinou et al. proposed in [17,18] a production-ready solution for RDFizing a digital repository content based on the R2RML language. The information processing flow mainly use the relational database, a R2RML parser tool[10] and an R2RML mapping file consisting of SQL queries (or views) and respective RDF classes/properties that transforms repository records as an RDF graph. System evaluation showed performance improvements compared to D2RQ-based solutions.

Koutsomitropoulos et al. [3] presented a process to extract and improve the University of Patras DSpace digital repository by harvesting the metadata content through the OAI-PMH protocol and RDFizing the information using the OAI-PMH RDFizer tool from the MIT SIMILE project[11]. Later, Koutsomitropoulos et al. describe in [19] a process for extracting and publishing Linked Data out of DSpace resources that follow an on-the-fly two-step replication strategy: (a) perform a curated metadata extraction process through the OAI-PMH interface; and (b) translate ingested metadata into RDF/OWL using an Extensible Stylesheet Language (XSL) transformation file. Additionally, authors presented *Semantic Search*, a DSpace plugin to combine a reasoning-based knowledge acquisition mechanism with the Linked Data service and provide new content discovery capabilities, however, targeted users must have some familiarity with semantic web concepts and Manchester Syntax for building queries.

Piedra et al. proposed in [20,21] a lifecycle approach to extract and publish Open Educational Resources (OERs) in the semantic web with the aim to improve the integration and interoperability of OERs stored in digital repositories. They harvested the metadata from a DSpace repository using Harvester2 and stored the OAI triples in an intermediary database repository in order to perform necessary data cleaning tasks. Then, OERs metadata was transformed into RDF using a custom generator tool based on Apache Jena.

In [7], authors emphasised the use of the OAI-PMH protocol to harvest digital repositories metadata in order to obtain a more interoperable ecosystem for publishing OERs as Linked Data and enhance the discoverability and reuse of academic resources. However, they only outlined an integration method used for combining resources from different sources but does not compare and contrast their extraction process with other approaches.

---

[9] http://wifo5-03.informatik.uni-mannheim.de/bizer/silk/.
[10] https://www.w3.org/2001/sw/wiki/R2RML_Parser.
[11] http://simile.mit.edu/wiki/OAI-PMH_RDFizer.

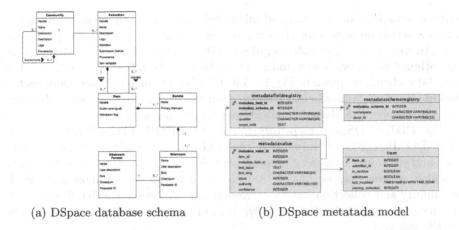

(a) DSpace database schema   (b) DSpace metatada model

Fig. 1. DSpace data model

Following, we present our experience, lessons learned and the challenges found during the process of publishing the University of Cuenca DSpace digital repository on the Semantic Web using two data extraction approaches (database schema and OAI-PMH protocol), and then perform a benchmark study for identifying and evaluating certain features like performance and process complexity of each method, The steps involved for generating Linked Data are based on the methodological guidelines published by Villazon et al. [1].

3 Process for Generating Linked Open Data from a DSpace Digital Repository

In order to generate Linked Data for a digital repository, we use the methodology published by the O.E.G Working Group [1], together with the best practices that the W3C recommend [22], so the process steps are defined as follows: specification, modelling, generation, publication and exploitation. As a use case, we worked with the University of Cuenca *Centro de Documentacion Juan Bautista Vasquez* (CDJBV) DSpace digital repository[12] which is in charge of publishing institutional bibliographic resources like thesis, articles, magazines and other documents. DSpace is commonly used by all other member of the Ecuadorian Consortium for the Development of Advanced Internet (CEPRA), therefore a common extraction mechanism for interoperability is needed.

3.1 Specification

Data Model Analysis. The DSpace data schema, as shown in Fig. 1a, is composed by *communities*, that can be divided into sub-communities. These, in turn,

---

[12] http://dspace.ucuenca.edu.ec/.

contain *collections* of contents and might belong to more than one community. Each collection manage a set of *items*, and each item belongs to a unique collection. An item can also contain bundles of bitstreams with an associated format (e.g. original file, preview files, indexed text, license, etc.). On the other hand, the metadata schema is shown in Fig. 1b. The CDJBV DSpace instance includes the Dublin Core as default schema, plus an extension of new elements with identifier *ucuenca* to solve the library's context-specific requirements.

The CDJBV DSpace repository has an OAI-PMH service[13] registered on OPENDOAR registry[14]. In general, the OAI protocol allows to expose collections and communities as sets, allowing repositories to expose a hierarchy of sets in which records may be placed. A record can be in zero or more sets. Each community and collection have a corresponding OAI set identifier discoverable by harvesters via the *ListSets* verb, while item records can be harvested via the *ListRecords* verb.

As a stepping stone for the modelling stage, we generated a view script of the *metadatavalue* table to explore the uses of each metadata property on each type of bibliographic resource, and thus save some time by omitting the modelling of the complete set of terms available, so the generation process will use a model that only consider the terms used by the institution. Additionally, we analysed the different metadata formats that the OAI protocol provides by performing some data requests using the harvester instance, obtaining stream samples for each of the available formats. This process helped us conclude that the best format to extract *listSets* and *listRecords* streams are *dim* and *xoai* metadata formats respectively as they allowed us to retrieve all the existing information provided by the digital repository about a bibliographic resource, including a useful set of descriptive and qualified refinements that ease their classification.

URI Design. One of the principles of Linked Data tells that publishers need to identify resources using well-designed URIs, so we followed the best practices [23] defined by the *W3C Working Group*. The dataset namespace and URI representation for each type of bibliographic resource is shown in Table 1.

License. License information is mostly gathered from the attached licenses of each record under the DSpace repository, but for those items without a defined licence, we propose the use of the *Creative Commons Attribution 4.0 International Public License*[15]. On the other hand, a policy-based access control using the RDFLicenses dataset [24] is also integrated. The dataset contains over 100 licenses in a RDF representation using the Open Digital Rights Language (ODRL) 2.0[16] and Linked Data Rights (LDR) 2.0[17] vocabularies, and that can

---

[13] http://dspace.ucuenca.edu.ec/oai/request.
[14] http://v2.sherpa.ac.uk/id/repository/4186.
[15] http://creativecommons.org/licenses/by/4.0/legalcode.
[16] http://www.w3.org/ns/odrl/2/.
[17] http://purl.oclc.org/NET/ldr/ns#.

Table 1. URI design for the CDJBV DSpace RDF graph

Resource	URI design
namespace	http://{server-domain}/dspace/
Director	{namespace}/contribuidor/director/{name}
Assessor	{namespace}/contribuidor/asesor/{name}
Author	{namespace}/contribuidor/autor/{name}
Collaborator	{namespace}/contribuidor/colaborador/{name}
Coordinator	{namespace}/contribuidor/coordinador/{name}
Editor	{namespace}/contribuidor/editor/{name}
Other contributor	{namespace}/contribuidor/otro/{name}
Format	{namespace}/fileformat/{format}
Community	{namespace}/comunidad/name
Collection	{namespace}/coleccion/name
Bibliographic resource	{namespace}/recurso/{item-id}

Table 2. Vocabularies to be reused in the ontology model

Vocabulary	Description
foaf	Allows to model bibliographic resources contributors
dcterms	DC terms to model some bibliographic resources properties
bibo	For Bibliographic Resources and its properties
mrel	Represents different types of contributors as MARC21 codes
rdag1	Outlines some properties between contributors and bib. resources
rdaa	The Agent properties element set

be linked to a resource using the standard Dublin Core license metadata element
to provide a simplified rights representation for both humans and machines.

3.2 Modeling

The data analysis made on the previous step gave us an idea on the existing
ontologies, from those available in the Linked Open Vocabularies (LOV) librarian
space[18], that we can reuse to model the vocabulary needed to represent each
property of a resource. The selected ontologies are described on Table 2, while
fully qualified URIs for each vocabulary can be found by querying the *prefix.cc*[19]
lookup service.

---

[18] http://lov.okfn.org/dataset/lov/details/vocabularySpace_Library.html.
[19] http://prefix.cc/.

3.3   Generation

Based on previous experiences found in the related work, we decided to evaluate two of the most commonly used approaches to generate a Linked Data graph from the CDJBV DSpace repository. The first generates an RDF document directly from the repository database using the D2RQ platform, while the second uses the OAI protocol and a modified version of *oai2rdf* where we developed a few improvements[20]. It is worth to mention that at the time of writing this paper, no other study has covered a benchmark study to evaluate the performance of both approaches.

Database Approach: Transformation and Data Cleaning. Prior generating the RDF graph, we performed a literature review about the current available tools for generating Linked Data sets from database schemas. D2RQ was chosen as it allowed us to automatically generate an initial RDF mapping schema that can serve as the baseline to map all the existing entities/properties to RDF subjects/objects. Among the main features it offers we can mention:

- Direct SPARQL queries to non-RDF databases, also knows as *Virtualized Generation*
- Web access to database contents as Linked Data
- RDF generation from a database schema, also known as *Materialized Generation*.

To execute the RDF generation process using D2RQ, we executed an initial entity mapping file with the automated generation tool. This mapping was defined using the *D2RQ Mapping Language*: a *Turtle* descriptive language based on the R2RML specification. Then, the mapping file was modified to establish the different relations between each type of bibliographic resources with its properties and the database schema.

During a first extraction process where all the mappings were included in one definition file, the tool raised the following errors:

- Since most of the data (DC metadata) are located on a single table of the database schema, the generated dataset produce too many repeated triples and duplicated misinformation. After, analysing the tool logs, we found that the problem was given by trying to represent different entities with the same subject/property on a single mapping file.
- The dataset extraction on *.rdf* format generate too many junk information like repeated triples including some with wrong information (e.g. title data repeated n times, being n the total number of entity properties), which results in complex cleaning processes.

Due to all metadata information is contained in a single database table inside DSpace, an intermediate data normalisation step to another database schema

---

[20] https://github.com/santteegt/oai2rdf

should be performed if we want to avoid this problem. However, to avoid these problems without much overhead, we created separate mappings files for each pair of bibliographic resource types as well as an appropriate mapping file for the other descriptive metadata entities that need of a controlled vocabulary to be defined like contributors, communities/collections and file formats. We chose *Turtle* as generation format, as the tool generates the cleanest information with this serialisation, and thus enabling easier cleaning processes.

OAI-PMH Approach: Transformation and Data Cleaning. To extract data through the DSpace OAI protocol, we used an improved version of the *OAI-PMH RDFizer* tool developed by MIT SIMILE project. Our coding modifications include allowing the extraction of ListSets data, and to save the generated RDF in one single file. By default, the tool generates a file for every 100 records harvested, which becomes problematic when having to consolidate a repository of ten of thousand of records in an RDF graph.

After harvesting records through the protocol, the tool performs a transformation process based on *Extensible Stylesheet Language Transformations* (XSLT) files defined by the user. For our use case, we defined 4 different XSLT files for transforming data from list sets, contributors, file formats and bibliographic resources respectively into RDF.

3.4 Linking

With the purpose of improving the discovery of resources, we created linkages between the resource from the CDJBV generated RDF dataset and contributors from other DSpace Linked Data repositories from institutions member of CEPRA. To generate those links (using *owl:sameAs* property), we used *Silk* as a link discovery framework. Silk allows to define a threshold for finding similar links through syntactic metrics, and then validate those links by establishing a semantic relation between related attributes. On the other hand, to enrich the contents of the generated RDF graph, we used *DBpedia Spotlight*[21] API for the discovery and annotation of information related to topics and/or keywords within the DSpace digital records. External resources found through the API are then appended to the RDF using the Web Annotation Model[22]. The specific properties of interest for our annotation model are:

- @URI: link to the related DBPedia article.
- @types: entity type.
- @surfaceForm: entity in plain text.
- @offset: the entity position in the input string.

---

[21] http://www.dbpedia-spotlight.org/.
[22] https://www.w3.org/TR/annotation-model/.

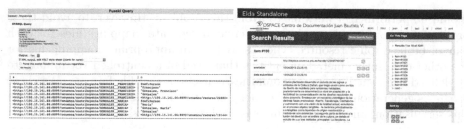

(a) Query example in SPARQL endpoint   (b) Elda LinkedData API instance

Fig. 2. Interfaces used to publish and exploit the linked data set

3.5 Publication

In order to publish the generated CDJBV DSpace Linked Data set to make it publicly available to users as well as other services and repositories, we deployed a SPARQL endpoint using *Apache Fuseki*, which serves as a storage, query, and data interaction interface. Moreover, it was used by other repositories as a support for the linking process. The advantages of using Fuseki against other similar technologies such as Virtuoso or Apache Marmotta are its small size and its support to special features as federated queries and text indexing. Figure 2a shows an example of using our deployed instance[23] to query the dataset for contributors and related bibliographic resources with a specific last name.

3.6 Exploitation

To allow the consumption of the generated RDF dataset, we deployed an instance[24] of the *Elda* framework[25] as a *Linked Data API* solution to enable dereferenceable URIs as well as for publishing a user-friendly RDF visualisation frontend (see Fig. 2b). Although the visualization features provided by ELDA are enough for this use case, some implementations might require more advanced exploitation strategies (e.g. geo-referencing and full text search).

4 Benchmarking

In this section, we outline the results of a benchmarking study that help us to conclude which linked data generation approach is the best for digital repositories. The study involved both a quantitative analysis of their performance in terms of the execution time taken for extracting the repository resources, and a qualitative analysis based on how many extra pre/post processing steps are needed to obtain a valid RDF graph. For the benchmarking, we used a machine with a 2.5 GHz Intel Core i5 processor, 8 GB of RAM, and an internet connection with 86 Mbps.

---

[23] http://190.15.141.102:8891/sparql.tpl.
[24] http://190.15.141.66:8899/ucuenca/recurso.
[25] https://github.com/epimorphics/elda.

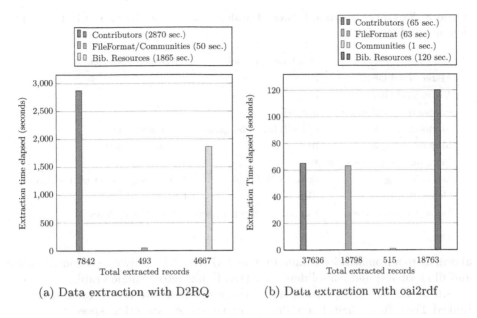

Fig. 3. Benchmarking results

4.1 Database Approach

To evaluate the performance of this method, we measured the average time elapsed during the generation processes and the total number of obtained records (triples in general: contributors, digital resources, etc.) without any transformation, cleaning and/or elimination of triples. For this approach in particular, we used a locally installed Postgres SQL server with an instance of the CDJBV DSpace database schema. Results are shown in Fig. 3a.

During the qualitative analysis of the generated Linked Data chunks, we found some inconsistencies such as incomplete, wrongly generated but unnecessary triples. Those triples had to be eliminated with various regex replacing tasks, and then, chunks were consolidated and validated in a single RDF graph using the Apache Jena tools.

4.2 OAI-PMH Approach

A similar quantitative analysis was performed for this approach, except that records were directly extracted from the CDJBV DSpace production instance using the OAI harvesting protocol and an internet connection. Results shown in Fig. 3b demonstrate that this approach offers a faster execution time compared to extracting bibliographic resources from a local copy of the database, mainly due to its lightweight data transformation mechanism.

On every generated RDF chunk, we had to use a regex sentence to clean unnecessary XML headers that the generation tool creates. Finally, Jena tools

Table 3. Feature comparison between Database and OAI-PMH Linked Data generation approaches

Features	Database approach	OAI-PMH approach
Materialized Gen.	✓	✓
Virtualized Gen.	✓	✗
Supported serializations	.rdf .ttl .n3	.rdf
Mapping definition	R2RML-based language	XSLT stylesheet
Mapping complexity	High	Medium to High
Mapping Lang. extension	✗	✓
Data cleaning	Basic (SQL-based)	XSLT complete set of functions
Generation time	High	Low
Dataset update process	Full dataset regeneration	Differential updates

allows us to automatically eliminate repeated triples (mainly about contributors and file formats) and consolidate all RDF chunks into a single graph.

All in all, the OAI protocol seems to be the best alternative for generating Linked Data from digital repositories in terms of extraction speed time and quality of the dataset (minimum extra cleaning processes after RDF generation). This approach was able to extract contributors 180 times faster than generating the same number RDF resources from the database schema, and 60x faster than *D2RQ* when extracting bibliographic resources. On the other hand, our use case only needed of one single (manual) regex task to clean inconsistencies generated by the *oai2rdf* tool, while *D2RQ* output needed of various manual regex tasks to eliminate wrongly generated triples.

5   Lessons Learned

Table 3 shows a features comparison between both generation approaches. We consider both as valid methods to transform a DSpace digital repository into RDF, but OAI-PMH generation approach was chosen as the best alternative due to the following technical and methodological arguments.

5.1   Technical

- The OAI-PMH approach offers an easily extendable mapping language (XSLT) offers a wide range of data manipulation methods and the capability to create new ones.
- It has the capability to define data cleaning/transforming processes right on the mapping definition file.
- Very low execution time for data extraction and RDF generation compared to the database approach considering that the tool requests data remotely to the DSpace repository via the OAI protocol and that it returns too many repeated triples on controlled vocabularies (however they can be easily removed using Apache Jena command line tool).

- Extracting data directly from the digital repository database schema allow us to retrieve unique correct triples by using the *disintct* statement, but the process takes longer periods of time due to multiple non-efficient (self) join queries performed by *D2RQ*.

5.2 Methodological

- Easy RDF update process: just need to execute the generation process for new records available from the last resumption token that DSpace OAI protocol returned in a previous generation.
- In the database approach, we must have to use separate mapping files and more static mapping sentences like *d2rq:uriPattern* instead of *d2rq:join* (e.g. to relate contributors and bibliographic resources) in order to decrease the generation of too many wrong and repeated triples.
- Due to the metadata stored in the DSpace schema comes from one single table, we experienced some issues such as the above mentioned. However, *D2RQ* output quality RDF representations when the meta-data tables are normalised. Schema transformation solutions will increase the RDF generation time as ETL[26] tasks must be run previously.

It is important to mention that neither approach is easy to perform by non-technical users such as librarians who mostly have little or zero understanding about Linked Data, Semantic Web technologies and/or data mining and data integration techniques. Linked Data generation process still requires of a multidisciplinary team formed by at least Semantic Web experts, software developers and specialists in the domain of data to be performed. However, our method still introduces some advantages such as it does no require to load the repository records into an intermediate relational database model in order to perform necessary data cleaning tasks (used by other approaches), which makes it more faster to execute and easier to use and integrate into a general purpose Linked Open Data generation framework as demonstrated in [25].

6   Conclusions and Future Work

Linked Data generation of the CDJBV DSpace digital repository opened up new possibilities for students and researchers by facilitating the visibility and access of digital bibliographic material as well as by easing the information discovery based on the relationships between digital content, contributors, topics, and other entities of interest for the user.

During the generation process, we concluded that the best way to extract data from a digital repository is through the standard OAI-PMH protocol. Even though this approach generates a lot of repeated triples on such as contributor entities (extracting data directly from the digital repository database schema allow us to retrieve unique correct triples) its performance in terms of execution

---

[26] Extract, Transform, Load (ETL) process in data warehousing.

time is much shorter than the database approach, while additional data cleaning tasks are minimal.

During the benchmarking study, the latter showed that its execution time takes much longer periods of time due to multiple inefficient join queries built by the *D2RQ* tool. Moreover, a database approach generates too many junk information which increases the number of data cleaning processes (that need to be manually performed in some cases). All of this happened due to the denormalised nature of the DSpace database schema.

Future contributions will include the research and development of a platform solution able to cover the complete lifecycle and automate the generation and publication of digital repositories (or any data source) in the Semantic Web. This architecture will allow to non LD expert users to publish their data sources as an enriched Linked Data graph without the need of having strong skills on the Semantic Web technologies, thus increasing the usability and the user experience when facing the LD methodological process. Additionally, the platform will also help to automate the generation process of every DSpace repository of every institution member of CEDIA.

Finally, to improve the user experience when querying to multiple Linked Data digital repositories (through SPARQL query federation presented in [8]), we will work on a novel web interface that aims to enhance the discovery and visualisation of bibliographic resources from any source available on the Linked Data cloud.

References

1. Villazón-Terrazas, B., Vilches-Blázquez, L.M., Corcho, O., Gómez-Pérez, A.: Methodological guidelines for publishing government linked data. In: Wood, D. (ed.) Linking Government Data, pp. 27–49. Springer, Heidelberg (2011). https://doi.org/10.1007/978-1-4614-1767-5_2
2. Alexopoulos, A.D., Koutsomitropoulos, D., Papatheodorou, T.S., Solomou, G.D.: Digital repositories and the semantic web: semantic search and navigation for DSpace. Georgia Institute of Technology (2009)
3. Koutsomitropoulos, D., Solomou, G.D., Papatheodorou, T.S.: Semantic interoperability of dublin core metadata in digital repositories. In: 2008 International Conference on Innovations in Information Technology (2008)
4. Koutsomitropoulos, D.A., Solomou, G.D., Domenech, R.: Dspace semantic search v2. 0: what's new and current status. In: Proceeding of the 7th International Conference on Open Repositories (OR 2012), 9–13 July, Edinburgh (2012)
5. Koutsomitropoulos, D.A., Solomou, G.D., Papatheodorou, T.S.: Semantic query answering in digital repositories: semantic search v2 for DSpace. Int. J. Metadata Semant. Ontol. 8(1), 46–55 (2013)
6. Haslhofer, B., Schandl, B.: The OAI2LOD server: exposing OAI-PMH metadata as linked data. In: International Workshop on Linked Data on the Web (LDOW2008), Co-located with WWW 2008, Beijing, April 2008
7. Piedra, N., Chicaiza, J., Lopez-Vargas, J., Caro, E.T.: Guidelines to producing structured interoperable data from open access repositories. In: 2016 IEEE Frontiers in Education Conference (FIE), pp. 1–9. IEEE (2016)

8. Segarra, J., Ortiz, J., Espinoza, M., Saquicela, V.: Integration of digital repositories through federated queries using semantic technologies. In: 2016 XLII Latin American Computing Conference (CLEI), pp. 1–9. IEEE (2016)

9. Vila-Suero, D., Villazón-Terrazas, B., Gómez-Pérez, A.: Datos. bne. es: a library linked dataset. Semant. Web **4**(3), 307–313 (2013)

10. Lampert, C.K., Southwick, S.B.: Leading to linking: introducing linked data to academic library digital collections. J. Libr. Metadata **13**(2–3), 230–253 (2013)

11. Southwick, S.B.: A guide for transforming digital collections metadata into linked data using open source technologies. J. Libr. Metadata **15**(1), 1–35 (2015)

12. Berners-Lee, T.: Linked Data - Design Issues, July 2006. http://www.w3.org/DesignIssues/LinkedData.html. Accessed 12 Jan 2017

13. Latif, A., Scherp, A., Tochtermann, K.: LOD for library science: benefits of applying linked open data in the digital library setting. KI-Künstliche Intelligenz **30**(2), 149–157 (2016)

14. Das, S., Sundara, S., Cyganiak, R.: R2RML: RDB to RDF mapping language, September 2012. http://www.w3.org/TR/r2rml/. Accessed 13 June 2017

15. Hidalgo-Delgado, Y., Estrada-Nelson, R., Xu, B., Villazon-Terrazas, B., Leiva-Maderos, A., Tello, A.: Methodological guidelines for publishing library data as linked data. In: 2017 IEEE International Conference on Big Data (2017)

16. Anibaldi, S., Jaques, Y., Celli, F., Stellato, A., Keizer, J.: Migrating bibliographic datasets to the semantic web: the AGRIS case. Semant. Web **6**(2), 113–120 (2015)

17. Konstantinou, N., Spanos, D.E., Houssos, N., Mitrou, N.: Exposing scholarly information as linked open data: Rdfizing DSpace contents. Electron. Libr. **32**(6), 834–851 (2014)

18. Konstantinou, N., Spanos, D.-E.: Creating linked data from relational databases. In: Konstantinou, N., Spanos, D.-E. (eds.) Materializing the Web of Linked Data, pp. 73–102. Springer, Cham (2015). https://doi.org/10.1007/978-3-319-16074-0_4

19. Koutsomitropoulos, D.A., Solomou, G.D., Kalou, A.K.: Herding linked data: semantic search and navigation among scholarly datasets. Int. J. Semant. Comput. **9**(04), 459–482 (2015)

20. Piedra, N., Chicaiza, J., Quichimbo, P.: Integración semántica de recursos educativos abiertos cosechados con oai-pmh. proceso aplicado al servicio de búsqueda de oers en la red esvial. de Formación virtual inclusiva y de calidad para el siglo XXI CAFVIR, pp. 337–351 (2015)

21. Piedra, N., et al.: Marco de trabajo para la integración de recursos digitales basado en un enfoque de web semántica. RISTI-Revista Ibérica de Sistemas e Tecnologias de Informação, pp. 55–70 (2015)

22. Hyland, B., Stones, R., Atemezing, I.G., EURECOM, Villazón-Terrazas, B., iSOCO, S.A., I.S.C.: Best practices for publishing linked data, January 2014. http://www.w3.org/TR/ld-bp/. Accessed 12 June 2017

23. Sauermann, L., Cyganiak, R., Ayers, D., Völkel, M.: Cool URIs for the semantic web, December 2008. http://www.w3.org/TR/cooluris/. Accessed 12 June 2017

24. Rodríguez Doncel, V., Gómez-Pérez, A., Villata, S.: A dataset of RDF licenses. In: Legal Knowledge and Information Systems: JURIX 2014: The Twenty-Seventh Annual Conference (2014)

25. Saquicela, V., et al.: LOD-GF: an integral linked open data generation framework. In: Botto-Tobar, M., Barba-Maggi, L., González-Huerta, J., Villacrés-Cevallos, P., S. Gómez, O., Uvidia-Fassler, M.I. (eds.) TICEC 2018. AISC, vol. 884, pp. 283–300. Springer, Cham (2019). https://doi.org/10.1007/978-3-030-02828-2_21

Author-Topic Classification Based on Semantic Knowledge

José Segarra[✉][iD], Xavier Sumba[iD], José Ortiz[iD], Ronald Gualán[iD],
Mauricio Espinoza-Mejia[iD], and Víctor Saquicela[iD]

Department of Computer Science, University of Cuenca, Cuenca, Ecuador
{jose.segarra,xavier.sumba93,jose.ortizv,ronald.gualan,mauricio.espinoza,
victor.saquicela}@ucuenca.edu.ec

Abstract. We propose a novel unsupervised two-phased classification model leveraging from semantic web technologies for discovering common research fields between researchers based on information available from a bibliographic repository and external resources. The first phase performs coarse-grained classification by knowledge disciplines using as reference the disciplines defined in the UNESCO thesaurus. The second phase provides a fine-grained classification by means of a clustering approach combined with external resources. The methodology was applied to the REDI (Semantic Repository of Ecuadorian researchers) project, with remarkable results and thus proving a valuable tool to one of the main REDI's goals: discover Ecuadorian authors sharing research interests to foster collaborative research efforts.

Keywords: Author-topic classification · Knowledge base ·
Data mining · Semantic web · Linked data · Data integration ·
Query languages

1 Introduction

In today's WWW (World Wide Web), the massive amount of bibliographic resources available through a number of digital repositories hinders data discovery and causes that many publications to go unnoticed due to the lack of interpretability of their databases. To overcome this limitation and take advantage of all kind of text resources available on the web, the scientific community has devised text processing technologies specialized in analysis and identification of bibliographic resources content. NLP (Natural Language Processing) and clustering are two well known of such technologies. However, most technologies perform syntactic analysis only and ignore the semantic analysis. This incomplete approach lead to poor results unable to fulfill users' expectations. Semantic web technologies have the potential to fill this missing gap, by preserving the meaning of language elements and make them processable and understandable for people and machines. Likewise, following the aforementioned principle, semantic knowledge bases such as DBpedia have emerged to try and preserve complete

B. Villazón-Terrazas and Y. Hidalgo-Delgado (Eds.): KGSWC 2019, CCIS 1029, pp. 56–71, 2019.
https://doi.org/10.1007/978-3-030-21395-4_5

knowledge by means of structures aimed to maintain not only meanings but also relationships between elements.

In this paper, we focus on the author-topic classification problem, i.e. modeling authors and their respective research fields based on their publications, by means of semantic web technologies. These models are useful to support interactive and exploratory queries over bibliographic resources, including analysis of topic trends, finding authors who are most likely to write on a given topic, discovering potential collaborative groups, among others [9]. Our proposed approach consists of a two-phase classification model: the first phase tries to associate authors to classes obtained from a thesaurus using semantic metrics to assess matching quality; while the second phase leverages clustering techniques to identify research fields associated to authors using information extracted from knowledge bases. The results from this phases are used as inputs to classify authors of scientific publications within automatically generated research areas.

The remainder of the paper is organized as follows. Section 2 reports the related work. Section 3 describes the proposed methodology. Next, Sect. 4 discusses the results obtained after applying the proposed methodology inside the REDI project. Finally, Sect. 5 presents the conclusions and future work.

2 Related Work

To the best of our knowledge, no unsupervised methods for author-topic classification exploiting semantic knowledge have been found. On the other hand, there is plenty of research about document classification, which might serve as a previous step to author classification systems [6]. Text classification methods have become very popular nowadays because of the increasing amount of documents published in digital format and the need to properly exploit them. For this reason, these techniques are very popular in tasks such as text mining, knowledge recovery, information retrieval, among others. There is an extense variety of text classification models; most of them mainly belonging to clustering models and machine learning algorithms, such as SVM, Naive Bayes, k-nearest neighbor, Neural Networks, Boosting strategies, etc. [8]. Leveraging knowledge bases has also been considered as an alternative to the traditional text classification models, and is mainly used to strengthen the process of document classification and clustering. In [12], for example, ontological models are used to improve the distance calculation of fuzzy classification techniques. Other proposals such as [1, 2] harnessed popular knowledge bases such as WordNet[1] as the basis to identify the structure of sentences (e.g. nouns, verbs, adjectives) and extend their meaning during the classification process. In [5], the authors also use Wordnet plus a domain ontology to demonstrate how these knowledge bases help to overcome gaps associated with the syntactic representation of words and obtain better results in the task of documents clustering.

---

[1] https://wordnet.princeton.edu/.

In recent years, Wikipedia[2] has also supported a number of proposals related to text processing, information enrichment, and semantic classification as can be seen in [3,7,10]. This has been possible thanks to the huge amount of information available in Wikipedia and thanks to its growing community support. Thus, recognizing the relevance of Wikipedia in the semantic web domain, the project DBpedia emerged[3] as a semantic knowledge base harnessing most of Wikipedia's information but with an emphasis on using appropriate representation structures designed to facilitate querying and processing by both people and machines. Since its appearance, DBpedia has supported a considerable number of proposals for a variety of applications particularly in the information retrieval field. For instance [4] leverages DBpedia and page-rank techniques to semantically enrich meaning and structure (associated nodes) of data, to offer document categorization methods. Most of the proposals in the same line than [4], focus on document classification, mainly using categorization and clustering techniques according to the scope of the problem to be solved. However, most of those models present a great limitation in their practical application: they require large volumes of data for training. The need for pre-classified text is not trivial, especially when the classification problem does not consider predefined classes. For this reason, we propose an approach to author-topic classification based on the application of heuristics with the help of knowledge bases to offer a two-phased methodology. The proposed method was successfully used to classify authors based on their publications taking as use case the REDI project [11].

3   Author-Topic Classification

The approach presented in this section aims to classify an author to his corresponding research field, by means of a two-phase classification process. The proposed approach is depicted in Fig. 1. Two input parameters feed the process: the first one is a value that allows the unique identification of the author, while the second parameter is a set of keywords of publications in which he has worked. These data are common and easy to obtain for research scenarios, where all publications have associated keywords. For scenarios where there are not keywords, an alternative is to perform a pre-processing step of keyword extraction, which can usually be found in NLP frameworks.

As can be seen in Fig. 1, the result is a two-phased or two-level classification. The first phase is a classification by knowledge disciplines, while the second phase is more specific and includes a classification by research areas. These phases are further described next.

3.1   Phase 1: Classification Based on an External Taxonomy

The first phase of the proposed approach for author-topic classification begins with a general classification with respect to an external taxonomy such as the

---

[2] https://www.wikipedia.org/.
[3] https://wiki.dbpedia.org/.

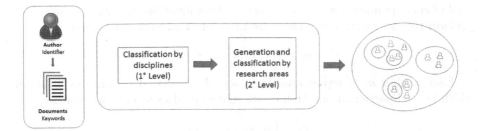

Fig. 1. Overall author-topic classification approach

UNESCO thesaurus[4]. Since the classification is done with respect to a controlled vocabulary (thesaurus), this first phase aims to reduce the number of possible groups or categories in a classification process. We have chosen the UNESCO thesaurus because it is worldwide known and is oriented to the classification of knowledge mainly related to research projects, thus covering several areas of knowledge. The UNESCO taxonomy contains a hierarchical three-level categorization:

- Fields: They refer to the most general sections and comprise several disciplines. They are encoded in two digits.
- Disciplines: They assume a general description of groups of specialties, and are encoded with four digits. Despite being different between themselves or disciplines with cross-references, it is assumed they have common features.
- Subdisciplines: These are the most specific entries in the nomenclature and represent the activities that are carried out within a discipline. They are encoded with six digits.

Initially, the classification process envisaged the use of a single-phase classification process, using an association with the subdisciplines of the UNESCO thesaurus. However, since the subdisciplines were outdated, many recent research areas might be left out. For this reason, it was decided that the UNESCO classification process would be the first classification phase. Additionally, instead of using the most specific subdisciplines, we decided to take as reference the disciplines (second level in the hierarchy), which are more general and remain valid for the intended use.

There are several ways to access the UNESCO thesaurus; however, in this work the SPARQL access point[5] was used. To classify the authors according to UNESCO's second level categories (disciplines), a relatively simple strategy has been chosen: comparing authors, represented by their keywords (from their publications), with each of the disciplines and subdisciplines of the UNESCO thesaurus. This is exemplified in Fig. 2. In this way, the disciplines with a higher

---

[4] http://skos.um.es/unescothes.
[5] http://skos.um.es/sparql/.

level of correspondence will be the one that best identifies the author's work. To perform this operation the authors are therefore represented as follows:

$$a_i = \{d_1, d_2, d_3, ..., d_m\}$$

Each author a_i is represented by a set of associated documents d_i about which he had participation. And, d_i are represented as a set of keywords s_i

$$d_i = \{s_1, s_2, s_3, ..., s_n\}$$

Finally, this implies that the authors a_i can be represented as combined set of the keywords from all their documents in the following way.

$$aS_i = \{s_1, s_2, s_3, ..., s_k\}$$

So that the results do not depend solely on the syntactic representation of keywords, the comparison is also made using semantic metrics (*SemSim*). This semantic metric is provided by the service of cortical.io[6]. Cortical.io, a company focused on *machine learning* and *big data*, has proposed a new data processing and representation methodology known as *Semantic Folding*. Within this representation, concepts are expressed by *semantic fingerprints* able to preserve multiple meanings and contexts and able to be used in several tasks including concept comparison. Cortical has started supporting multiple languages; however, in order to maintain homogeneity in the data and achieve better results, these are translated into English prior to comparison. The calculation of the score for each author with respect to a UNESCO's discipline is represented as follows:

$$ScoreAutorDisc(aS_i, Unesco_j) = \sum_{l=0}^{k} SemSim(s_l, Disc_j)$$

Where $Disc_j$ are the UNESCO's disciplines represented by the concept of the discipline j and the set of subdisciplines that underlies it.

$$Disc_j = \{disc, sub_1, sub_2, sub_3, ..., sub_p\}$$

Once each author has been compared to each of the UNESCO's disciplines and a score has been obtained, the disciplines are ordered such that the highest scored disciplines are associated with the author.

$$Clasf(aS_i) = \{(Unesco_j, ScoreAutorDisc(aS_i, Unesco_j)) \mid Unesco_j \in UNESCO\}$$

For example, according to the first phase of the classification approach, the author exemplified at Fig. 2 is correctly associated with the highest scored disciplines, namely computer science and computer technologies.

---

[6] https://www.cortical.io/.

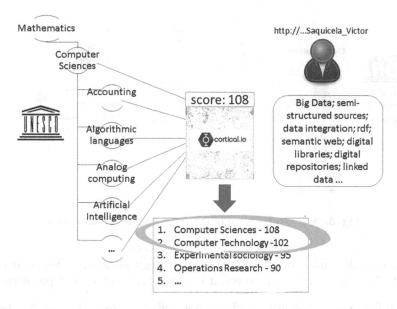

Fig. 2. Example of a semantic association of UNESCO's disciplines with an author

3.2 Phase 2: Classification to a Research Area

The second-level classification is meant to improve the first-level classification presented in the previous section, by providing a more specific approach. As can be seen in Fig. 3, this additional phase aims to group the authors according to their research areas based on their publications. To achieve this goal and given that the clusters (classification groups) are unknown, we intend to use the publications' keywords available to the authors, through a selection and filtering process to identify those that are suitable to be converted into valid classification groups.

The publications' keywords are quite suitable alternatives to be identified as research areas because they are generally relevant words placed by the author to try and reflect the scope of research covered by his work. However, this strategy was not considered as the only classification method because the set of keywords compiled by all the authors and even for the same author is extensive, which makes it difficult to identify valid groups in the face of a large number of possibilities.

To address this problem, firstly the clusters previously formed are taken into account to reduce the universe of keywords to analyze for generating second-level clusters. Taking the keywords from the first-phase clusters (previously identified classification groups) considerably increases the possibilities of finding common or closely related second-phase clusters. The second strategy is to identify the most relevant keywords within the incoming clusters to provide more representative research areas. For this, the most frequent keywords of each first-level

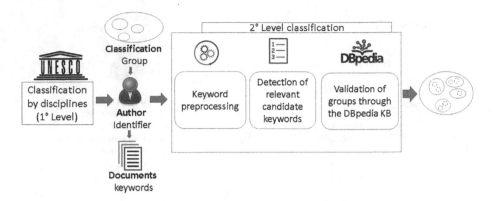

Fig. 3. A general scheme of the second phase classification

cluster are taken into consideration. This strategy alone provides good candidates to form new clusters; however, it is susceptible to the next problems:

- High-frequency keywords which do not reflect a research area: Sometimes high-frequency keywords reflect trivial data. For example, the location "Ecuador" or a word associated with the field "scientific article" may have high occurrence.
- Repeated words with different representation: It may be the case that keywords representing the same concept are repeated several times with different forms or languages. For example "Linked Data" with "Datos enlazados" or "Digital TV" with "Digital Television".

To address the aforementioned problems and select the most suitable keywords as valid research areas in the author classification, we propose using a semantic knowledge base for its validation. Specifically for this task, it is recommended to use DBpedia, which is suitable for the intended purpose because it contains a large amount of information of general nature. Additionally, DBpedia offers services such as *DBpedia Spotlight* to allow associating set of words with DBpedia concepts. Through the use of these tools, we intend to filter those keywords that are of interest for the classification, excluding those that represent very specific entities such as locations, people, among others. Furthermore, the structure containing the knowledge base can be used to refine keywords and detect those that are structurally close or represent the same concept with another representation. To accomplish the second-phase classification it is necessary to execute the following steps:

Data Extraction. The second phase classification begins by collecting keywords from the documents of all the authors listed in the first-phase clusters (UNESCO's disciplines). For example, all the authors belonging to the *computer science* cluster will be queried, and the corresponding keywords will be extracted. Thus obtaining a bag of words or set of words for this cluster.

$$BoW(Cluster_g) = \{aS_1, aS_2, aS_3, ..., aS_i\}$$

In this case, the classification process will not be done by author as in the previous phase, but by cluster. The results of this process will be assigned to the authors.

Keyword Preprocessing. The keywords extracted in the previous step are passed through a series of transformations aimed to correct some problems and help improve the results of this classification. The transformations applied are as follow:

- foreign characters removal (i.e. removing quotation marks, curly brackets, etc.),
- to-lowercase transformation,
- translation to English, and
- duplicated keyword removal (for each author).

Some of these preprocessing steps, such as translation and lowercase transformation, are mainly oriented to improve detection by the DBpedia Spotlight service.

Relevant Keyword Detection. To obtain the most relevant keywords from the words collected above, each one is counted and scored based on its frequency of appearance. From the most often words, the first 50 words are extracted and passed for the next step. If the number of words is less than 50, all of them pass. The defined number is arbitrary and was chosen to reduce the number of possible clusters that must be processed. The idea behind this step is that the keywords selected as research areas are the most relevant within each discipline; and therefore, include the largest number of authors.

Validation of Candidate Clusters Through a Knowledge Base. From the obtained set of keywords, a filtering and refining process is carried out to identify which keywords are suitable as research areas in the classification. To carry out this refinement process, the following tools are used: DBpedia Spotlight service for the detection of DBpedia entities, and DBpedia SPARQL endpoint to expand the information provided by the entities. The inputs feeding this step are the most relevant keywords. DBpedia Spotlight recognizes the input keywords and associates them with DBpedia entities that represent them. This service has the advantage of detecting common entities independent of their syntactic representation. Additionally, when there are multiple possible concepts for a given word, DBpedia Spotlight returns the closest one according to the context. For instance, if it finds *Apple* for computer science keywords, it will return the concept associated to the computer company's brand, instead that of the fruit.

Once the DBpedia concepts associated with the keywords are obtained, this link is used to carry out some additional validation and generalization processes.

Validation consists of recognizing only the keywords that can represent valid research areas. On the other hand, generalization aims to enforce that specific concepts are grouped together into a more general one and therefore the research area envelops the largest number of authors. For example, although concepts such as 'linked data' and 'semantic web' are different, through the structure of the knowledge base it can be discovered that they are close and that one of them encompasses the other. With this strategy, therefore, it is intended to prioritize the most general clusters, i.e. those that would contain the greatest number of elements. For the validation and generalization process the following strategies are followed:

Entity Filtering. Entities identified as persons or locations are ignored as candidate keywords. This is achieved through the type relationship (rdf:type) available to each entity.

Detection of Academic Type Relationships. In DBpedia there is a relationship between two entities known as *academicDiscipline*[7] that is used to identify an academic discipline or field of study and associate it with a scientific journal that contains it. By checking the existence of this relationship, it can be verified that the concept associated with the keyword analyzed can represent a valid area of research and thus obtain more congruent clusters. To detect this type of relationship, several strategies are performed as described below:

1. Direct verification: Checks if the entity has academicDiscipline relationships. If available, it will be marked as a valid research area.
2. Enrichment with parent categories: The parent entities are extracted from the current entity, and then it is checked if they have an academicDiscipline relation. If the entity has only one parent entity, the keyword is automatically identified as a research area.
3. Enrichment with sibling categories: sibling entities having the academicDiscipline relation are extracted from the current entity. If it has a single sibling entity, it is identified as research areas.
4. Direct classification: When there are no other possibilities, it is checked whether the concept is represented as a category independently whether or not it has an academicDiscipline relationship.

The strategies mentioned above are depicted in Fig. 4 and make the best effort to find the relationship of academic discipline both directly and through the knowledge structure. As a secondary result of this step, the possibility of finding common general concepts that encompass other concepts is also increased.

---

[7] http://dbpedia.org/ontology/academicDiscipline.

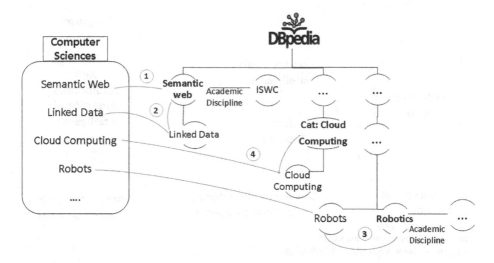

Fig. 4. Validation through the DBpedia structure.

If, after processing all the possibilities, an entity or set of entities that represent the processed keyword has not yet been found, a second pass is made where the following is done:

1. The entities that successfully passed the previous process are stored and identified as research areas.
2. Entities that have not been recognized are processed again, this time taking the parents and siblings of the previous process as a means of comparison. If they coincide with any research area previously obtained, this concept is linked to the matching areas.

An example of the process aforementioned is the cluster of *computer science* (See Fig. 5). In this case, it can be seen that although there is no direct relationship of the concept *mobile robots* with any research area, an indirect relationship through the structure of concepts (*skos:broader*) can be found. The previous proposal aims to maximize the possibility of relating concepts to common research areas among the authors, both directly and indirectly, using the knowledge base structure. The research areas finally obtained are associated with the authors of the keywords which resulted in those research areas. To achieve this, the history of changes applied to the author's keyword until it relates to a valid research area is stored. An example that represents this process is presented in Fig. 6.

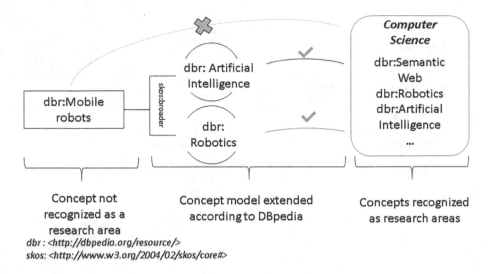

Fig. 5. Example of indirect association (Second pass)

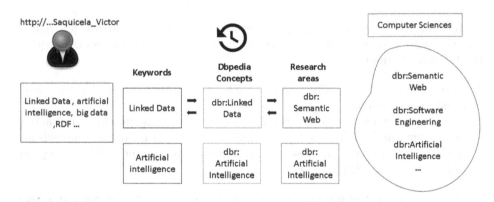

Fig. 6. Example of second-phase cluster assignment to authors

4   Discussion

The described method has been implemented within the REDI project (Semantic Repository of Ecuadorian Researchers), which compiles information related to Ecuador's scientific production. The information encompasses authors, publications, journals, etc. In this case, the main objective of the classification has been to recognize the most relevant research areas of the repository on which the researchers have focused their efforts. Through the execution of the process described in Sect. 3, up to two levels of classification have been achieved. The first based on UNESCO's disciplines, which was identified within the project as a knowledge area. The second-level classification was obtained from the same data with the support of DBpedia and has been recognized as the research area.

Most relevant resulting knowledge areas with their respective research areas are shown in Table 1.

Table 1. Main knowledge areas with their research areas obtained from REDI database

Knowledge areas	Research areas
Computer Sciences	Algorithm, Applied Mathematics, Artificial Intelligence, automation, Big data, Biomedical Engineering, Cloud Computing, Computer Network, Computer Simulation, Computer Vision, Control System, Control theory, Data mining, Data transmission, Decision Theory, Human-Computer Interaction, Image Processing, Information Technology, Machine learning, Mathematical Optimization, Pattern recognition, Risk Management, Robotics, Semantic web, Signal Processing, Social Science, Software Engineering, Systems Engineering, technology, Telecommunication, Theoretical Computer Science, World Wide Web
International Economics	Capitalism, Economic development, economic liberalism, economic policy, foreign direct investment, governance, human rights, international relations, microeconomics, monetary economics, public policy, social justice, social policy, sociology, unemployment
Policy Sciences	Education, Social science, Technology, Agriculture, Ecology, International development, Ethnology, Culture, Economic development, Health, Governance, Social policy, Public policy, Academic publishing, Capitalism, Politics, Environmental policy, Sociology, Youth, Globalization, Poverty, Environmental sociology, Cooperation

Based on the results shown in Table 1, it can be concluded that most of the classifications obtained are acceptable considering that no human intervention was necessary for the identification of the groups and their labeling. However, it can not be omitted that some results are not very intuitive and seem to be incorrect. Analyzing the latter highlights some Research areas not much related to the Knowledge areas. For instance: Biomedical Engineering, Social Science to Computer Sciences; Human Rights, Sociology to International Economics; Education, Technology, Agriculture to Policy Sciences. A further review of these cases reveals that they emerged due to very relevant authors on multidisciplinary works, whereby their keywords relate to several research areas. Another factor

Table 2. Example of authors belonging to the Computer Vision research area

Author	Main keywords
PONGUILLO INTRIAGO RONALD ALBERTO	Kalman filter, robotics, fpga, inertial navigation system, fuzzy logic, unmanned aerial vehicle, computer vision
CHILUIZA GARCIA KATHERINE MALENA	Learning analytics, multimodal learning analytics, human computer interaction, gamification, computer visión, user-centered design, educational data mining
CHANG TORTOLERO OSCAR GUILLERMO	Deep learning, artificial intelligence, image processing, artificial neural networks, machine visión, robotic visión, artificial vision

Table 3. Example of possible authors belonging to Computer Vision excluded by the algorithm

Author	Main keywords
RUEDA AYALA VICTOR PATRICIO	Fuzzy logic, image analysis, mapping, selectivity, site-specific harrowing, machine learning, remote sensing
OCHOA DONOSO DANIEL ERICK	Segmentation, feature extraction, recognition, hyperspectral imaging, image analysis, gene expression, fuzzy logic, unmanned aerial vehicle, social media, tracking
BENALCAZAR PALACIOS MARCO	Pattern recognition, machine learning, hand gesture recognition, image processing, mathematical morphology, neural networks

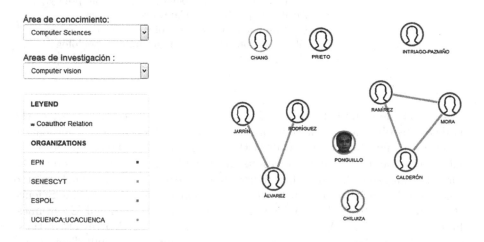

Fig. 7. Example of authors clustering

producing this kind of miss-classification is the lack of precision in the classification of first level authors because the semantic comparison algorithm is still in development and is not mature enough to cover all the topics with enough accuracy. This could be improved by placing minimum requirements on both the quality of the keywords representing an author during pre-processing, and the application of a threshold for the first-level classification process, which filters out ambiguous or low-trust authors.

Also, some sub-disciplines have been found too general and therefore can be placed at the same level of disciplines. Examples of such cases are: Mathematics, Energy, Electronics, Physics, Theory within Computer Sciences; Politics, Sociology within Policy Sciences. This happens because there is no model able to inform and limit the level of granularity in the process of grouping and labeling at the second-level phase (sub-discipline). This could be avoided by mapping the results of the sub-disciplines with respect to the UNESCO model or another standard model which provides a reference for the granularity. These problems will be further analyzed in a future work.

Regarding the conformation of the clusters, it has been noted that most of the authors belonging to these clusters do contain keywords associated with the tag of the generated cluster. This indicates that there is a high probability of membership between authors and the inferred sub-discipline. An example of some authors associated with the Knowledge area of *Computer Sciences* and the research area of *Computer Vision* are presented in the Table 2 keywords has been included as part of the author's name to provide context. On the other hand, it has also been noted that there is a chance the proposed method might leave authors out of their appropriate cluster due to author's keywords do not linked to cluster's relevant keywords. This can be due to multiple factors such as limitations on the knowledge bases or a high level gap between the keyword and a research area that does not allow knowing that they are related. An example of these cases can be seen in Table 3 which lists authors who were not clustered in the *Computer Vision* cluster. A more extensive and rigorous review of the quality of the groups obtained will be carried out in future work.

Finally, the result of clustering authors in the REDI web tool is presented. In this case, it can be seen how the authors are related with the knowledge area of *Computer science* and the *Computer Vision* research area (See Fig. 7). In addition, a complete list of clusters and authors can be found on the official website of the REDI project (https://redi.cedia.edu.ec/#/group/area).

5   Conclusions and Future Work

A two-phased author classification method is proposed. The approach defines 2 levels for generating clusters based on research areas around publications. The method showed remarkable results on the use case of the REDI project, contributing to the main objective of the project: discover authors sharing research interests. Although so far the proposed method has been tested in the scientific field only, with minor adjustments it has the potential to model author classifications in other applications, e.g. bibliography or institutional classifications.

Nevertheless, a notable limitation of the proposed method is that it can not guarantee successful classifications for all the cases. It can not be guaranteed that all authors belong at least to a second level group. As future work, we plan to evaluate the results against other proposals or using a gold standard which provides more clues about the quality of the obtained results. Additionally, it is planned to integrate state-of-art text classification methods and taxonomies to further improve the proposed strategy.

Acknowledgement. This manuscript was funded by the project "Repositorio Ecuatoriano de Investigadores" of the "Corporación Ecuatoriana para el Desarrollo de la Investigación y la Academia" (https://www.cedia.edu.ec/) (CEDIA, Spanish Acronym).

References

1. Bawakid, A., Oussalah, M.: A semantic-based text classification system. In: 2010 IEEE 9th International Conference on Cyberntic Intelligent Systems, pp. 1–6, September 2010
2. Celik, K., Güngör, T.: A comprehensive analysis of using semantic information in text categorization. In: 2013 IEEE INISTA, pp. 1–5, June 2013
3. Ciesielski, K., Borkowski, P., Kłopotek, M.A., Trojanowski, K., Wysocki, K.: Wikipedia-based document categorization. In: Bouvry, P., Kłopotek, M.A., Leprévost, F., Marciniak, M., Mykowiecka, A., Rybiński, H. (eds.) SIIS 2011. LNCS, vol. 7053, pp. 265–278. Springer, Heidelberg (2012). https://doi.org/10.1007/978-3-642-25261-7_21
4. Dostal, M., Nykl, M., Ježek, K.: Exploration of document classification with linked data and pagerank. In: Zavoral, F., Jung, J., Badica, C. (eds.) Intelligent Distributed Computing VII, pp. 37–43. Springer, Cham (2014). https://doi.org/10.1007/978-3-319-01571-2_6
5. Hotho, A., Staab, S., Stumme, G.: Ontologies improve text document clustering. In: Third IEEE International Conference on Data Mining, pp. 541–544, November 2003
6. Korde, V.: Text classification and classifiers: a survey. Int. J. Artif. Intell. Appl. **3**, 85–99 (2012)
7. Milne, D., Witten, I.H.: An effective, low-cost measure of semantic relatedness obtained from Wikipedia links (2008)
8. Sebastiani, F.: Machine learning in automated text categorization. ACM Comput. Surv. (CSUR) **34**(1), 1–47 (2002)
9. Steyvers, M., Smyth, P., Rosen-Zvi, M., Griffiths, T.: Probabilistic author-topic models for information discovery. In: Proceedings of the Tenth ACM SIGKDD International Conference on Knowledge Discovery and Data Mining, pp. 306–315. ACM (2004)
10. Strube, M., Ponzetto, S.P.: Wikirelate! computing semantic relatedness using Wikipedia. In: Proceedings of the National Conference on Artificial Intelligence, vol. 2, 01 2006

11. Sumba, X., Segarra, J., Ortiz, J., Villazón-Terrazas, B., Espinoza, M., Saquicela, V.: REDI: a linked data-powered research networking platform. In: Gangemi, A., et al. (eds.) ESWC 2018. LNCS, vol. 11155, pp. 121–125. Springer, Cham (2018). https://doi.org/10.1007/978-3-319-98192-5_23
12. Zhang, H., Song, H.: Fuzzy related classification approach based on semantic measurement for web document. In: Sixth IEEE International Conference on Data Mining - Workshops (ICDMW 2006), pp. 615–619, December 2006

A General Process for the Semantic Annotation and Enrichment of Electronic Program Guides

Santiago Gonzalez-Toral[1]([✉])(iD), Mauricio Espinoza-Mejia[1],
Kenneth Palacio-Baus[2], and Victor Saquicela[1]

[1] Department of Computer Science, University of Cuenca, Cuenca, Ecuador
{hernan.gonzalezt,mauricio.espinoza,victor.saquicela}@ucuenca.edu.ec
[2] Department of Electrical, Electronic Engineering and Telecommunications,
University of Cuenca, Cuenca, Ecuador
kenneth.palacio@ucuenca.edu.ec

Abstract. Electronic Program Guides (EPGs) are usual resources aimed to inform the audience about the programming being transmitted by TV stations and cable/satellite TV providers. However, they only provide basic metadata about the TV programs, while users may want to obtain additional information related to the content they are currently watching. This paper proposes a general process for the semantic annotation and subsequent enrichment of EPGs using external knowledge bases and natural language processing techniques with the aim to tackle the lack of immediate availability of related information about TV programs. Additionally, we define an evaluation approach based on a distributed representation of words that can enable TV content providers to verify the effectiveness of the system and perform an automatic execution of the enrichment process. We test our proposal using a real-world dataset and demonstrate its effectiveness by using different knowledge bases, word representation models and similarity measures. Results showed that DBpedia and Google Knowledge Graph knowledge bases return the most relevant content during the enrichment process, while word2vec and fast-text models with Words Mover's Distance as similarity function can be combined to validate the effectiveness of the retrieval task.

Keywords: Electronic programming guides · Semantic enrichment · Natural language processing · Word embeddings

1 Introduction

Nowadays public and private TV stations, as well as cable/satellite TV companies, provide Electronic Program Guides (EPG) among their services to inform the audience about programming content being transmitted. These guides, previously created and distributed by a small group through closed-source protocols are now usually published at their websites or mobile applications using

B. Villazón-Terrazas and Y. Hidalgo-Delgado (Eds.): KGSWC 2019, CCIS 1029, pp. 72–86, 2019.
https://doi.org/10.1007/978-3-030-21395-4_6

non-structured description formats such as HTML. However, this approach of exposing information to the user implies two main issues: (i) provided unstructured information can only be understood by humans, and (ii) developed ad-hoc information extraction mechanisms might stop working if the website structure is modified.

Different traditional approaches used to tackle the EPG enrichment problem by applying manual or semiautomatic processes. For example, Ibrahim et al. [1] proposal aimed to improve specific TV program information by using manual and pattern-based annotation tasks to link external data sources to a programming guide. Nevertheless, new mechanisms for EPG annotation and content enrichment are needed with the aim to automate this process.

Motivated by the example above, the present work introduces an improved implementation of the EPG information enrichment method presented in [2]. As main contributions, we propose a general process for the semantic annotation and enrichment of EPGs using external information sources, and assess different evaluation approaches using distributed text representation models [3] and similarity measures that can help to verify the effectiveness of the system without the need of generating a *ground-truth* dataset and/or other additional manual post-processing steps to validate the precision of the retrieval task.

This article is organised as follows. First, Sect. 2 introduces some background concepts and related work about the enrichment of EPGs. Section 3 outlines the problem that needs to be tackled on a typical scenario of EPGs in Latin America. A general process and system architecture for the semantic annotation of EPGs are then described in Sect. 4. Different strategies for evaluating the effectiveness of the approach are shown and discussed in Sect. 5. Finally, Sect. 6 presents some conclusions and future lines derived from this work.

2 Background and Related Work

The advent of digital television has facilitated the management of services and applications provided to users. The service that enables TV content providers to stream information is one of the most important and it is directly related to an electronic programming guide. This (non-)interactive guides usually allow users to either browse for specific TV program information by providing basic metadata values such as title, genre, emission date, etc., and perform keyword-based searches. Results are then presented using static and/or semistructured formats that do not allow the discovery of additional content related to what the user is interested in. The use of ontologies on the other hand allow a smart way for managing data and knowledge sharing among different objects [4], which facilitates the execution of knowledge discovery and enrichment techniques on a dataset.

Different approaches to tackle the EPG enrichment process problem have been proposed during the last years. The European project called NoTube implemented a set of TV content enrichment services using existing web services, a shared background knowledge base, and a middleware for workflow coordination [5]. The enrichment process implied the recognition of entities extracted from EPGs and their annotation through semantic links to concepts and/or entities from other Linked Open Data repositories such as DBpedia, SKOS, and IMDB, while EPG metadata was used to discover additional semantic links that improve the TV programming information.

Some authors have proposed an ontology-based automatic video categorisation method that is used as the mechanism for information retrieval. In [6], a genre-based video classifier was modelled using support vector machines, while in [7], video content is organised by building a hierarchical structure using video frames and a knowledge database. In [8], multimodal concepts were used to represent different categories over the latent semantic space, and then a semisupervised learning approach is employed for ad classification using visual and textual features. The methods described above, however, cannot identify potential relationships between related content unless they have matching metadata.

Kunjithapatham et al. [9] proposed a semantic enrichment of TV programs that maps keywords within EPG metadata to specific topics found on Freebase and an EPG maintained by a private provider, while topic type and related attributes were incorporated as secondary data. Macedo et al. [10] on the other hand enriched soccer events and TV series in Portuguese by extracting related news articles from pre-defined sources using scrappers, and then semantically annotate them using DBpedia. Narducci et al. [11] introduced a semantically enhanced Vector Space Model (eVSM) based on the Rocchio discriminative model [12] which combines keywords and Wikipedia concepts in order to extend and enrich the representation of TV contents and then return the top-N TV programs with highest similarity score. Even if the approach improved a model's recall it did not increase precision.

Zhang et al. [13] introduced a cross-lingual semantic annotation, search and recommendation system, whose data model is defined using a vocabulary similar to the Web Annotation Model,[1]. The annotation module supports interfaces for annotating media data with resources in knowledge bases and performs an offline exploitation of multilingual Wikipedia to extract the cross-lingual groundings of entities. Then a semantic search module applies a data retrieval process to calculate the semantic similarity between items using standard cosine similarity measure and finally rank retrieved media items. The system, however, was built and tested using large datasets contributed by commercial partners.

3   Problem Definition and Motivation

When TV users are enjoying their favourites series or just looking for an interesting program, they usually want to know further details about the content that are about to watch, such as the number of episodes for each season, the actor's biography, related programs, etc. However, current EPGs published by a broadcaster and/or TV service providers in Latin America often provides limited and even incomplete or mismatched content about each TV program. Users are then forced to disturb from what they are watching and make use of a third device (i.e.

---

[1] http://www.w3.org/TR/annotation-model/.

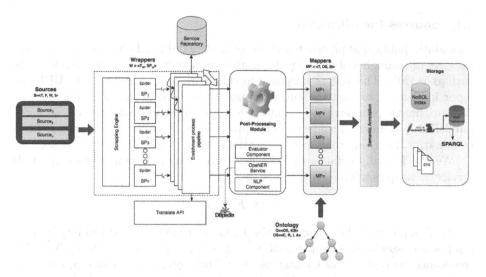

Fig. 1. EPG semantic enrichment system architecture

smartphone, laptop, etc.) in order to get more information from search engines, resulting in information overloading and poor TV experience. Therefore, new system approaches are needed to solve the problem associated with the lack of immediate availability of related information about TV programs, and thus enhance the user experience.

4   General Process for the Enrichment and Semantic Annotation of Electronic Programming Guides

This section presents an overview of our proposed approach for automating the EPG enrichment process using semantic technologies. A description of the system architecture is shown in Fig. 1. The system prototype, inspired by the general model for data mining using Linked Open Data presented in [14], is mainly composed of the following seven components:

(1) *Sources identification*, aimed to retrieve basic information about programming guides from TV content providers; (2) *Wrappers*, used to transform the raw data into formatted information; (3) *Enrichment module*, with a pipeline architecture that allows to plug-in external services and knowledge bases to be used in the enrichment process; (4) *Services Repository*, employed to register external services (web services, SPARQL endpoints, and/or APIs); (5) *Evaluation/Post-processing module*, to perform an evaluation of the enrichment process using Natural Language Processing (NLP) techniques, and subsequently, apply a named-entity recognition post-processing; (6) *Mapping module*, which delineates the retrieved metadata content so far with ontological concepts; and finally, (7) *Semantic Annotation module*, populates the ontology with EPG information and the underlying metadata obtained from different sources.

4.1   Sources Identification

Nowadays, public and private television providers publish EPG contents at their websites or through mobile applications using non-structured description formats such as HTML. The system proposed in this work takes these website URLs as input in order to extract the initial dataset to be used in the following steps of the enrichment process. For demonstration purposes, we make use of the EPG published by *Directv Ecuador*[2], which provides basic content information from both national and international TV stations.

We can formally define an EPG data source (coming from a web page, web service, set-top box, etc.) with the tuple:

$$S = \langle T, F, W, \boldsymbol{I} \rangle \tag{1}$$

where T represents the schema of the EPG, F represents the format, W represents an associated wrapper and $\boldsymbol{I} = \{I_1, I_2, ..., I_j \mid 1 \leq j \leq k; \forall k \in \mathbb{N}\}$ represents the finite set of k instances of S. Therefore, a datasource S_i can have an associated data structure with *schema* T_{S_i} and *format* F_{S_i}, which are common across all pages since this kind of content is usually generated by a system's backend. Then, a *wrapper* W is assigned to it to extract the underlying data from each *j-th* instance I_j of S_i.

4.2   Wrappers

In order to extract the semistructured content of an EPG, scraping techniques need to be implemented. Web scraping is the process that allow data collectors to harvest heterogeneous data of interest from the web. The web crawler framework we opted in to use is *Scrapy*[3], as it allows us to define how a certain (group of) website(s) will be scrapped, including how to perform the crawl (i.e. navigation through links) and how to obtain structured data from their pages (different output formats available). Additionally, we use *Scrapyd* as an application server to deploy a scraping engine that will be in charge of scheduling spiders and executing jobs in multiple processes in parallel.

Therefore, the *wrapper* component is in charge of parsing the semistructured HTML content and transform this into a model that describes the EPG. As soon as an EPG source is registered, the system parses the associated URL and subsequently assigns and schedules a *spider* based on certain parameters. We formally define a wrapper W by the tuple:

$$W = \langle T_W, SP_W \rangle \tag{2}$$

where T_W is a target schema, and SP_W is the corresponding spider program that extracts data with unstructured format F_{S_i} and output instances I_j with schema T_W. Then, the resulting EPG schema $T_{W_{\mathrm{DTV}}}$ is composed by a set of attributes $T = \{t_1, t_2, \ldots, t_n\}$.

---

[2] https://www.directv.com.ec/movil/ProgramGuide/ProgramGuide.
[3] https://scrapy.org/.

4.3   Enrichment Process Using External Sources

The enrichment of an EPG is understood as the process of incorporating new information related to TV programs through the use of knowledge bases and related API services. This process makes use of data fields obtained from previous stages, in addition to an enrichment module with a pipeline architecture that allows to plug-in any external REST/API service. The output will provides useful information such as genre, actors, program categories, etc. that will be employed in next steps to enrich the EPG ontology as well as to evaluate the retrieval task. An indiscriminate execution of these REST/API requests might imply several runtime issues such as limited number of accesses constrained by the service provider. Therefore before these services can be automatically invoked, they must be registered in a *service repository* such that input/output and service parameters can be easily found. The model used for the semantic annotation of RESTful services is documented in [15].

The system's enrichment pipeline in our implementation uses four data service providers as core knowledge bases:

- *Google Knowledge Graph (GKG)*: introduced in [16] as a probabilistic knowledge base that provides a REST API based on standard *schema.org* vocabulary types to find entities in the Google Knowledge Graph.
- *DBpedia Spotlight*: is a REST API that provides a solution framework [17] for linking unstructured information sources to the Linked Open Data cloud through DBpedia knowledge base [18].
- *The Movie Database (TMDb)*: it is a community built movie and TV database with a free and open access REST API that allows the extraction of a varied set of TV content features.
- *DBpedia SPARQL endpoints*: leverages a gigantic source of knowledge bases extracted from Wikipedia in multiple languages[4] through different SPARQL query endpoints.

The order of invocation of the registered services in the enrichment process starts with a batch job in charge of delivering key attributes from each extracted TV program instance in the queue to the next enrichment pipeline processes. In this step, our implementation only uses the title attribute from $T_{W_{\text{DTV}}}$ as required input. Final output is composed by all the new enriched content attributes obtained through the pipeline and transmitted to the following modules using a JSON schema. Each service provider can be formally defined as an external source with the following tuple:

$$ ES = \langle E_I, E_O \rangle \tag{3} $$

where $E_I = \{e_{i_1}, \ldots, e_{i_n}\}$ represents a finite set of terms that are used as input (notice that $E_I = T_W$), whereas $E_O = \{e_{o_1}, \ldots, e_{o_n}\}$ denotes the set of key-value terms $e_{o_i} = \langle label, value \rangle$ obtained from different knowledge bases, being *label* a literal identifier, and *value* a set of results $value = \{v_1, \ldots, v_n \mid \forall n \in \mathbb{N}\}$.

---

[4] http://wiki.dbpedia.org/about/language-chapters.

4.4   Evaluation/Post-processing

Although up to this point an EPG might be already highly enriched, an evaluation of the retrieval process must be performed in order to automatically validate the quality of obtained information to semantically annotate a programming guide. Such task is addressed by implementing a module using *gensim*[5] that applies NLP techniques to process the EPG textual data obtained until the present stage, and which consists of the following components.

Evaluation Submodule. It constitutes of an algebraic model that represent textual documents in the vector space [19]. Each document d within a corpus can be represented as a point in a textitn-dimensional vector space, where n is the number of the distinct terms that occur in the entire corpus:

$$d = \{w_1, w_2, \ldots, w_n\} \tag{4}$$

where w_i is the weight of term t_i in document d. This term weight can be computed using different weighting techniques ranging from simple counting, one-hot vector encoding, up to even more complex models such as TF-IDF and distributed representation of words, known as *word embeddings* [20]. In the latter, words or phrases from a large vocabulary are mapped to a reduced vector representation of real numbers using neural networks and dimensionality reduction techniques.

In our implementation, we experimented with two pre-trained model approaches for word representation:

- *word2vec*: provides an efficient model implementation of the continuous bag-of-words (CBOW) and skip-gram architectures for computing the vector representations of words [21]. We used a pre-trained model with 300-dimensional vectors published by Cardellino [22], which has been trained using a Spanish language corpora of 1.5 million words from different sources.
- *fasttext*: implements a vector representation model for words that takes into account *subword* information, namely, the relationships between characters, within characters and so on, using character-based n-grams [23]. In order to perform text classification, we make use of a pre-trained model in Spanish published by Facebook Research [24]. It is composed of 300-dimensional vectors trained using the Wikipedia corpus.

The main reason of experimenting with both models is because *word2vec* embeddings have reported being slightly better than *fastText* embeddings at the semantic tasks, while the latter performs significantly better on the syntactic analogies, being especially useful for morphologically rich languages and when these words rarely occur. A performance evaluation of both approaches under the retrieval task of TV contents is exposed in Sect. 5.

---

[5] https://radimrehurek.com/gensim/.

In order to measure the relatedness between a ground-truth EPG document d_g and the underlying content extracted during the enrichment process d_e, different geometrical models that rely on the distributional hypothesis [25] can be used. We have adopted to compute the *cosine similarity* SIM_C, using an averaged representation of document terms in the VSM. Document similarity $SIM_C : \mathbb{R}^n \times \mathbb{R}^n \to [0,1] \in \mathbb{R}$ can be calculated using Eq. 5.

$$SIM_C(d_g, d_e) = \frac{d_g \cdot d_e}{\|d_g\|_2 \times \|d_e\|_2} \tag{5}$$

However, the information available for each scraped TV program is composed by a short textual description. In this situation, their vector representation are very sparse and have few or no common words, which results in similarities close to zero even if both documents have similar meanings, as SIM_C does not capture the distance between individual words, but as an averaged representation of words in the whole document.

The *Word Mover's Distance* (WMD) [26] metric (Eq. 6) is able to solve this problem by capturing the dissimilarity between two documents as the cost required to move all words from d_g to d_e, where $\mathbf{T}$ is a sparse flow matrix representing how much of word i in d_g travels to word j in d_e, while $c(i,j) = \|w_i - w_j\|_2$ denotes the Euclidean distance in the word embedding space. We can then use $Sim_{WMD} : \mathbb{R} \to [0,1]$ defined in Eq. 7 to calculate the document similarity using the negative of the distance. This method has reported to perform well at finding short documents that are similar to each other.

$$D_{WMD} = \min_{\mathbf{T} \geq 0} \sum_{i,j=1}^{n} \mathbf{T}_{ij} c(i,j) \tag{6}$$

$$Sim_{WMD} = \frac{1}{1 + D_{WMD}} \tag{7}$$

NER Submodule. Once the extracted EPG data is validated, it can be further semantically improved by using a process to recognize a variety of entities within TV program descriptions. To achieve this, we integrated OpeNER, a language analysis toolchain that includes different NLP components such as Name Entity Resolution (NER) and Named Entity Disambiguation (NED) based on DBpedia Spotlight API and DBpedia knowledge bases. Finally, extracted entities are then used to semantically annotate the EPG ontology.

4.5   Ontology Mapping

At this stage, the EPG content needs to be described using a structured knowledge graph representation, such that its main features can be semantically annotated through described concepts. The required model must be applicable to the audiovisual content domain and must contain at least some basic TV content descriptors. Using a similar definition provided in [27], we can formally define a language mapping between an ontology and the EPG content by the following tuple:

$$O = \langle OS, KB \rangle \qquad (8)$$

where OS represents the ontology schema and KB represents the knowledge base. Furthermore, the ontology schema OS can be defined through the following tuple:

$$OS = \langle C, A, R \rangle \qquad (9)$$

where $C = \{c_1, \ldots, c_m\}$ is a finite set of concepts or classes, $A = \{a_1, \ldots, a_m\} \mid a_i \in C \times L$ is a finite set of attributes of class C and literal value L, and $R = \{r_1, \ldots, r_m\} \mid r_i \in C \times C$ is a finite set of relations between concepts.

On the other hand, the knowledge base KB has a tuple structure in the form:

$$KB = \langle I, f_C, f_A, f_R \rangle \qquad (10)$$

where I is a set of instances with instance identifiers $\{i_1, \ldots, i_n\}$, a function $f_C : C \rightarrow I_C$ for ontology class instantiation, a function $f_A : A \rightarrow I_A$ for attribute instantiation, and a function $f_R : R \rightarrow I_C \times I_C$ for relations instantiation.

From different ontologies for EPG modelling proposed in the literature, we chose the *BBC Programmes Ontology*[6] as it provides a simple mixture of general and specific classes and properties for TV program description. In order to relate the information obtained from previous stages with the selected ontology, we implemented a static mapping process to match entities and properties found for each TV program with the corresponding ontology concepts and attributes. This mapping process MP is then defined as a declarative specification of the semantic overlap between an external source ES and a target ontology O_T with schema OS. It can be denoted with the tuple:

$$MP = \langle ES, OS, M \rangle \qquad (11)$$

where ES and OS were introduced in Definitions 3 and 9 respectively, and $M = \{m_1, \ldots, m_n\}$ is a finite set of mapping elements between the set of TV program descriptors and ontology classes, attributes and relations. We call the elements of M as *one-to-one mappings* because they relate one element of external source ES with schema T_W to one element in the ontology schema OS.

A similar process is also required to map the entities recognized through the NER component with proper relations in the EPG ontology. Therefore, we defined a mapping process $MPER$ in the form:

$$MPER = \langle ES, OS, MER \rangle \qquad (12)$$

where ES is the NER service described in Sect. 4.4, OS represents the annotation model schema, and $MER = \{mper_1, \ldots, mper_n\}$ is a finite set of mappings between a set of entities $\{er_1, \ldots, er_n\}$ and vocabulary relations $\{r_1, \ldots, r_n\}$.

---

[6] http://purl.org/ontology/po/.

Algorithm 1. General process for the enrichment and semantic annotation of electronic programming guides

---

```
EnrichmentProcess (T_s, F_s, M, Sim_score, O_epg, O_ner);
Input: T_s → EPG source schema, F_s → EPG format, M → Word repr. model, Sim → Similarity measure,
       O_epg → Ontology for EPG repr., O_ner → Ontology for NER
S ← new EPGSource(T_s, F_s)
W_S ← get_wrapper(S)
/* W_S is run asynchronously                                                              */
I_S ← W_S.schedule_and_exec_spider()
while TV_show in I_S do
    /* text descriptors to be used as query                                              */
    q ← extract_fields(TV_show)
    lang_q ← lang_detection(q)
    /* Enrichment process                                                                */
    for ES in the pipeline do
        /* Translates only if lang differ from ES language                               */
        ES.E_I ← do_translate(q, lang_ES, lang_q)
        ES.E_O ← ES.execute_extraction()
        if contains_dbpedia_uris(ES.E_O) then
        |   ES.E_O.append(extract_dbp_entities(ES.E_O))
        end
        /* transform text to the VSM for evaluation using model M                         */
        d_g ← M.to_model_representation(Inst_j)
        d_e ← M.to_model_representation(ES.E_O)
        score ← Sim(d_g, d_e)
        if score > threshold then
            ES_ner ← execute_NER(ES.E_O)
            /* Proceeds to ontology mapping                                              */
            M_epg ← get_mappings(OS_epg)
            /* Executes MP                                                               */
            triples_epg ← generate_annotations(ES, OS_epg, M_epg)
            M_ner ← get_mappings(OS_ner)
            /* Executes MPER                                                             */
            triples_ner ← generate_annotations(ES_ner, OS_ner, M_ner)
            store(triples_epg + triples_ner)
        end
    end
end
```

For this scenario, we use the Open Annotation Data Model[7] for semantic entity annotation, and the NERD[8] ontology to manage a unified set of entity class types.

4.6 Semantic Annotation and Storage

Once the mapping process concludes, an ontology is populated with new information obtained from the scrapping, enrichment and entity recognition stages. This procedure is performed by executing SPARQL update sentences on an *Apache Marmotta*[9] triple store. Nevertheless our storage architecture was thought to be extended with the aim to support additional types of storage, such as a NoSQL indexing database to provide further data integration and query capabilities for future client applications.

Algorithm 1 outlines the overall process for enriching and generating semantic annotations on electronic programming guides, while summarizing the formal definition of the system described throughout this sections.

---

[7] http://www.openannotation.org/spec/core/20130208.

[8] http://nerd.eurecom.fr/ontology.

[9] http://marmotta.apache.org/.

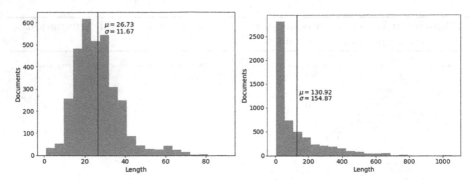

(a) Document length distribution on the initial dataset

(b) Document length distribution of the enriched content dataset

Fig. 2. Word-based document length distribution of datasets

5   Evaluation

In previous sections, we presented a system approach for enriching electronic program guides using semantic technologies and external knowledge bases. This section aims to provide a brief description of the initial EPG dataset extracted during system initialization, and the different experimental setups we defined for our evaluation module. Results of the retrieval task in terms of precision are then shown and compared among experiments. Finally, we present an analysis of the effectiveness of each knowledge base to provide relevant contents for EPGs from Latin America.

5.1   Dataset and Experimental Setup

As mentioned in Sect. 4.1, EPG data was extracted from the Ecuadorian *DirecTV* programming guide available online. To perform an evaluation of the EPG enrichment process, we filtered out content related to sports and news as well as those TV shows with no description provided by the broadcaster. Overall, we obtained 3335 total TV programs from 99 TV stations, distributed in 295 (9%) national and 3040 (91%) international TV shows. During evaluation of the retrieval task, we used *title and synopsis* fields as they can be found on the initial and the enriched content datasets. Document corpus is then built-in using either, or the concatenation of both properties.

Prior to the execution of the experiments, we analyzed the difference between datasets distribution in terms of document length, which is crucial when measuring document similarities. As shown in Fig. 2, the difference is considerable, having in average, short textual descriptions in the scraped EPG and more extensive synopsis in the enriched content. Their distribution reported a *Cohen's d* value of 0.49 standard deviations, which evidenced the difference between document sizes. For this reason, we proceed to experiment with different configurations

Table 1. Configuration properties for experiments

Configuration	Approach	Experiment				
		E1	E2	E3	E4	E5
Text descriptors	Title	✓	✓	✓	✓	✓
	Synopsis	✗	✗	✓	✓	✓
Text pre-processing	Tokenization	✓	✓	✓	✓	✓
	Stopwords removal	✗	✗	✓	✓	✓
Text repr. model	word2vec	✗	✗	✓	✗	✓
	Fasttext	✗	✓	✗	✓	✗
Similarity measures	Pure lexical	✓	✗	✗	✗	✗
	Cosine similarity	✗	✓	✓	✓	✗
	WMD	✗	✗	✗	✗	✓

that allow us to choose the best setup for the evaluation module that can be able to automate the assessment of the EPG enrichment process.

Table 1 presents an overview of the configuration properties for each of the experiments carried out. Specifically, we defined a set of five experiments with different flavours of text descriptors for TV program representation, text pre-processing tasks, document model representation and similarity metrics. For the latter, we adopted the following approaches:

- *Pure lexical similarity*: known as *Ratcliff-Obershelp algorithm*, it computes the similarity of two strings as the number of matching characters divided by the total number of characters in the two strings [28]. We use it as our baseline model to validate the effectiveness of the other approaches.
- *Cosine similarity*: using the *gensim n_similarity* built-in function to compute the cosine similarity (Eq. 5) using an averaged vector representation of document words.
- *WMD*: it first uses the *gensim wmdistance* built-in function (Eq. 6) to compute the Word Mover's Distance between two documents, and then use Eq. 7 to determine the similarity score.

5.2 Experimental Results

Table 2 presents a comparison of the precision score obtained by each of the experiments, as well as the (overall) effectiveness reported by each knowledge base when retrieving national and international TV programs. A TV program is marked as relevant if the similarity score, defined as $sim_{score}(d_e, d_g) \in [0, 1]$, between its content and the gold record surpasses a threshold. In addition, *Max-precision* in our context was defined as the system's capability of retrieving at least one relevant document per TV show from any knowledge base.

Using the *fasttext* model to find similar content based on the concatenation of title and synopsis (E4) obtained the worst performance, with a max-precision

Table 2. Comparison of precision results between experiments and external knowledge bases

Exp.	External knowledge base									Max. precision
	DBpedia			GKG			TMDB			
	Nat	*Int*	*Overall*	*Nat*	*Int*	*Overall*	*Nat*	*Int*	*Overall*	
E1	20.22%	39.69%	28.67%	22.47%	47.62%	33.98%	7.86%	58.33%	37.35%	**57.76%**
E2	34.83%	51.19%	33.33%	23.59%	52.38%	31.89%	5.62%	64.28%	34.78%	**69.67%**
E3	46.29%	49.05%	50.37%	22.39%	23.33%	23.88%	5.97%	30.48%	25.75%	**61.37%**
E4	34.33%	36.19%	45.62%	13.43%	20.95%	24.42%	4.48%	29.05%	29.96%	**50.54%**
E5	40.30%	38.10%	31.10%	40.30%	53.81%	40.70%	20.9%	39.05%	28.20%	**68.95%**
Avg.	35.19%	42.84%	37.82%	24.44%	39.62%	30.97%	8.97%	42.16%	31.21%	

that could not improve the score reported by the baseline (E1). However, this model outperformed all other setups obtaining a max-precision score of 69.67% when finding the similarity of TV content using only their TV program title information (E2). On the other hand, the *word2vec* model with *WMD* as similarity measure (E5) nearly approximated to the score of our best evaluation method even if it also uses TV synopsis during evaluation, which evidence the robustness of this approach when using longer text descriptors to find similar items. Nevertheless, in terms of algorithm complexity, WMD requires $O(p^3 log p)$, where p denotes the number of unique words in the documents, which does not scale under scenarios with large number of documents with unique words.

In terms of the effectiveness for each knowledge base in providing relevant content for EPGs in Latin America, *DBpedia* obtained the highest number of relevant TV program entities in general and for content related to national TV shows, while *TMDB* demonstrated not to be a good knowledge base for local contents. Nonetheless, it obtained, on average, slightly more relevant documents than the other external sources when only considering international TV programs. Finally, it is important to mention that even if the *GKG* knowledge base did not return as many relevant contents than the other information sources, it was very useful to find a more concise synopsis and relevant linkages to Wikipedia entities that could not be directly retrieved using the *DBpedia Spotlight* API.

6   Conclusions and Future Work

In this work, we propose a general process for the semantic annotation of EPGs in Latin America, as well as an evaluation method of the enrichment process that enables an automatic execution of the retrieval task. Experimental findings demonstrated that the *fasttext* model with cosine similarity obtained the best performance (almost 12% better than the baseline) when finding similar TV programs by their title, which is an expected result since it was reported to perform well on syntactic tasks. On the other hand, the *word2vec* model with WMD obtained nearly the same precision score than *fasttext* by using both title and synopsis information to compute the similarity score. Therefore, either model and/or an ensemble of both are then recommended to be used in a module that evaluates the enrichment process of an EPG, however a more scalable implementations of WMD to linear complexity should be considered [29].

We believe that almost 70% precision can be thought as a considerable but not sufficiently enough for a retrieval system. One of the main reasons we obtained such score is mainly due to the large difference in content between the gold description and the retrieved synopsis information even if they relate to the same TV program. An analysis of the data obtained by our system showed that while many of the short descriptors contain a concise overview of what an TV episode is about, synopsis from *DBpedia* usually contains more information about the cast, producers, release date, number of seasons and episodes, etc. To overcome this problem, we should consider adding other knowledge base data properties and linkages (e.g. DBpedia links to TV program seasons information).

As a future work, we will explore other evaluation approaches to measure the semantic similarity between TV contents such as cross-lingual explicit semantic analysis and graph-based similarity measures. Additionally, we will experiment with other text representation models such as *Doc2Vec* and *RDF2Vec*. Next system iteration will integrate a real-time data streaming module to allow the semantic annotation and enrichment of live audio/video content to provide recommendations to the users *on-the-go*.

References

1. Ibrahim, A., Choi, H.J.: Role of annotation in electronic process guide (EPG). In: Future Generation Communication and Networking (FGCN 2007), vol. 2, pp. 569–572. IEEE (2007)
2. Saquicela, V., Espinoza-Mejía, M., Palacio, K., Albán, H.: Enriching electronic program guides using semantic technologies and external resources. In: 2014 XL Latin American Computing Conference (CLEI), pp. 1–8. IEEE (2014)
3. Bengio, Y., Ducharme, R., Vincent, P., Jauvin, C.: A neural probabilistic language model. J. Mach. Learn. Res. **3**(Feb), 1137–1155 (2003)
4. Gruber, T.R.: A translation approach to portable ontology specifications. Knowl. Acquisition **5**(2), 199–220 (1993)
5. Aroyo, L., Nixon, L., Miller, L.: Notube: the television experience enhanced by online social and semantic data. In: 2011 IEEE International Conference on Consumer Electronics-Berlin (ICCE-Berlin), pp. 269–273. IEEE (2011)
6. Yuan, X., Lai, W., Mei, T., Hua, X.S., Wu, X.Q., Li, S.: Automatic video genre categorization using hierarchical SVM. In: 2006 IEEE International Conference on Image Processing, pp. 2905–2908. IEEE (2006)
7. Smoliar, S.W., Zhang, H.: Content based video indexing and retrieval. IEEE Multimedia **1**(2), 62–72 (1994)
8. Wang, J., Duan, L., Xu, L., Lu, H., Jin, J.S.: TV ad video categorization with probabilistic latent concept learning. In: Proceedings of the International Workshop on Workshop on Multimedia Information Retrieval, pp. 217–226. ACM (2007)
9. Kunjithapatham, A., Rathod, P., Gibbs, S.J., Sheshagiri, M.: Enabling topic-based discovery of television programs. In: Proceedings of the International Workshop on Cross-Media Information Access and Mining (CIAM 2009), p. 43 (2009)

10. Macedo, P., Cardoso, J., Pinto, A.M.: Enriching electronic programming guides with web data. In: Proceeding of the 2nd International Workshop on Linked Media (LiME2014), Crete, Greece (2014)
11. Narducci, F., Musto, C., de Gemmis, M., Lops, P., Semeraro, G.: TV-program retrieval and classification: a comparison of approaches based on machine learning. Inf. Syst. Front. **20**, 1157–1171 (2017)
12. Rocchio, J.J.: Relevance feedback in information retrieval. In: The Smart Retrieval System-Experiments in Automatic Document Processing (1971)
13. Zhang, L., Thalhammer, A., Rettinger, A., Färber, M., Mogadala, A., Denaux, R.: The xLiMe system: cross-lingual and cross-modal semantic annotation, search and recommendation over live-TV, news and social media streams. J. Web Semant. **46**, 20–30 (2017)
14. Ristoski, P., Paulheim, H.: Semantic web in data mining and knowledge discovery: a comprehensive survey. Web Semant.: Sci. Serv. Agents World Wide Web **36**, 1–22 (2016)
15. Saquicela, V., Vilches-Blázquez, L.M., Corcho, O.: Adding semantic annotations into (geospatial) restful services. Int. J. Semant. Web Inf. Syst. **8**(2), 51–71 (2012)
16. Dong, X.L., et al.: Knowledge vault: a web-scale approach to probabilistic knowledge fusion. In: The 20th ACM SIGKDD International Conference on Knowledge Discovery and Data Mining, KDD 2014, 24–27 August 2014, New York, NY, USA, pp. 601–610 (2014)
17. Daiber, J., Jakob, M., Hokamp, C., Mendes, P.N.: Improving efficiency and accuracy in multilingual entity extraction. In: Proceedings of the 9th International Conference on Semantic Systems (I-Semantics) (2013)
18. Auer, S., Bizer, C., Kobilarov, G., Lehmann, J., Cyganiak, R., Ives, Z.: DBpedia: a nucleus for a web of open data. In: Aberer, K., et al. (eds.) ASWC/ISWC -2007. LNCS, vol. 4825, pp. 722–735. Springer, Heidelberg (2007). https://doi.org/10.1007/978-3-540-76298-0_52
19. Baeza-Yates, R., Ribeiro-Neto, B., et al.: Modern Information Retrieval, vol. 463. ACM Press, New York (1999)
20. Hinton, G., McClelland, J., Rumelhart, D.: Distributed representations. Inparallel distributed processing: explorations in the microstructure of cognition (1986)
21. Mikolov, T., Chen, K., Corrado, G., Dean, J.: Efficient estimation of word representations in vector space. arXiv preprint arXiv:1301.3781 (2013)
22. Cardellino, C.: Spanish Billion Words Corpus and Embeddings, March 2016. http://crscardellino.me/SBWCE/
23. Bojanowski, P., Grave, E., Joulin, A., Mikolov, T.: Enriching word vectors with subword information. arXiv preprint arXiv:1607.04606 (2016)
24. Joulin, A., Grave, E., Bojanowski, P., Mikolov, T.: Bag of tricks for efficient text classification. arXiv preprint arXiv:1607.01759 (2016)
25. Mohammad, S.M., Hirst, G.: Distributional measures of semantic distance: A survey. arXiv preprint arXiv:1203.1858 (2012)
26. Kusner, M., Sun, Y., Kolkin, N., Weinberger, K.: From word embeddings to document distances. In: International Conference on Machine Learning, pp. 957–966 (2015)
27. Scharffe, F., de Bruijn, J.: A language to specify mappings between ontologies. In: SITIS, pp. 267–271 (2005)
28. Ratcliff, J.W., Metzener, D.E.: Pattern-matching-the gestalt approach. Dr Dobbs J. **13**(7), 46 (1988)
29. Atasu, K., et al.: Linear-complexity relaxed word mover's distance with GPU acceleration. CoRR abs/1711.07227 (2017). http://arxiv.org/abs/1711.07227

Extraction of RDF Statements from Text

Jose L. Martinez-Rodriguez[1]([✉]), Ivan Lopez-Arevalo[1], Ana B. Rios-Alvarado[2],
Julio Hernandez[1], and Edwin Aldana-Bobadilla[1]

[1] Cinvestav Tamaulipas, Victoria, Mexico
{lmartinez,ilopez,nhernandez,ealdana}@tamps.cinvestav.mx
[2] Faculty of Engineering and Sciences, UAT, Victoria, Mexico
arios@uat.edu.mx

Abstract. The vision of the Semantic Web is to get information with
a defined meaning in a way that computers and people can work col-
laboratively. In this sense, the RDF model provides such a definition
by linking and representing resources and descriptions through defined
schemes and vocabularies. However, much of the information able to be
represented is contained within plain text, which results in an unfea-
sible task by humans to annotate large scale data sources such as the
Web. Therefore, this paper presents a strategy for the extraction and
representation of RDF statements from text. The idea is to provide an
architecture that receives sentences and returns triples with elements
linked to resources and vocabularies of the Semantic Web. The results
demonstrate the feasibility of representing RDF statements from text
through an implementation following the proposed strategy.

Keywords: Semantic Web representation · RDF representation ·
Entity linking · Relation extraction · RDF statements

1 Introduction

The Semantic Web refers to an extension of the traditional Web, which has an
important goal of providing a formal data representation that enables the sharing and reuse of information by people and applications [1]. This goal is being
addressed by varied standards and protocols, such as the Resource Description
Framework (RDF) and the Linked Open Data (LOD) principles [2]; on which the
data are represented through basic units of information called RDF triples, each
one composed of *Subject-Predicate-Object* elements. In consequence, the data are
organized into a knowledge graph where the nodes correspond to information
resources (such as real-world objects, *aka* "entities") and edges to descriptions
(that adopt formal vocabularies or ontologies[1]) or relationships between such
resources. Additionally, every resource (node/edge) must be individually identified through Internationalized Resource Identifiers (IRI) and retrieved (deref-
erenced) via the HTTP protocol to provide more information of the resource
through the Internet (as is done on the traditional Web).

---

[1] An ontology defines the concepts, terms, classes, taxonomies, and rules of a
domain [11].

© Springer Nature Switzerland AG 2019
B. Villazón-Terrazas and Y. Hidalgo-Delgado (Eds.): KGSWC 2019, CCIS 1029, pp. 87–101, 2019.
https://doi.org/10.1007/978-3-030-21395-4_7

The Semantic Web information representation usually follows a process focused on extracting knowledge elements[2] to later associate them with (unambiguous) identifiers (IRIs) based on ontology descriptions and standards of the RDF model. In consequence, the information represented through RDF triples can be used to create or enrich a Knowledge Base (KB) that can be queried using the SPARQL language[3]. Hence, in order to represent plain text sentences[4] as RDF triples, relevant elements should be extracted from text (e.g., named entities and their relationships) to then associate them with the elements of the RDF triple. For instance, the sentence *"Ciudad Victoria is a town located in the state of Tamaulipas"* can be represented by RDF triples in two ways as depicted in Fig. 1. While the option (a) uses a binary statement (two resources linked by a property), the option (b) relies on an n-ary statement (more than two resources linked to various properties) [15].

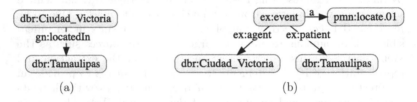

(a)   (b)

Fig. 1. Example of a sentence represented through RDF triples. (a) Indicates a binary statement; (b) Indicates an n-ary statement.

From the Fig. 1, both representations are used to describe the same idea within the sentence. In this way, binary statements link two resources (or a resource and a literal value) through a property from a KB. On the other hand, n-ary statements allow a resource to be linked to one or more resources and/or literal values. n-ary statements are useful for describing particular events/situations involving diverse actors; for example, in a product sale we may find actors such as the buyer, seller, and the product. However, it is often difficult to know the exact role of the actors in a sentence. Hence, in the example of Fig. 1b the actors of the event (`ex:event`) are denoted by semantic roles[5], in which the *causer* of the event (or action) is denoted by the property `ex:agent`, the *undergoer* by the property (`ex:patient`), and the type of event by the letter

---

[2] In this context, knowledge elements refer to Conceptual Knowledge [22] in terms of things or concepts and the way they are related to each other with the support of an ontology.

[3] https://www.w3.org/TR/sparql11-overview/. All URLs in this paper were last accessed on 2019/04/15.

[4] Different to formatted text, plain text does not contain any style information or graphical objects and refers to only readable characters.

[5] Semantic roles identify the participants in an event guided by a verb and its underlying relationship [13].

a or rdf:type, to mention a few. Note that we model n-ary statements according to the reification options presented by Hernández *et al.* [15], where a relation is modeled through a resource instead of a property, which can be annotated with meta-information. Note that particular implementations (through tools or strategies) of the tasks involved within the proposed methodology depends on the modeler decisions according to the type of addressed statement (i.e., binary or n-ary).

According to the previous example, the representation of sentences as RDF triples faces varied difficulties and challenges to detect the two main elements of a statement: named entities and their semantic relations. Moreover, in the context of the Semantic Web, such elements must be associated with resources and properties from an existing ontology (or KB) respectively. Therefore, this paper proposes a methodology for the extraction and representation of RDF statements from text. Particularly, binary and n-ary RDF statements from plain text sentences. The aim is to provide a way to represent such statements through a methodology that encompasses the interaction of diverse tasks from areas such as Information Extraction (IE) and Natural Language Processing (NLP). As a proof of concept, we present a strategy for the extraction and representation of n-ary statements from plain text, where specific tools and strategies are configured and implemented in order to fulfill the tasks presented in the proposed methodology. This implementation is useful for presenting an initial evaluation of the proposal, which involves the participation of human judges on topics such as news and tourism.

2   State of the Art

General strategies and recommendations for the information representation on the Semantic Web have been performed so far. In this regard, Bizer and Heath [14] described the Linked Data operation sequence for publishing semantic information. Their architecture is organized into three stages that receive distinct input sources. First, a preparation stage parses structured text or processes unstructured data through NLP tools. The second stage is intended to extract and store entities and parsed elements obtained from the text. Finally, the information is published using a web server. The difficulty of this approach relies on the lack of association of resources with Semantic Web resources.

Another representation strategy is provided by the FOX (*Federated knOwledge eXtraction*) framework[6], which generates RDF data by using Named Recognition (NER), Keyword Extraction (KE) and Relation Extraction (RE) algorithms within an architecture composed of three layers: Automatic Learning layer, for training a module with the best-performing tools and categories; Controller layer, to coordinate information and parsing tools; and Tools layer, containing a repository of tools such as NLP services and data mining algorithms.

Similarly, Auer *et al.* [3] identified three branches for extracting features used for representing RDF triples from unstructured text: NER to extract entity labels

---

[6] FOX framework. http://aksw.org/Projects/FOX.html.

from text, KE to recognize central topics, and RE to extract properties that link entities. Moreover, authors also state that a disambiguation task is necessary to obtain adequate URIs for every resource within the extracted RDF triples. This task is conducted employing entity matching over KBs like DBpedia[7] or FreeBase[8]. Along these lines, based on the previous steps, approaches such as [5, 10,17,25] obtain entities through NLP tools, apply morphosyntactic analysis and lexical databases like WordNet[9] to extract and disambiguate elements from text using existing vocabularies.

On the other hand, according to the type of extraction, we distinguished three groups of approaches that extract RDF statements from text using NLP and/or machine learning techniques. First, discourse-based approaches [5,12] employ a framework for describing lexical meaning in terms of a set of predicates (Frames) and their arguments (Frame Elements)[10], where the elements are directly mapped to properties of a KB through n-ary statements. Second, pattern-based approaches [9] generate patterns (pattern induction) that describe conventional relations from the text, where properties could be directly mapped to a KB or obtained by semantic similarity matching. Third, machine learning-based approaches [4] use semantic and syntactic annotations together with information from a KB to obtain features used for training a machine learning algorithm (mainly a supervised strategy), where properties of binary relations are directly associated through the training data.

The above approaches are consistent regarding the stages such as the extraction of features from text, named entities, and semantic relations. However, such approaches provide only a brief overview of basic architectures to extract and publish information as RDF statements, which do not state stages for the association of relations with properties and the organization of elements that should be part of the final statements. Thus, the following section provides the proposed methodology containing the tasks and components involved in the representation of RDF statements on the Semantic Web.

3   Methodology

This section presents the proposed methodology for the representation of RDF statements from text. It consists of the architecture presented in Fig. 2, which is composed of three main stages: Data Layer, Knowledge Extraction Layer, and Representation Layer. Such stages cover several tasks and components involved in the representation of statements on the Semantic Web such as the diverse types of input data (domains), representation structures (RDF reification), and representation formats.

A description of the stages within the proposed architecture is presented in the following subsections.

---

[7] https://wiki.dbpedia.org.

[8] https://developers.google.com/freebase/.

[9] WordNet is a lexical database for English http://wordnet.princeton.edu.

[10] From a First Order Logic perspective, the predicate of a sentence corresponds to the main verb and any auxiliaries surrounding it.

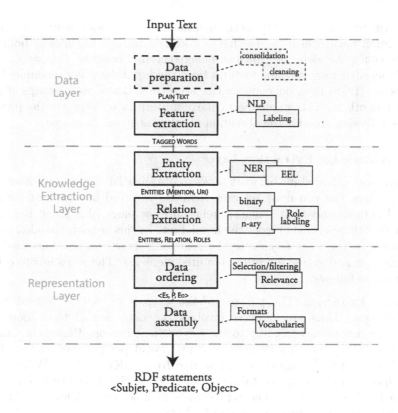

Fig. 2. Architecture for the representation of RDF statements from text

3.1 Data Layer

The first stage of the architecture refers to operations performed over the initial data in order to clean and obtain features used in further steps. In this sense, we only consider unstructured text (plain text) as input data to the architecture[11]. This stage is composed of the following steps:

- Data preparation. The input data might be given in diverse formats (e.g., PDF, Word). The purpose of this step is to merge the diverse sources that could be presented for the architecture in order to get a homogenized data source. Moreover, the input data often contains superfluous annotations that are not useful for the proposed strategy. For example, formatting tags (e.g., HTML). In this sense, this step is aimed at applying cleaning and parsing operations over the input text, so that plain text is finally obtained. Note that this step is optional because the text might be provided as plain text.

---

[11] Although the architecture only admits plain text as input data, there are several types of data that could be considered such as structured data (e.g., databases, tables), images, or raw data (e.g., data from sensors).

– Feature extraction. As previously mentioned, we consider plain text sentences as input data, which means that it does not include features or boundaries describing the elements that can be extracted. Therefore, this step is aimed at identifying and tagging features from the input data. For example, Part of Speech (POS) tags, dependency tree structures that denote groups of nouns, among others. This step is particularly important to facilitate the process of the following step for the obtention of relevant items from text.

3.2 Knowledge Extraction Layer

The strategy followed in this work seeks to obtain RDF binary and n-ary statements. Thus, the two most relevant elements involved in such statements are named entities and their semantic relation. Therefore, this stage is aimed at extracting these elements from the input text. In this regard, the idea is to get support from the *Data Layer* stage by providing structures and tags used in the organization and extraction of the required elements. The steps involved in this stage are as follows:

– Entity Extraction. The purpose of this step is to extract Named Entities from text. Thus, this process involves the detection of those nouns that can be described according to their type (i.e., Person, Place, etc.) and the resources representing them from a real-world perspective; that is, linking a found entity[12] mention to a resource from a KB such as Wikidata[13] or DBpedia. This complete task is known as *Entity Extraction and Linking* (EEL). The output of this step consists of a set of Entities, in which each element contains the mention and its URI.
– Relation Extraction. A subsequent and important process is to detect how those previously found entities are related to each other. Thus, this step is aimed at detecting semantic relations between entities from text. However, as presented in the introduction, there are different types of statements according to the level of detail and context that needs to be extracted; binary and n-ary relationships. While the former lead to declare two resources joined by a property, the latter involves an exhaustive analysis to get several resources involved in the same idea and the correct relationship among them[14]. Together with the set of entities, the output of this step contains the identified relation between entities and the roles that denotes the activity of entities (e.g., the causer of an action).

3.3 Representation Layer

Once the entities and their relationships are extracted from the input text, the next task is to order such elements to make the final representation of statements using standards of the Semantic Web. This stage involves the following steps:

---

[12] In this work, we indistinctly refer to named entities as only entities.
[13] www.wikidata.org.
[14] This process is often supported by the Semantic Role Labeling task, which helps to determine the role or action performed by an entity within a statement.

– Data ordering. The previous stage considers the identification of entities and their role on the statement –as performed by Semantic Role Labeling (SRL)–. Thus, this step is in charge of determining the correct position of an entity within the final RDF triple. That is, positioning an entity as the subject/object within a binary statement or as the agent/patient within an n-ary statement (as described in Fig. 1b). In any case, the relationships on both statements must be linked to properties in a KB, on a process known as *property selection*. Thus, a property can be obtained from a KB by an entity matching comparison [9] or by direct string mappings [12], to mention two. Moreover, the property selection is often accompanied by a score that measures the level of matching between the predicate of a semantic relation and a property from a KB. Thus, this step also involves filtering irrelevant statements according to a score or function. Note that the complete process of extracting semantic relations and linking the components to resources and properties from a KB is known as *Relation Extraction and Linking* (REL) [21]
– Data assembly. This final step involves the formatting of statements. Therefore, it should be able to export the information on diverse formats (e.g., Turtle, XML/RDF). In some cases (e.g., n-ary statements), the representation also involves the declaration of descriptions through defined vocabularies. For example, including provenance information that allows the represented data to be evaluated according to the original data.

The next section provides the implementation of a version of the proposed methodology, where n-ary statements are extracted and represented from text.

4 Implementation Focused on n-ary RDF Statements

This section presents the steps followed for the implementation of a version of the proposed methodology. This is because several IE and NLP approaches are involved in the process, which can be replaced by others that cover the same purpose. Although such a methodology provides the steps involved in the representation of either binary and/or n-ary statements, we only cover the extraction and representation of n-ary statements (see Fig. 1), which is useful for describing the resources and their performed role within an action/event stated in a text sentence (we plan to include a strategy to extract binary statements in a future work). In this regard, the implementation was developed as a Java application. Thus, some internal configuration details of the Information Extraction and NLP tools and services used by the application are provided in this section with respect to the architecture depicted in Fig. 2.

Data layer. Although we assume that the input data is given as plain text that does not require further cleaning operations, the following tasks were applied:

– Feature extraction. This step is intended to perform NLP tasks through the Stanford CoreNLP tool [19], where models for English[15] were used in the

---
[15] Stanford CoreNLP models https://stanfordnlp.github.io/CoreNLP/.

configuration. Hence, this step performs the following tasks: tokenization of words, sentence segmentation, Part of Speech (POS) tagging, and structural parsing (*constituency tree* parsing). Additionally, we also performed a strategy to expand language contractions; for example, converting words such as *aren't* into *are not*.

Knowledge Extraction Layer. We performed tasks for the extraction of entities and semantic relations as follows:

- Entity Extraction. Entities were extracted and linked to a KB by following the strategy presented in [20], where four EEL systems were configured (DBpedia Spotlight, TagMe, Babelfy, and WAT) and integrated into an ensemble-like system. Additionally, it was developed a Java module that takes as input a sentence (and its constituency tree extracted by the feature extraction step) and the entities extracted in the EEL step to return entities grouped by noun phrases (NP); which is intended to preserve the coherence of ideas (in order to not decompose entities that belong to the same unit of information).
- Relation Extraction. The extraction of semantic relations was performed through the OpenIE tool ClausIE [8], which was configured using default parameters to obtain only binary relations. Additionally, Mate-Tools[16] was used for obtaining semantic roles (SRL) associated with entities and predicates (verbs) of the identified semantic relations. In this regard, predicates and arguments provided by Mate-Tools are based on annotations of the lexical resource PropBank. The data models used by Mate-Tools for internally parsing, lemmatizing and tagging were the CoNLL2009 models for English[17]. Note that, although we extract binary relations, the final representation results in n-ary statements by representing the thematic roles (i.e., agent, patient, predicate) and additional elements (e.g., original sentence).

Representation Layer. The final representation of entities and relations was as follows:

- Data ordering. Entities in the input sentence were selected according to the roles detected by the SRL tool (Mate-Tools). However, if the role is not identified, the entity near to the verb (within the semantic relation) is selected. Moreover, to obtain an identifier for the event/action expressed in the semantic relation, we leverage the predicate sense identified by Mate-Tools to perform a SPARQL query over the Premon KB[18], requesting the resource with the label (`rdfs:label`) matching the identified predicate sense. For such purpose, a Jena[19] module was implemented, using the SPARQL 1.1 syntax.

---

[16] MatePlus https://github.com/microth/mateplus.
[17] Data models downloaded from https://code.google.com/archive/p/mate-tools/downloads.
[18] https://premon.fbk.eu/query.html.
[19] Jena https://jena.apache.org.

– Data assembly. A Jena module was implemented for organizing all event-based information obtained from sentences and documents throughout the pipeline. In other words, this step represents events that contain a predicate and its arguments (*Agent* and *Patient*), which are represented by an *n*-ary reification model using the TriG[20] format.

5   Evaluation

This section presents the evaluation of the method for the representation of RDF statements. In this sense, two types of evaluation were performed, quantitative and qualitative. First, we obtained the total number of RDF triples represented by the method (including entities and relations). Second, we evaluated the precision of such data. The experiments were performed over a computer with OS X Yosemite, Intel Core i5, and 8 GB RAM. The next section provides details of the datasets used for the experiments.

5.1   Datasets

The experiments were performed over three datasets:

– IT news. It contains 605 documents regarding the IT domain manually extracted from sites such as DailyTech[21] and ComputerWeekly[22].
– LonelyPlanet[23]. It consists of 1801 webpage documents containing descriptions of places such as countries, cities, and so on. The HTML content of the retrieved webpages have been cleaned and converted to plain text, it contains over one million of tokens. This dataset was used by Cimiano [7] for the ontology learning task.
– BBC news. This dataset contains 2225 documents extracted from the BBC news website[24] corresponding to stories categorized in five topics: business, entertainment, politics, sport, and tech.

A description of the datasets used for the experiments is presented in Table 1. Note that the BBC dataset was divided according to document topics.

5.2   RDF Quantitative Evaluation

This section presents the quantitative experiment of the RDF *n*-ary representation produced from the three datasets. The aim of this experiment is to analyze the information that can be extracted from text and represented as RDF triples

---

[20] https://www.w3.org/TR/trig/.
[21] https://dailytech.page.
[22] https://www.computerweekly.com.
[23] The LonelyPlanet dataset was originally downloaded by Martin Kavalec from the site http://www.lonelyplanet.com/destinations.
[24] http://mlg.ucd.ie/datasets/bbc.html.

Table 1. Description of datasets used for RDF representation experiments.

Dataset	Domain	Documents	Sentences
IT news	News	605	12015
LonelyPlanet	Tourism	1801	16540
BBC	Business	510	5988
BBC	Entertainment	386	4482
BBC	Politics	417	5902
BBC	Sport	511	6514
BBC	Tech	401	6901
Total		4631	58342

by following the proposed representation approach. This experiment consisted of the execution of the strategy described in Sect. 4 over the three selected datasets (IT news, LonelyPlanet, and BBC news). Hence, for this analysis, every document was submitted to tasks such as entity extraction, relation extraction and ordering until RDF n-ary statements were represented.

The results obtained through the execution of the proposed representation approach are presented in Table 2, where the column *Documents* refers to the number of documents on each dataset, *Rep. Sent.* refers to the represented sentences (with at least one event), *Entities* refers to the extracted and linked entities, *Relations* refers to the extracted relations, *Events* refers to the number of events represented in an n-ary fashion (every event contains elements such as Agent, Patient, predicate sense, location, and so on), and *Triples* refers to the total number of represented triples.

Table 2. Result of the RDF triple representation on the three datasets.

Dataset	Rep. Sent.	Relations	Triples	Events	Entities
IT news	4262	41190	89486	7606	20536
LonelyPlanet	4312	37657	63553	5059	12014
BBC (business)	3181	17651	51561	4451	10352
BBC (entertainment)	1984	12930	32456	2747	6928
BBC (politics)	2850	18499	46217	4057	9770
BBC (sport)	2538	19023	40184	3498	8935
BBC (tech)	3213	19376	50956	4451	8894
Total	**22340**	**166326**	**374413**	**31869**	**77429**

Discussion. According to the results presented in Table 2, it has to be noticed that the input data was not completely represented as RDF. The proportion of represented information as RDF statements is shown in Table 3, where the second column indicates the ratio of represented sentences regarding the original ones, and the third column represents the ratio of semantic relations represented as events. These facts are produced because diverse NLP strategies are involved in the representation strategy. Hence, the following facets regarding the representation strategy can be mentioned:

- Feature extraction. Although the NLP tool's accuracy has improved during the years [23], elements in the text are often difficult to segment or annotate, particularly large sentences or text with typos.
- Recognition. Mentions of entities and relations need to be found. However, such tasks often depend on the segmentation and annotation of words provided by the previous aspect, which in turn, might produce wrong element extractions. Moreover, while OpenIE tools do not depend on a particular domain to obtain semantic relations, not all types of relationships are covered by the rules and patterns employed by such tools. On the other hand, EEL systems used for providing entities from text are often associated with a domain and/or KB. In consequence, the proposed method can represent only those sentences that contain semantic relations in which entities appear both in subject and object.
- Representation. The representation only covers RDF triples with object properties. That is, only those relationships containing resources (named entities) in *subject* and *object* are represented in RDF (e.g., `dbr:New_York_City rdf:type dbr:Location`). Although literal values can be assigned to the object of an RDF triple (e.g., `dbr:New_York_City rdfs:label"New York"`), such cases are not within the focus of this work.

Table 3. Ratio of represented information.

Dataset	Ratio Sent./R. Sent.	Ratio Rel./Events
IT news	35.47	18.47
LonelyPlanet	26.07	13.43
BBC (business)	53.12	25.22
BBC (entert.)	44.27	21.25
BBC (politics)	48.29	21.93
BBC (sport)	38.96	18.39
BBC (tech)	46.56	22.97
Total	38.29	19.16

Given the previous facets and results, it can be observed that, from the total of input sentences of the three datasets, only 38.29% was represented as RDF statements and only 19.16% of the extracted relations was represented using RDF events. The most affected dataset (regarding the level of representation) was LonelyPlanet, which contains text on the tourism domain. Note that such a dataset is in English but some elements such as names of things and places are expressed in diverse languages (e.g., Spanish, African-based) around the world that can difficult the recognition of entities. On the other hand, the BBC dataset corresponding to the business domain obtained the higher proportion of information represented. This is due to the kind of data from the domain, which contains several relations between well-known companies/organizations, people and places.

5.3   RDF Qualitative Evaluation

After counting the number of represented RDF triples, the following step consisted of evaluating the quality of such triples. Hence, this subsection presents a qualitative evaluation based on the strategy proposed by Dutta et al. [9], in which a set of triples is presented to a human judge for evaluation. Thus, every element of the triple must be marked as correct (including the semantic relation) to deem the whole statement as precise. Details of this evaluation were as follows:

- This evaluation was conducted by four human judges from an IT-based engineering college. Given that the proposed representation method processes English sentences to represent events, the judges must have (at least) an intermediate level of English (e.g., to read and understand news in English). Likewise, judges have notions of the terminology and structure used for the RDF representation (e.g., RDF triples, thematic roles).
- A total of 50 events were randomly selected from the IT-news dataset (presented in Subsect. 5.1). Each event contains triples for describing elements such as Agent, Patient, Action/Predicate, Semantic Relation, and the original sentence.
- The selected events were presented to the judges via a web application, where every element of the event had to be judged as "Correct" or "Incorrect".

We obtained the precision values for the events evaluated by the four judges. The values obtained for each element were: Agent (0.72), Predicate/Action (0.89), Patient (0.64), Semantic Relation (0.82), Total (0.51). Note that the Total value refers to those cases where the event is marked as correct for all its elements. Additionally, the results of the agreement among judges were obtained through the kappa score [24] as follows: Agent (0.45), Predicate (0.65), Patient (0.31), Semantic Relation (0.70), and Total (0.38). This evaluation demonstrates that human judges depict a fair to a moderate agreement that the represented data is not given by chance [18].

5.4   Discussion

Although the evaluation of the accuracy of represented sentences could sometimes be guided by the subjectivity of the judges, the obtained results can be also influenced by aspects such as the complexity of the evaluated sentences, the dependency of NLP and IE tools (that could be inaccurate), and the understanding of concepts by the judges. However, the recognition of entities for the Agent and Patient demonstrates encouraging results in comparison to other approaches with similar purpose [12]. Moreover, the implementation also demonstrates the capability of the methodology to cover the stages needed for the representation of n-ary statements. It is worth mentioning that there is a lack of gold standard datasets that limits a fair comparison regarding existing works. Thus, we plan to include a more consistent evaluation under a scenario that considers diverse approaches, domains, and type of extractions.

6 Conclusions

The information represented on the Semantic Web has been used in tasks related to question answering [26], semantic annotation [6], and information retrieval [16], to mention a few. Thus, the main motivation of this research work is to formally represent unstructured data on the Semantic Web in order to support the consumption and dissemination of information through the integration of tools from areas such as Information Retrieval (IR), Information Extraction (IE), Machine Learning, Natural Language Processing (NLP), among others. This paper presented a methodology for the representation of RDF binary and n-ary statements. This is based on the steps followed by general Relation Extraction and Linking (REL) approaches for obtaining named entities and relations to then link them using data and standards of the Semantic Web. As a proof of concept, we presented an implementation of the proposed methodology for the representation of RDF n-ary statements from plain text. The experiments demonstrate the feasibility of the proposed architecture for the representation of statements in terms of the number of represented triples and the factors influencing their quality. Moreover, we also noted that diverse standards and scenarios are needed for the evaluation of these types of representation approaches.

Acknowledgments. This work was funded in part by the Fondo SEP-Cinvestav, Project No. 229. We would like to thank the reviewers for their comments on this paper.

References

1. Antoniou, G., Groth, P.T., van Harmelen, F., Hoekstra, R.: A Semantic Web Primer, 3rd edn. MIT Press, Cambridge (2012)
2. Auer, S., Bryl, V., Tramp, S. (eds.): Linked Open Data - Creating Knowledge Out of Interlinked Data - Results of the LOD2 Project. LNCS, vol. 8661. Springer, Heidelberg (2014). https://doi.org/10.1007/978-3-319-09846-3
3. Auer, S., Lehmann, J., Ngonga Ngomo, A.-C., Zaveri, A.: Introduction to linked data and its lifecycle on the web. In: Rudolph, S., Gottlob, G., Horrocks, I., van Harmelen, F. (eds.) Reasoning Web 2013. LNCS, vol. 8067, pp. 1–90. Springer, Heidelberg (2013). https://doi.org/10.1007/978-3-642-39784-4_1

4. Augenstein, I., Maynard, D., Ciravegna, F.: Distantly supervised web relation extraction for knowledge base population. Semant. Web **7**(4), 335–349 (2016). https://doi.org/10.3233/SW-150180

5. Augenstein, I., Padó, S., Rudolph, S.: LODifier: generating linked data from unstructured text. In: Simperl, E., Cimiano, P., Polleres, A., Corcho, O., Presutti, V. (eds.) ESWC 2012. LNCS, vol. 7295, pp. 210–224. Springer, Heidelberg (2012). https://doi.org/10.1007/978-3-642-30284-8_21

6. Chabchoub, M., Gagnon, M., Zouaq, A.: Collective disambiguation and semantic annotation for entity linking and typing. In: Sack, H., Dietze, S., Tordai, A., Lange, C. (eds.) SemWebEval 2016. CCIS, pp. 33–47. Springer, Heidelberg (2016). https://doi.org/10.1007/978-3-319-46565-4_3

7. Cimiano, P.: Ontology Learning and Population from Text - Algorithms. Evaluation and Applications. Springer, Heidelberg (2006). https://doi.org/10.1007/978-0-387-39252-3

8. Del Corro, L., Gemulla, R.: Clausie: clause-based open information extraction. In: International Conference on World Wide Web, pp. 355–366. ACM (2013). https://doi.org/10.1145/2488388.2488420

9. Dutta, A., Meilicke, C., Stuckenschmidt, H.: Enriching structured knowledge with open information. In: Gangemi, A., Leonardi, S., Panconesi, A. (eds.) World Wide Web Conference (WWW), pp. 267–277. ACM (2015)

10. Exner, P., Nugues, P.: Entity extraction: from unstructured text to DBpedia RDF triples. In: The Web of Linked Entities Workshop (WoLE 2012), pp. 58–69. CEUR-WS (2012)

11. Fensel, D., et al.: Enabling Semantic Web Services. Springer, Heidelberg (2007). https://doi.org/10.1007/978-3-540-34520-6

12. Gangemi, A., Presutti, V., Recupero, D.R., Nuzzolese, A.G., Draicchio, F., Mongiovì, M.: Semantic web machine reading with FRED. Semant. Web **8**(6), 873–893 (2017). https://doi.org/10.3233/SW-160240

13. Gildea, D., Jurafsky, D.: Automatic labeling of semantic roles. Comput. Linguist. **28**(3), 245–288 (2002). https://doi.org/10.1162/089120102760275983

14. Heath, T., Bizer, C.: Linked Data: Evolving the Web into a Global Data Space. Synthesis Lectures on the Semantic Web. Morgan & Claypool Publishers, San Rafael (2011). https://doi.org/10.2200/S00334ED1V01Y201102WBE001

15. Hernández, D., Hogan, A., Krötzsch, M.: Reifying RDF: what works well with wikidata? In: Liebig, T., Fokoue, A. (eds.) International Workshop on Scalable Semantic Web Knowledge Base Systems Co-located with ISWC, pp. 32–47. CEUR-WS.org (2015)

16. Waitelonis, J., Exeler, C., Sack, H.: Linked data enabled generalized vector space model to improve document retrieval. In: NLP & DBpedia Workshop in Conjunction with ISWC 2015. CEUR (2015)

17. Kertkeidkachorn, N., Ichise, R.: An automatic knowledge graph creation framework from natural language text. IEICE Trans. **101**(D(1)), 90–98 (2018). https://doi.org/10.1587/transinf.2017SWP0006

18. Landis, J.R., Koch, G.G.: The measurement of observer agreement for categorical data. Biometrics **33**, 159–174 (1977)

19. Manning, C.D., Surdeanu, M., Bauer, J., Finkel, J.R., Bethard, S., McClosky, D.: The Stanford CoreNLP natural language processing toolkit. In: Annual Meeting of the Association for Computational Linguistics (ACL), pp. 55–60 (2014)

20. Martinez-Rodriguez, J.L., Hernandez, J., Lopez-Arevalo, I., Rios-Alvarado, A.B.: A strategy for the integration of named entity extraction and linking results. In: Proceedings of the 3rd International Workshop on Semantic Web 2018 Co-located with 15th International Congress on Information (INFO 2018), 7 March 2018, Havana, Cuba, pp. 13–20. CEUR-WS.org (2018)
21. Martinez-Rodriguez, J.L., Hogan, A., Lopez-Arevalo, I.: Information extraction meets the semantic web: a survey. Semant. Web J. (2018, to appear)
22. Milton, N.R.: Knowledge Acquisition in Practice: A Step-by-Step Guide. Springer, Heidelberg (2007). https://doi.org/10.1007/978-1-84628-861-6
23. Pinto, A.M., Oliveira, H.G., Alves, A.O.: Comparing the performance of different NLP toolkits in formal and social media text. In: 5th Symposium on Languages, Applications and Technologies, SLATE, pp. 3:1–3:16 (2016)
24. Randolph, J.J.: Free-marginal multirater kappa (multirater k [free]): An alternative to fleiss' fixed-marginal multirater kappa. In: Joensuu Learning and Instruction Symposium (2005)
25. Rusu, D., Fortuna, B., Mladenic, D.: Automatically annotating text with linked open data. In: Bizer, C., Heath, T., Berners-Lee, T., Hausenblas, M. (eds.) WWW2011 Workshop on Linked Data on the Web. CEUR-WS.org (2011)
26. Unger, C., Freitas, A., Cimiano, P.: An introduction to question answering over linked data. In: Koubarakis, M., et al. (eds.) Reasoning Web 2014. LNCS, vol. 8714, pp. 100–140. Springer, Cham (2014). https://doi.org/10.1007/978-3-319-10587-1_2

Meta-Modelling Ontology Design Pattern

Edelweis Rohrer[1(✉)], Paula Severi[2], and Regina Motz[1]

[1] Instituto de Computación, Facultad de Ingeniería, UdelaR, Montevideo, Uruguay
erohrer@gmail.com
[2] Department of Computer Science, University of Leicester, Leicester, England

Abstract. In the last decades, the meta-modelling problem has received increasing attention in the conceptual modelling and semantic web communities. We have proposed a solution to this problem in the context of ontological modelling which consists in extending a fragment of the Web Ontology Language OWL with a meta-modelling constructor to equate instances to classes. Even though there are methodologies and patterns that help the ontology engineer to conceptualize a domain using ontologies, there is a lack of such guides for the meta-modelling approaches that extend OWL. In this work we introduce a design pattern that guides in the conceptualization of domains for which there are requirements at different knowledge levels, in particular for different user perspectives.

1 Introduction

Meta-modelling is the conceptual modelling problem of having classes that could be instances of other classes (called metaclasses) or form part of metaproperties (properties between metaclasses). This is a relevant problem for many areas such as model-driven engineering (MDE) and ontology design. MDE promote models as artifacts for the domain conceptualization in the development process [27]. Following the MDE approach, the meta-object facility (MOF) [2] is a standard that describes modelling languages such as UML [4] for representing object oriented models, that are implemented by frameworks such us Eclipse Modeling Framework (EMF) [1]. It is a structure of layers of models which in the end describes an application domain in terms of classes (or types) and instances of classes. But there are real application domains for which it is needed to represent several layers or knowledge levels (as classes with instances that also are classes) within the domain itself. For example, some applications have at least two user levels: (i) one for domain experts, who visualize the whole organization landscape and are in charge of defining work procedures and business rules, naturally represented as *instances* and (ii) another for operators, who daily apply a defined procedure many times, which is better represented as a *set of instances*.

Some MOF-based modelling approaches propose extensions to conceptualize domains with meta-modelling [6,21], and some of them use ontologies to model constraints on such languages [9]. But in general, these meta-modelling approaches do not propose mechanisms to generate (automatically) constraints on the final implementation, from the intended conceptualization.

© Springer Nature Switzerland AG 2019
B. Villazón-Terrazas and Y. Hidalgo-Delgado (Eds.): KGSWC 2019, CCIS 1029, pp. 102–117, 2019.
https://doi.org/10.1007/978-3-030-21395-4_8

There are other approaches that adopt ontologies as a (broadly proved) modelling artifact to represent a domain, with the definition of classes, instances and relations, in particular the W3C standard ontology language OWL [13]. Moreover, they enable the automatic validation of constraints on the final application, by providing implementations of reasoners that check consistency and draw inferences from a domain conceptualization (given by an ontology) [3,24]. In this last direction, there are different approaches that extend the OWL ontology language to give solution to the domain meta-modelling [8,12,14,19,20,23,25]. In particular, we have proposed an extension of the description logic $\mathcal{SHIQ}$ (and the reasoner algorithm) with a meta-modelling constructor that equates instances to classes, and recently, we introduced another meta-modelling constructor called MetaRule that allows to create rules by relating instances at an upper level, which are translated as restrictions on the lower level [25,26,28]. The main advantage of these meta-modelling approaches is the capability of automatically validating the modelling

As well as there are object oriented design patterns [11], there are methodologies, guidelines and patterns to conceptualize a domain using ontologies [17,29]. In particular, the Neon methodology presents a set of ontology design patterns for different scenarios, however it does not address the problem of modelling different views (as instances and as concepts) of the same domain. As far as we know there is a lack of guidelines for modelling a domain using meta-modelling approaches that extend OWL (or a fragment of it), including our approach [25,28].

The main contribution of this work is to introduce the first design pattern that helps the ontology engineer in conceptualizing domains for which there are requirements at different knowledge levels, in particular different user perspectives. The motivation for this pattern is given by a real three-level user scenario from the educational domain, for the users institution, professor and student, where higher level users define rules for the lower level users. Our aim is to provide a practical and useful mechanism to discern how and in what scenarios to apply our meta-modelling approach. We also show another suitable scenario to apply the proposed pattern, in the accounting domain.

The remainder of this paper is organized as follows. Section 2 present some related work. A motivating case study is detailed in Sect. 3. Then, the design pattern is introduced in Sect. 4 and its application on a real case study about accounting is presented in Sect. 5. Finally, Sect. 6 give some conclusions and future work.

2   Related Work

According to Guizzardi, "ontology-driven conceptual modeling is the utilization of ontological theories to develop engineering artifacts (e.g. modeling languages, methodologies, design patterns and simulators) for improving the theory and practice of conceptual modeling" [15,16]. Some authors go further and formalize meta-modelling as Atkinson et al. that coined the term *clabject* to emphasize that there are classes that are also objects [5], and Carvalho et al. that present a first order logic theory, MLT [7].

Related work on description logics (the logical foundations of OWL) extended with meta-modelling capabilities has an extense literature, due to space restrictions, we refer to [25, 28] for a thorough comparison. These meta-modelling approaches have the advantage of automatically validating the modelled constraints on the final application, through reasoners that check the knowledge base consistency and draw inferences.

Regarding design patterns Gamma et al. propose a set of patterns to model a domain using object oriented languages [11]. It sets a standard to specify design patterns that has been broadly adopted in different approaches and languages. Suarez-Figueroa et al. propose a complete methodology of design using ontologies that covers all engineering activities from ontology requirements, design patterns and also ontology evaluation, but they do not cover ontology-based approaches with meta-modelling [29]. Falbo et al. address the ontology engineering process by defining three main phases, (i) conceptual modelling, (ii) design and (iii) implementation, in a processable language as OWL [10]. They present a classification of patterns based on the ontology engineering process. Our pattern would fit in their classification either as design or architectural pattern. Falbo et al. do not address ontology meta-modelling approaches neither. However, Carvalho et al. and Lara et al. describe a set of meta-modelling design patterns for MOF-based approaches. Carvalho et al. present a pattern expressed by a first order theory, which assigns a level to each class, bounded by three levels [9]. Lara et al. address the problem of dynamically create object types that both have instances and are instances of other types [21]. Our meta-modelling approach also give solution to the same problem by extending the description logic $\mathcal{SHIQ}$ with two constructors, one that equates instances to classes and another one that translates rules from higher to lower knowledge levels, but moreover it enables the automatic validation of the modelled constraints [25, 28].

3   A Motivating Real-World Case for the Design Pattern

In this section we present an educational real-world scenario from the project DIIA at the public university of Uruguay[1]. It is about the management of learning activities such as modules and workshops, and the associated services, as learning platforms and classrooms. Moreover, an important aspect is the interaction of students with different work environments in degree modules. Bellow we present the main requirements, which are associated to three different levels of users: *institution, professors* and *students*.

The *institution* defines all possible the learning activities that can be developed in the university and assigns the services that can be used in each activity. For instance, for a module the institution enables the use of services such as equipment and work environments. If the activity is a conference, it moreover

---

[1] Descubrimiento de Interacciones que Impactan en el Aprendizaje - Creación de un ambiente de software para descubrir patrones semánticos de interacción.

allows to hire a catering service, but it does not allow the use of such service for a module. According to different factors (as the economical policy, or change of authorities) services assigned to activities can vary over the time, although at least one service must be enabled so that the activity can work.

For each module of the degree structure, every year *professors* are in charge of defining what particular services (within those enabled by the institution) they will use to develop the module. For example, if modules are enabled to use work environments, the professor of the module of Basic Programming can decide to use two work environments: the classroom and the web platform, and the professor of Data Base Foundations can define to use the web platform and the computer laboratory. These decisions can vary in each edition of the same module depending on factors such as the number of enrolled students or the physical space in classrooms. However, they only can take such decisions for the services enabled by the institution, which also can change over the time. However, it is a policy of the university of many years ago that at least two different work environments must be available for all modules.

Basically, *students* enroll in different modules, and for each module they must attend at least one of the work environments enabled by the professor.

Figure 1 illustrates the scenario with three ontologies, one for each user level. Ovals represent classes, arrows represent properties and bullets instances.

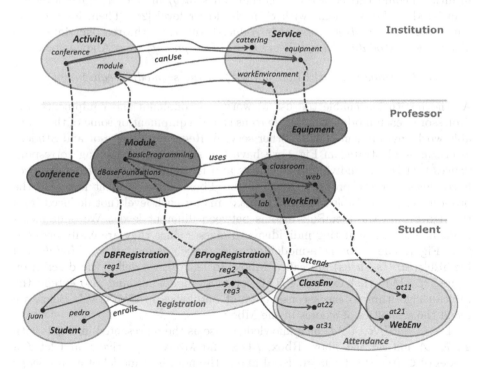

Fig. 1. Example of educational model

In the Institution level, each activity is represented by the individuals *module* and *conference* as instances of the class *Activity*, whereas in the Professor level they are represented by the classes *Module* and *Conference*. It would not be correct to define *Module* as a subclass of *Activity*, since it does not represent the Institution perspective of a module, as one of its activities. This equality between individuals and classes is illustrated in the figure by dotted lines. Moreover, services are represented by the individuals *workEnvironment* and *equipment* in the Institution level, whereas classes *WorkEnv* and *Equipment* represent them at the Professor level. Our extension to $\mathcal{SHIQ}$ provides a *meta-modelling* constructor that allows to represent this correspondence between individuals and classes by introducing the axiom *module* $=_m$ *Module*, and similar axioms for *conference* and *Conference*, *workEnvironment* and *WorkEnv*, and *equipment* and *Equipment* [25]. Moreover, in the Institution level the property *canUse* connects activities to the enabled services. So, according to the requirements described above, in the Professor level individuals of the class *Module* only can be related to individuals of the classes *WorkEnv* and *Equipment* by the property *uses*, since the individual *module* is linked to individuals *workEnvironment* and *equipment* by the property *canUse*. In order to explicitly declare this kind of correspondence between properties (such as *canUse* and *uses*) at different levels, we also provide another meta-modelling constructor MetaRule(R, S) for properties R and S. The intuition behind this constructor is that pairs (a, b) in R in a higher level are translated as TBox axioms with S in the lower level [28]. Then, for the case study MetaRule($canUse, uses$) is introduced and then the reasoner infers the Tbox axiom $Module \sqsubseteq \forall uses.(WorkEnv \sqcup Equipment)$ from Abox axioms:

$$canUse(module, workEnvironment) \quad canUse(module, equipment)$$

As the institution enable the use of work environments and equipments, the professor of each module can decide to use some equipment or some of the available work environments but no other service. Regarding Professor and Student levels, as is illustrated in Fig. 1 we have the same meta-modelling correspondences that equate individuals to classes and translate the Abox from the Professor level (for the property *uses*) to the Tbox of the Student level (on the property *attends*). Table 1 shows Tbox axioms for each level (not deduced from the figure) and the MetaRule axioms between different levels. We omit meta-modelling axioms equating individuals to classes since they are easily deduced from Fig. 1. The set of meta-modelling axioms such as *module* $=_m$ *Module* and MetaRule($canUse, uses$) are called Mbox. In [25,28], we define the description logic $\mathcal{SHIQM^*}$ that extends $\mathcal{SHIQ}$ for meta-modelling, and also extend the tableau algorithm to check consistency of ontologies in $\mathcal{SHIQM^*}$. Below we recall the semantics of axioms in the Mbox.

Let $\mathcal{O} = (\mathcal{T}, \mathcal{R}, \mathcal{A}, \mathcal{M})$ be a knowledge base as the represented in Fig. 1, with $\mathcal{T}$, $\mathcal{R}$, $\mathcal{A}$ and $\mathcal{M}$ the Tbox, Rbox, Abox and Mbox respectively, and let $\mathcal{I}$ a model of $\mathcal{O}$ (see [18] for more detail about the notion of model of a knowledge base). The semantics of the meta-modelling axioms $a =_m A$ and MetaRule(R, S) is defined as follows.

- $a^{\mathcal{I}} = A^{\mathcal{I}}$ holds for each equality statement $a =_m A$.
- $A^{\mathcal{I}} \subseteq (\forall S.(\sqcup X))^{\mathcal{I}}$ holds for each role characteristic $\mathsf{MetaRule}(R, S)$ and each equality statement $a =_m A$, where $X = \{B \mid (a^{\mathcal{I}}, b^{\mathcal{I}}) \in R^{\mathcal{I}}$ and $b =_m B \in \mathcal{M}\}$.

At the moment OWL and its reasoners (as Pellet or Hermit) cannot handle meta-modelling with neither equalities between concepts and individuals nor the MetaRule role characteristic [28]. Applying our meta-modelling approach to the educational case study has some advantages. On the one hand, the kind of requirements for the Professor level such as at least two different environments must be available for each module is represented by the Tbox axiom (2) in Table 1. On the other hand, the kind of requirements such as modules (and other activities) can use the services enabled by the institution, that can vary over the time, are represented by Abox axioms as $canUse(module, workEnvironment)$ in the Institution level and the Mbox axiom $\mathsf{MetaRule}(canUse, uses)$ (axioms (4) in Table 1) that connects properties of Institution and Professor levels, inferring restrictions in the Professor level. The MetaRule constructor provides a flexible mechanism for introducing dynamic rules in the Abox (which are data for the Institution user) avoiding the engineer has to declare Tbox axioms at the Professor level (that can change over the time) since they are inferred by the reasoner.

Table 1. Educational domain Tbox and Mbox.

Axiom	Description
(1) $Activity \sqsubseteq \exists canUse.Service$	All activities have enabled at least one service
(2) $Module \sqsubseteq\, \geq 2uses.WorkEnv$	All modules use at least two different environments
(3) $Registration \sqsubseteq \exists attends.Attendance$	All students attends at least one work environment for each module they are enrolled
(4) $\mathsf{MetaRule}(canUse, uses)$ $\mathsf{MetaRule}(uses, attends)$	The services enabled to activities by the institution determine the definition of what particular services are used in each activity, by professors. The work environments defined for modules by professors determine the attendance of students

4 A Meta-Modelling Design Pattern for Different User Views

In this section we introduce a design pattern for the application of our meta-modelling approach [25,28], following the style of Gamma et al. [11].

Pattern Name. Meta-modelling ontology pattern.

Intent. Taking ontologies as modelling artifacts, to conceptualize a domain by modelling two or more knowledge levels associated to different user views. For each level, there are static requirements (that rarely change) and also dynamic requirements that are changed by the immediate upper user level.

Motivation. The motivation for applying the *meta-modelling ontology pattern* is given by the scenario about the educational domain described in Sect. 3.

Applicability. The *meta-modelling ontology pattern* applies instead of single-level modelling approaches, when it is needed to conceptualize two or more knowledge levels for different user views. This pattern gives solution to the representation of some business rules at each knowledge level. There are rules that rarely change over the life cycle of the application, that we call *static rules*. There are also rules more sensitive to different factors that influence the business, such as the economical situation or new organization leaders, so they probably change. We call them *dynamic rules*. As was illustrated in Sect. 3, in general, changes in rules on a given knowledge level are defined by users at the immediate upper level. This pattern consider dynamic rules that restrict relations between sets of objects (as learning modules and working environments for the Professor level) which are defined as relations on atomic objects in the immediate upper level (as the Institution level). Hence, given a *knowledge user level*, the kind of *dynamic rules* that the *meta-modelling ontology pattern* solves are those *defined at the immediate upper level as relations on objects.*

Proposed Solution. Figure 2 illustrates the structure of the proposed pattern, showing the different knowledge user levels which were assigned natural numbers.
     Given the knowledge level n, the *meta-modelling ontology pattern* suggests the modelling of the rules as follows.

- *Static rules* are represented in the Tbox and Rbox of the level n.
- *Dynamic rules* that restrict the relation between classes A and B by a property S are represented as follows.
    - Abox axioms in the level $n+1$, that relate individuals a, b by a property R.
    - Mbox axioms $a =_m A$, $b =_m B$ from the level $n + 1$ to the level n.
    - The Mbox axiom $\mathsf{MetaRule}(R, S)$ from the level $n + 1$ to the level n.
- Any other kind of rule (for example cardinality restrictions) on the level n, that are not the focus of the presented pattern, are represented in the Tbox or Rbox of the level n.

Regarding dynamic rules, users of the level $n+1$ in charge of define business rules for the level n, can add and change their definitions by introducing Abox axioms. The Mbox axioms equating individuals at the level $n + 1$ to classes at the level n allow to express that individuals and corresponding classes are the same real entities that are visualized with different granularity by different users. Finally, the Mbox axiom $\mathsf{MetaRule}(R, S)$ express that relations on the property R at the

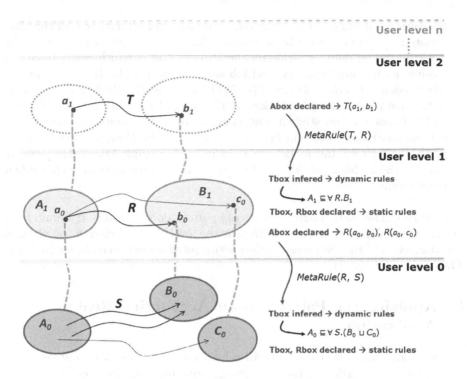

Fig. 2. Multi-level ontology pattern

level $n+1$ are constraints for the property S at the level n, on classes semantically equivalent than individuals related by R. Hence, the reasoner extended for Mbox axioms will infer the Tbox axioms that express dynamic rules on the level n, as is showed in Fig. 2.

Consequences. The application of the *meta-modelling ontology pattern* has some advantages that are described below.

- In general, *static rules* are accepted and agreed aspects of the domain. For this reason, it is more likely to be reused, and the fact that they are modelled in the Tbox favors the reuse of a structure, which later is populated with instances.
- As *dynamic rules* for the level n are modelled in the Abox of the level $n+1$, this kind of rules are treated as data for the user of the level $n+1$, what makes it a flexible approach.
- When *static rules* (as Tbox axioms) on a level n, $n > 0$, restrict individuals related by a role R that is in an axiom MetaRule(R, S), these static rules on the level n are in fact *rules on rules* on the level $n-1$, since Abox axioms with R are translated as rules (Tbox) for the level $n-1$.
- Expressing *rules for a level n on rules for the level $n-1$* (as described above) have the advantage of checking for a condition only once over an individual of

the level n, avoiding to check the same condition for all instances of the class equated to that individual by meta-modelling. For example, let's consider for the educational domain a rule on the Professor level which restricts that a module do not use both web and lab work environments. Hence, there is a Tbox axiom $Module \sqsubseteq \forall uses.\neg(\{web\} \sqcap \{lab\})^2$ at the Professor level. This restriction (and others) is checked at the level of each instance of $Module$, which forces that no student who is enrolled on a module can attend (for this module) both web and lab work environments. However, if we do not apply the pattern and model the domain with a single knowledge level we have to check this condition (and many others) at the level of each student registration.

Limitations. The *meta-modelling ontology pattern* does not solve dynamic rules for a level n different from those defined at the level $n+1$ as relations on objects, and translated to the level n as restrictions on relations between classes (inferred Tbox axioms of Fig. 2).

5   Applying the Pattern to an Accounting Real Application

We have identified other domains for which the *meta-modelling ontology pattern* applies, in particular the accounting domain. Our decision of choosing this domain comes from the analysis of some weaknesses of a real implemented application, the accounting module of the information system called "Integrated Rental Guarantee Management System" (SIGGA) at the General Accounting Agency of the Ministry of Economy and Finance in Uruguay[3]. Whereas the educational scenario results a more "day-to-day" business, the accounting domain is more technical and challenging with regard to the identification of the requirements for each knowledge level. Besides showing the pattern application to the accounting domain, in this section we also present a solution for the same domain that does not apply the pattern, to better visualize the pattern usefulness.

A detailed description of the SIGGA accounting domain can be obtained in [26]. The underlying business is about that Uruguayan government acts as a guarantor for employees who want to rent a property. The application helps manage renter payments, as salary discounts or direct cash payment, and the payments to landlords. The accounting module is in charge of recording the accounting entries for the business rules of SIGGA, which was modelled by the relational scheme depicted in Fig. 3.

From a conceptual point of view, there are two levels of the business: (i) a *definitional level*, related to the task of expert users on accounting who define

---

[2] Note that even though our extension of $\mathcal{SHIQ}$ does not consider nominals, we declare a Tbox axiom including them, for the sole purpose of illustrating the usefullness of the rules on rules.

[3] Sistema Integrado de Gestión de Garantía de Alquileres, Contaduría General de la Nación, www.cgn.gub.uy.

what kind of accounting entry (with debit and credit accounts) must be done for each financial movement, and (ii) an *operational level* related to the task of users that operate the application, and register concrete accounting entries. In the definitional level, different kinds of accounting entries are identified, called *entry definitions*, which are specified according to the business rules by a set of valid details at debit and credit, called *detail definitions*, over accounts that represent the essence of the financial movement. For example, Fig. 3 shows the entry definition 10, "Renter payment", with two detail definitions at debit (for accounts Cash and Bank) and two at credit (for accounts Renter Debt and Renter Fee). Whereas, in the operational level, particular *accounting entries* and *details* are registered, for example, the "Juan Perez payment" (252) on 14/12/2017 of $6,000 in cash, for the accounts "Renter Debt" ($4,500) and "Renter Fee" ($1,500), according to the entry definition 10. A detailed description of the relational scheme of SIGGA is presented in [26], along with the complete set of the domain requirements and how they are verified by the scheme of Fig. 3.

EntryDefs

entryDef	description
10	Renter payment
20	Monthly calculation of rent
30	Home damage expenses

DetDefs

entryDef	detailDef	account	D/C
10	1	11111	'D'
10	2	11112	'D'
10	3	11211	'C'
10	4	11311	'C'
20	1	11211	'D'
20	2	11311	'D'
20	3	21111	'C'
30	1	12222	'D'
30	2	21111	'C'

Accounts

account	description
11111	Cash
11112	Bank
11211	Renter Debt
21111	Landlords
12222	Damage Expenses
11311	Renter Fee

Entries

entry	entryDef	date	Observations
250	20	01/12/2017	Juan Pérez calc. of rent
251	10	13/12/2017	María García payment
252	10	14/12/2017	Juan Pérez payment

Dets

entry	detail	entryDef	detailDef	amount
250	1	20	1	4,500
250	2	20	2	1,500
250	3	20	3	6,000
252	1	10	1	6,000
252	2	10	3	4,500
252	3	10	4	1,500

Fig. 3. Relational tables for the accounting application and some few entries as example

A retrospective looking of the implemented application showed as a main drawback that the focus of the conceptualization was satisfying the requirements at the level of operators whereas relevant requirements of expert users were not considered. In the present work, with the aim of capitalizing the identified weaknesses and give a better understanding of the pattern application, we group some of the main requirements in *functional* and *non functional*, and classify functional requirements according to the following criteria: (i) the user (expert or operator) associated to the requirement, and (ii) if the requirement is static (rarely change) or dynamic (it probably changes during the application life). Below we present the *functional requirements*.

ReqF. 1. Each accounting entry has at least one debit detail and one credit detail, and each detail corresponds to a unique accounting entry. Moreover, each detail is either a debit or a credit (but not both) and has associated a single account. This set of requirements are associated to concrete accounting entries recorded during the operation of the application, so they correspond to the *operator user*, at the operational level. Since they come from the ALE-based accounting model of debits and credits (universally adopted) [22], they are *static*.

ReqF. 2. Accounting entries have details for accounts in accordance with the definitional level. For instance, each time a renter pays a debt in cash, the recorded accounting entry must have details for accounts "Cash", and "Renter Debt" or "Renter Fee" in accordance with the "Renter payment" entry definition. This requirement also is associated to the *operator user*. However, the definition of what debit and credit accounts can be associated to each concrete accounting entry (as the payment of Juan Perez) is in charge of expert users, who can decide to change these definitions. For instance, depending on information needs, may be experts decide separate "Renter Debt" in two accounts: one for debts of renters in Montevideo and the other for the remaining renters. So this requirement is *dynamic*.

ReqF. 3. Provide facilities to validate the correctness of accounting entry definitions. For instance, if the renter "Juan Pérez" incurs in a debt for damages in the house, it must be registered according to the entry definition 30 of Fig. 3 with a debit for the "Damage Expenses" account and a credit for the "Landlords" accounts. But as there is no row in the table DetDefs associating the entry definition 10 (Renter payment) to the account "Damage Expenses", so the "renter payment" entry (to register that "Juan Pérez" pays the damage expenses) cannot be registered. What happens is that the expert did not include the "Damage Expenses" account at credit in the entry definition 10. So, we should validate that the "renter payment" entry definition to have credit details for all accounts that are debits in some entry definition (that generates a renter debt). This requirement is associated to the *expert user* since it is a constraint on the accounting entry definitions, and this is *static* because, provided that a renter incurs in a debt he/she should be able to pay it.

Besides functional requirements, the identification of *two different knowledge levels* (definitional and operational) as well as dynamic business rules (as the ReqF. 2) also leads to identify some *non functional requirements or quality attributes* that contributes to improve the quality of the domain conceptualization. They are described below.

ReqNF. 1. With the aim that the domain conceptualization to be clear and explicit, it must differentiate definitional and operational views as two abstraction levels. Besides a greater expressiveness, a model with the capability to represent that tables EntryDefs, DetDefs and Accounts are in the definitional level whereas tables Entries and Dets are in the operational level, avoids errors of design that can arise from misinterpretations. For example, at the moment of reusing the SIGGA relational schema, it is useful to distinguish a foreign key from the table Entries to the table EntryDefs of Fig. 3 (that links conceptually equivalent knowledge at different levels) from a foreign key from DetDefs to Accounts (that links two conceptually different objects at the same level). In particular, the relational model has not the expressibility to differentiate both abstraction levels.

ReqNF. 2. Provide mechanisms to facilitate the conceptualization evolution, in particular, minimize the impact of changing entry definitions. Suppose that at a certain time, experts decide that for the definition of the "Renter payment" entry instead of the account "Renter Debt", another account "Rental Debt" must be used. The change must impact at definitional level, because the new renter payment entries must be done in accordance to the new definition. But at the same time, old "renter payment" entries must continue being classified as such, even though they do not follow the new definition.

In [26] we present two ontology-based modelling solutions for the accounting domain described above, the first one in OWL2 (called OM) and the other in the description logic $\mathcal{SHIQ}$ extended with meta-modelling (called OMM), and an analysis of how the relational model, OM and OMM accomplish the complete set of requirements. In the present work we only compare the ontology-based solutions OM and OMM, to show the application of the pattern in OMM. Figure 4 illustrates the OM solution. Subclasses of *Entry* represent all accounting entries of a given kind. They have details that belong to a subclass of *Det* and are associated to a given account (class *Account*) at debit (property *detailD*) or credit (property *detailC*), according to definitions of expert users. Axioms below model the definition for the "Renter Payment" entries (see Fig. 3), by defining the subclass *RenterPayEnt* of *Entry* and the corresponding subclasses of *Det*. These axioms represent the definitional level, they have to be declared for each kind of accounting entry such as those identified by 10, 20 and 30 in Fig. 3.

$$
\begin{aligned}
RenterPayEnt &\sqsubseteq \forall detailD.(PayCashDet \sqcup PayBankDet) \\
RenterPayEnt &\sqsubseteq \forall detailC.(PayDebtDet \sqcup PayRentFee) \\
PayCashDet &\sqsubseteq \forall detail^{-}.RenterPayEnt \\
PayBankDet &\sqsubseteq \forall detail^{-}.RenterPayEnt \\
PayDebtDet &\sqsubseteq \forall detail^{-}.RenterPayEnt \\
PayFeeDet &\sqsubseteq \forall detail^{-}.RenterPayEnt \\
PayCashDet &\sqsubseteq \exists account.\{cash\} \\
PayBankDet &\sqsubseteq \exists account.\{bank\} \\
PayDebtDet &\sqsubseteq \exists account.\{renterDebt\} \\
PayFeeDet &\sqsubseteq \exists account.\{renterFee\}
\end{aligned}
\tag{1}
$$

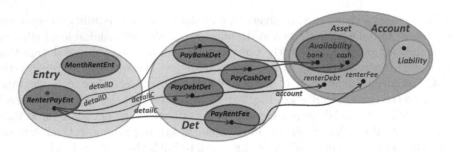

Fig. 4. Example of SIGGA OM design

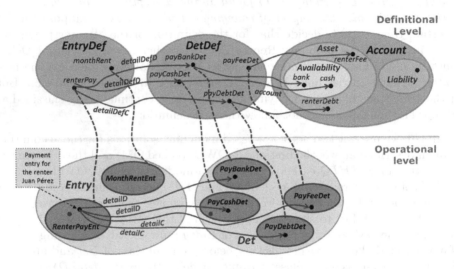

Fig. 5. Example of SIGGA OMM design

The OMM solution, illustrated in Fig. 5, applies the *meta-modelling ontology pattern* to conceptualize the accounting domain. It extends OM with a new ontology at the definitional level, to explicitly represent the relations that hold between definitional and operational levels. In the definitional ontology, each kind of accounting entry is represented as an instance of *EntryDef* whereas in the operational ontology it is represented as a subclass of *Entry*, which agrees with a unique entry definition in *EntryDef*. Table 2 shows some of the Tbox and Mbox axioms of OMM. As in the educational domain, each ontology conceptualizes the same business at different knowledge level.

We summarize in Table 3 the advantages and drawbacks of OM and OMM, for the requirements presented above. Besides showing that OMM is conceptually more expressive than OM, the table depicts the advantage of using meta-modelling and moreover applying the *meta-modelling ontology pattern*.

For the static requirement 1 at the level of operators, following the pattern we have Tbox axioms on classes and properties of the operational ontology,

Table 2. SIGGA OMM Tbox and Mbox.

Axiom	Description
(1) $Entry \sqsubseteq \exists detailD.\top \sqcap \exists detailC.\top$	Entries are balanced double entry records
(2) $EntryDef \sqsubseteq \exists detailDefD.\top \sqcap$ $\exists detailDefC.\top$	Accounting entry definitions are balanced double entry records
(3) $Account \sqcap \neg Avalilability \sqcap$ $\exists account^-.(\exists detailDefD^-.\top) \sqsubseteq$ $\exists account.^-.(\exists detailDefC^-.(\exists detailDefD.$ $\exists account.Avaliability))$	All accounts that generate debts must be in the definitions that have availability accounts (cash, bank), at credit
(4) $renterPay =_m RenterPayEnt$ $monthRent =_m MonthRentEnt$ MetaRule($detailDefD, detailD$) MetaRule($detailDefC, detailC$)	An accounting entry definition is the same entity as the set of concrete accounting entries of this kind Accounting entries at operational level follow the rules rules introduced at definitional level

Table 3. Expressibility achieved in the SIGGA accounting module by OM and OMM.

Requirements	User	Static/ Dynamic	OM	OMM
ReqF. 1: Acc. entries with debit and credit. Details are of a unique entry, either debit or credit, and with a single account.	Operator	Static	✓	✓
ReqF. 2: Accounting entries agree with expert definitions	Operator	Dynamic	✓	✓
ReqF. 3: Validate correctness of definitions	Expert	Static	✗	✓
ReqNF. 1: Differenciate definitional and operational levels	N/A	N/A	✗	✓
ReqNF. 1: Minimize impact of changing definitions	N/A	N/A	✗	✓

such as (1) in Table 2. The dynamic requirement 2 at the level of operators is solved by combining meta-modelling axioms (that equate instances of *EntryDef* to subclasses of *Entry* and instances of *DetDef* to subclasses of *Det*) with the MetaRule constructor (axioms (4) in Table 2). The benefits of applying the pattern are clearly visualized looking at the OM model which has the drawback that axioms 1 must be declared for each kind of accounting entry (around 80 in the real system). Whereas for OM entry definitions are expressed in the TBox, for OMM they are registered in the ABox as "data", what turns the OMM solution more flexible for expressing dynamic business rules. Moreover, the fact that these rules are expressed in the Abox allows to satisfy the static requirement *ReqF. 3* at the level of expert users. For OM, to validate that all accounts that generate debts are in the accounting definitions as "renter payment" at credit, we would have to explore all axioms of the form 1. The problem is that the requirement is about validating definitions of experts, not "data", at the level of operators, i.e. *rules on rules*. Hence, by applying the *meta-modelling ontology pattern* we solve the requirement just adding the axiom (3) of Table 2. Regarding non functional requirements, they are satisfied only by OMM due to the capability of expressing two different abstraction levels.

6 Conclusions and Future Work

In this work we present a design pattern that guides in the application of an ontological meta-modeling approach, to conceptualize requirements for different user levels, such that users at higher levels determine (dynamically) some business rules for users at lower levels. The presented pattern help to discern how to represent these dynamic business rules and also static rules. We also apply the pattern through the re-design of an implemented real accounting application. After identifying some weaknesses in the original design, we apply the pattern and then could compare a one-level ontology solution and the two-level model obtained following the pattern. Mainly, we evaluate as positive the capability of representing more than one abstraction level as well as the inference of (dynamic) constraints on a given level from definitions introduced (as relations on instances) in the upper level.

As we applied the pattern to completely different domains (educational and accounting) to give solution to the same problem of modelling requirements for users at different levels, we visualize it as a flexible approach for representing dynamic rules as well as rules on rules.

As a future work we plan to extend an existing methodology of ontology (network) design such as Neon, for ontologies in OWL with meta-modelling. We aim to cover the whole life cycle of ontology development (ontology requirements, design, evaluation and so on) as is addressed by the Neon approach.

References

1. Eclipse Modeling Framework. https://www.eclipse.org/modeling/emf/. Accessed Jan 2019
2. Meta-object Facility. https://www.omg.org/mof/. Accessed Jan 2019
3. Pellet: a practical OWL-DL reasoner. Web Semant.: Sci. Serv. Agents World Wide Web **5**(2), 51–53 (2007)
4. Unified Modeling Language Specification Version 241. https://www.omg.org/spec/UML/2.4.1/About-UML/. Accessed Jan 2019
5. Atkinson, C., Gerbig, R., Kühne, T.: A unifying approach to connections for multi-level modeling. In: 2015 ACM/IEEE 18th International Conference on Model Driven Engineering Languages and Systems (MODELS) (2015)
6. Atkinson, C., Kühne, T.: In defence of deep modelling. Inf. Softw. Technol. **64**, 36–51 (2015)
7. Carvalho, V.A., Almeida, J.P.A., Fonseca, C.M., Guizzardi, G.: Multi-level ontology-based conceptual modeling. Data Knowl. Eng. **109**, 3–24 (2017)
8. Cima, G., De Giacomo, G., Lenzerini, M., Poggi, A.: On the SPARQL metamodeling semantics entailment regime for OWL 2 QL ontologies. In: Proceedings of the 7th International Conference on Web Intelligence, Mining and Semantics (2017)
9. Carvalho, V.A., Almeida, J.P.A.: Toward a well-founded theory for multi-level conceptual modeling. Softw. Syst. Model. **17**, 205–231 (2018)

10. Falbo, R., Guizzardi, G., Gangemi, A., Presutti, V.: Ontology patterns: clarifying concepts and terminology. In CEUR Workshop Proceedings (2013)
11. Gamma, E., Helm, R., Johnson, R., Vlissides, J.: Design Patterns: Elements of Reusable Object-Oriented Software. Addison-Wesley Longman Publishing Co., Inc., Boston (1995)
12. Giacomo, G.D., Lenzerini, M., Rosati, R.: Higher-order description logics for domain metamodeling. In: Proceedings of the Twenty-Fifth AAAI Conference on Artificial Intelligence, AAAI 2011. AAAI Press (2011)
13. Grau, B.C., Horrocks, I., Motik, B., Parsia, B., Patel-Schneider, P.F., Sattler, U.: OWL 2: the next step for OWL. J. Web Semant. **6**, 309–322 (2008)
14. Gu, Z., Zhang, S.: The more irresistible Hi(SRIQ) for meta-modeling and meta-query answering. Front. Comput. Sci. **12**(5), 1029–1031 (2018)
15. Guizzardi, G.: Ontological foundations for conceptual modeling with applications. In: Ralyté, J., Franch, X., Brinkkemper, S., Wrycza, S. (eds.) CAiSE 2012. LNCS, vol. 7328, pp. 695–696. Springer, Heidelberg (2012). https://doi.org/10.1007/978-3-642-31095-9_45
16. Guizzardi, G., Wagner, G.: A unified foundational ontology and some applications of it in business modeling. In: Workshops in connection with the 16th Conference on Advanced Information Systems Engineering, Knowledge and Model Driven Information Systems Engineering for Networked Organisations, CAiSE 2004 (2004)
17. Hitzler, P., Gangemi, A., Janowicz, K., Krisnadhi, A., Presutti, V.: Ontology Engineering with Ontology Design Patterns: Foundations and Applications. IOS Press, Amsterdam (2016)
18. Hitzler, P., Krötzsch, M., Rudolph, S.: Foundations of Semantic Web Technologies. Chapman & Hall/CRC (2009)
19. Jekjantuk, N., Gröner, G., Pan, J.Z.: Modelling and reasoning in metamodelling enabled ontologies. Int. J. Soft Inform. **4**(3), 277–290 (2010)
20. Kubincová, P., Kluka, J., Homola, M.: Expressive description logic with instantiation metamodelling. In: Proceedings of KR 2016 (2016)
21. Lara, J.D., Guerra, E., Cuadrado, J.S.: When and how to use multilevel modelling. ACM Trans. Softw. Eng. Methodol. **24**(2), 12 (2014)
22. Meigs, W.B., Meigs, R.F.: Financial Accounting, 4th edn. McGraw-Hill, New York (1983)
23. Motik, B.: On the properties of metamodeling in OWL. J. Log. Comput. **17**(4), 617–637 (2007)
24. Motik, B., Shearer, R., Horrocks, I.: Hypertableau reasoning for description logics. J. Artif. Intell. Res. **36**(1), 165–228 (2009)
25. Motz, R., Rohrer, E., Severi, P.: The description logic SHIQ with a flexible meta-modelling hierarchy. J. Web Semant. **35**(4), 214–234 (2015)
26. Rohrer, E., Severi, P., Motz, R.: Applying meta-modelling to an accounting application. In: ONTOBRAS (2018)
27. Schmidt, D.C.: Model-driven engineering. IEEE Comput. **39**(2), 25 (2006)
28. Severi, P., Rohrer, E., Motz, R.: A description logic for unifying different points of view. In: Written for KGSWC 2019 (2019)
29. Suarez-Figueroa, M.C., Gomez-Perez, A., Motta, E., Gangemi, A.: Ontology Engineering in a Networked World. Springer, Heidelberg (2012). https://doi.org/10.1007/978-3-642-24794-1

Automated Large Geographic Ontologies Generation Method from Spatial Databases

Manuel E. Puebla-Martínez[1] , José M. Perea-Ortega[2(✉)] ,
Alfredo Simón-Cuevas[3] , Francisco P. Romero[4] ,
and José A. Olivas Varela[4]

[1] Universidad de las Ciencias Informáticas, La Habana, Cuba
mpuebla@uci.cu
[2] Universidad de Extremadura, Badajoz, Spain
jmperea@unex.es
[3] Universidad Tecnológica de La Habana José Antonio Echeverría, La Habana, Cuba
asimon@ceis.cujae.edu.cu
[4] Universidad de Castilla-La Mancha, Ciudad Real, Spain
{franciscop.romero,joseangel.olivas}@uclm.es

Abstract. Ontologies have emerged as an important component in Information Systems and, specifically, in Geographic Information Systems, where they play a key role. However, the creation and maintenance of geographic ontologies can become an exhausting work due to the rapid growth and availability of spatial data, which are provided through relational databases most times. For this reason there has been an increasing interest in the automatic generation of geographic ontologies from relational databases in recent years. This work describes an automatic method to generate a geographic ontology from the spatial data provided by a relational database. The importance and originality of this study lie in that it is able to model two main aspects of a spatial database in the generated ontology: (1) The three main types of spatial data (point, line and polygon) are modelled as a data property and not as an object property. (2) Four data integrity constraints: First Normal Form, Not Null, Unique and Primary Key. Another contribution of our proposal is related to the support for generating large ontologies, which are not usually supported by traditional tools of ontological engineering such as Protégé or OWL API. Finally, some experiments were conducted in order to show the effectiveness of the proposed method.

Keywords: Spatial database · Geographic ontology ·
Automatic generation of ontology · Data integrity constraints · OWL2

1 Introduction

The main reason for the popularity of ontologies is its ease to structure, manage, share and process information in different fields such as Semantic Web, digital

© Springer Nature Switzerland AG 2019
B. Villazón-Terrazas and Y. Hidalgo-Delgado (Eds.): KGSWC 2019, CCIS 1029, pp. 118–133, 2019.
https://doi.org/10.1007/978-3-030-21395-4_9

corpora, electronic commerce and medical applications, among others. Ontologies manage to offer a common and shared knowledge of some domains, allowing people and computer applications to communicate effectively [7, 8]. Geographical ontologies or geontologies are considered a specialization of traditional ontologies that allow integrating and managing spatial data and their semantics, which represent 80% of the remaining data [25]. Due to the emergence and expansion of the Semantic Web, the use of geontologies has increased in recent years, thus favouring the development of Geographic Information Retrieval (GIR) systems [17, 18, 27].

Ontologies can be generated manually, semi-automatically or automatically. In this regard, manual generation of large ontologies represents an intensive work due to the knowledge evolution and data availability, making it difficult to generate, maintain and expand them with adequate quality [26]. Moreover, spatial data are usually provided by relational databases (Spatial Databases, SDB), so there is a renewed interest in the GIR research community for developing automatic methods to generate and maintain geographic ontologies that get data from relational databases. This has a particular significance when large ontologies should be managed, since current solutions (e.g. Protégé, OWL API) do not support them.

Regarding how to model geometric fields (points, lines and polygons) of a SDB through a data property in ontologies, previous published studies are limited. In addition, no research has been found that modelled the integrity constraints that can appear in a relational database. Therefore, this study makes a major contribution on this aspect by describing an automatic method to build a geographical ontology from the data provided by a relational SDB, with the novelty that it allows modelling their geometric fields and integrity constraints by using a powerful ontological engineering language like OWL2.

The remaining part of the paper proceeds as follows: Sect. 2 presents basic concepts and gives a brief overview of the related work. Section 3 describes the proposed method for automatic generation of a geontology. Section 4 shows the experiments carried out and their results and, finally, Sect. 5 presents the findings of the research.

2   Background

2.1   Relational Databases

A Relational Database (RDB) is a data model that includes sets of relationships, attributes and basic types [16, 28], which could be represented in the form of a RDB schema. A RDB schema defines the structure of a database and consists of the following main elements: *relationship* (database table with a set of columns, rows and constraints), *attribute* (column of a database table), *tuple* (record or row of a database table), *domain* (data type of a column of a database table, i.e., the type of values that a column can store, e.g., integer values), *primary key* (a constraint related to a column, which is established to maintain the integrity of the entity in the table, making rows unique and different in such a table), and *foreign key* (a restriction related to a column of a table in order to maintain referential integrity with data of other tables, i.e., a foreign key allows maintaining relationships between tables in the database, such as one-to-one, one-to-many or many-to-many).

2.2 Geographic Ontologies

This study follows the definition of ontology reported in [9], which states that an ontology is defined as a 4-tuple $O =< C, P, I, A >$, where C is a set of concepts, P is a set of properties, I is a set of instances and A is a set of axioms. There are different types of ontologies according to the data domain represented. This work focuses on geographic ontologies or geontologies, which are considered as an extension of a conventional ontology [10].

Vera and Garea [24] make an analysis of the definition of geontology given by Hess et al. [10]. Three main differences can be pointed out between geontologies and conventional ontologies: (1) spatial relations have a predefined and standardized semantics, while conventional relations are defined according to the concepts that they relate. (2) Each geographic concept is represented by its geometry and this plays a key role in the definition of new spatial relationships of the concept. (3) A geographic instance is represented by its spatial position on the surface by using pairs of coordinates expressed in a given coordinate system.

2.3 Related Work

Because most data are currently stored in RDB, numerous studies have been performed to develop techniques and tools to facilitate mapping between RDB and local ontologies. Generally there are two different approaches to perform the mapping between a RDB and a local ontology: (1) creating an ontology from a database. (2) Mapping a database to an existing ontology [21].

A considerable amount of literature has been published on generating ontologies semi-automatically from databases [1,2,4,6,11,12,15,16,19,22,23], but there are relatively few studies that address the geographical domain specifically [2,4,6,22]. The works presented in [4] and [3] describe a methodology to translate natural language queries into statements directly linked to database tables by exploiting a semantic enriched geospatial ontology developed from a SDB. Table 1 shows a comparison on the main features considered in the related work on spatial ontologies generation from SDB.

From the studies that address the geographical domain specifically, only in [2] is detailed how to model the three types of geometric fields of a SDB through a data property, while the rest of fields are modelled through object properties. This is an advantage compared to modelling through object properties, since it reduces the computational cost of future accessing the data for GIR systems. This issue can become even worse when large ontologies are managed, as common nowadays.

Finally, no research has been found that addresses how to model the integrity constraints that are usually represented in a spatial database. An and Park [1] try

Table 1. Comparison of related work on spatial ontologies generation from SDB

Criteria to be modelled	[3, 4]	[6]	[2]	[22]
1st NF	No	No	No	No
Field	No	No	No	No
Single field	No	No	No	No
Key field	No	No	No	No
Relations among tables	Yes	Yes	Yes	Yes
Tables, columns, tuples	Yes	Yes	Yes	Yes
Spatial data supported	Points, lines polygons with object properties	Points, lines polygons with object properties	Points, lines polygons with data properties	Points, lines polygons with object properties
Support for large ontologies	No	No	No	No

to give a solution by limiting the cardinality of the data properties, but they do not get to solve it completely due to the use of OWL1 as an ontological language. According to Riboni and Bettini [20], OWL1 is not adequate to model integrity constraints because it does not allow modelling the restrictions of the key fields or unique fields of databases. Connolly and Begg [5] state that the integrity constraints allow defining the way in which the database manager will automatically demand the integrity of the database. Restrictions define rules regarding the values allowed in the columns, and constitute the standard mechanism to force integrity. The requirement of data integrity guarantees the quality of the data of the SDB. For this reason, if the integrity constraints are not modelled by converting the SDB into ontology, the future system that uses the generated ontology as a data source will lack mechanisms that allow it to maintain the correctness and completeness of the information. When the information provided by the ontology is modified by the system, the integrity of the stored data may be lost in different ways, thus generating errors in the performance of the system such as loss of information.

3   Automatic Generation Method of the Ontology

The proposed method starts from a small preliminary ontology of the geographical domain[1] whose objective is to provide a general conceptualization of the geographical domain. Geonames[2] was used for this purpose. As shown in Fig. 1, several concepts, properties and spatial relationships are represented in the preliminary ontology, such as "*Road*" and "*Vegetation*" (concepts), "*longitude*" and "*latitude*" (data properties), or "*contains*" and "*overlap*" (spatial relationships as object properties), among others.

During the first phase of the proposed method, the preliminary ontology is automatically enriched from the information provided by a SDB, which should be in First Normal Form at least. Extractions of concepts, data properties, object

---

[1] The preliminary ontology is called *Ontobasic* and it is available at http://sinai.ujaen. es/ontobasic.

[2] http://www.geonames.org.

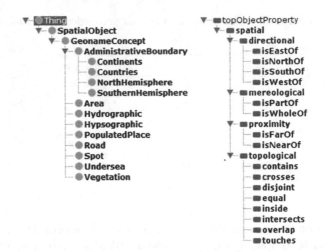

Fig. 1. Taxonomy and properties of the preliminary ontology

properties and their assertions, individuals and axioms for integrity constraints are carried out from the SDB. Optionally, the link between the concepts present in the preliminary ontology and the new concepts coming from the SDB can be performed with human intervention; otherwise the new concepts would not be considered. Finally, during the second phase, all the possible assertions of object properties (spatial relationships) are generated between the individuals previously extracted. Figure 2 shows an overview of the proposed method.

To support the exponential growth of the ontology we decided to use an Ontology-Based Database (OBDB), which allow storing and consulting ontologies with a large number of instances. The OBDB systems also take advantage of the functionalities provided by Relational Database Management (RDBM) systems, such as query performance, efficient storage of data, transaction management, among others. Section 3.3 describes in detail the procedure applied to manage the transformation of a large SDB into a geographic ontology.

The proposed method is characterized by three fundamental aspects: (1) the use of the WKT[3] string as an alternative to model the geometry field of the SDB. (2) The relationships between SDB tables are modelled in the ontology by using functional relationships defined in the preliminary ontology such as *"isPartOf"* or *"isWholeOf"*. (3) Modelling of four types of integrity constraints (First Normal Form, Not Null, Unique and Primary Key) that are usually supported by RDBM systems.

---

[3] Well-Known Text (WKT) is a text markup language for representing vector geometry objects on a map, spatial reference systems of spatial objects and transformations between spatial reference systems (Wikipedia).

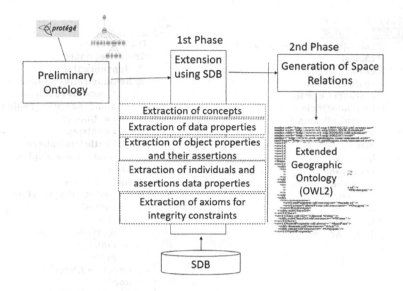

Fig. 2. Overview of the proposed method

3.1   Rule-Based Generation

During the first phase of the proposed method several rules were applied to generate the ontology:

1. **Concepts:** for each table of the SDB a concept with the same name is added to the ontology, with the exception of the tables generated by many-to-many relationships. These tables are modelled as object properties of type *"isPartOf"* or *"isWholeOf"*. The proposed method allows the user to establish manually the equivalence or inheritance between the new concept and those existing in the preliminary ontology. Figure 3 shows an example of the class hierarchy generated without (A) and with (B) human intervention.

2. **Data properties:** for each attribute A_i belonging to the table T_k, a new data property is added to the ontology, with the exception of the geometry attribute, for which the WKT string is used. The new data property becomes a sub-property of the data property called *"edbDataProperty"*, which is in the preliminary ontology. The concept corresponding to T_k would be the domain of the new data property, while the data type of A_i would be the range of the new data property. The name assigned to the new data property is composed by concatenating the name of T_k with the name of A_i.

3. **Objects properties and their assertions:** relationships between tables are converted into new object properties that will be sub-properties of "textitisPartOf" or *"isWholeOf"*. For each foreign key FK of the table T_i related to the table T_j, so that $i \neq j$, a new object property of the type *"isPartOf"* is added to the ontology. The concept corresponding to the table T_i would be the domain, while the concept corresponding to the table T_j would be the range.

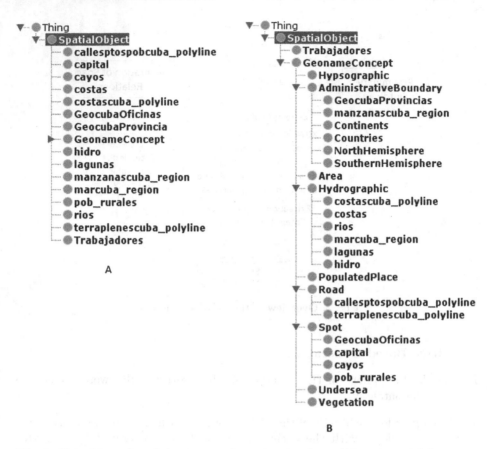

Fig. 3. Class hierarchy of the generated ontology without (A) and with (B) human intervention

The name of the new object property would be composed by concatenating the name of T_i with the string *"isPartOf"*, plus the name of the table T_j. For example, if a table is called *"Continents"* and another table called *"Countries"* has as a foreign key the primary key of *"Continents"*, the name of the new object property in the ontology would be *"Countries-isPartOf-Continents"*. Furthermore, the object property *"isWholeOf"* is the inverse of the *"isPartOf"* one, so for each object property of type *"isPartOf"* a new object property of type *"isWholeOf"* is generated analogously.

4. **Assertions object properties:** for each row F_i of the table T_i, related to row F_j of the table T_j, an assertion of object property is added to the ontology. In this way, we can relate the individual corresponding to F_i, the individual corresponding to F_j, and the object property corresponding to the relationship between the rows F_i and F_j. In the example above, all the individuals that represent countries would be related to the individual that

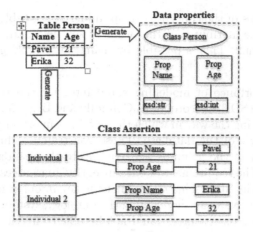

Fig. 4. Example of the construction of individuals and data properties assertions

represents their continent through the object property *"Countries-isPartOf-Continents"* and its inverse *"Continents-isWholeOf-Countries"*.

5. **Individuals and assertions data properties:** for each row F_i belonging to the table T_k, a new individual I_i is added to the ontology, becoming an instance of the concept corresponding to T_k. The name assigned to I_i is composed by the prefix *"DB-"*, the name of the table T_k, followed by a hyphen (-) and the value of the column F_i that represents the name of the spatial object. If the user does not specify the latter value, the concatenation of the values of the key attributes is used as the name of the spatial object.

6. **Assertions of data properties:** for each attribute A_x belonging to F_i, a new data property assertion is added to relate I_i, the data property corresponding to A_x and the value of A_x. Figure 4 shows an example of the construction of individuals and data properties assertions.

7. **Integrity constraints:**
   - All data properties from the SDB are restricted to maximum cardinality 1 (functional data properties). This is feasible because the SDB should be in First Normal Form at least, which guarantees no more than one value per attribute.
   - *Not Null*: for each table T_i an attribute A_k is identified if A_k cannot be null. In the affirmative case, the minimum cardinality of the data property that represents A_k in the concept corresponding to the table T_i becomes 1. This approach is similar to that proposed in [22].
   - *Unique*: for each table T_i the attributes that compose the unique restriction are identified. Then it is guaranteed that there are no instances of the concept corresponding to the table T_i with the same values in the attributes of the unique field. This is possible by using the *"DisjointDataProperties"* axiom provided by the OWL2 language.
   - *Primary Key*: for each table T_i the attributes that compose the primary key field are identified. Then it is guaranteed that there are no

two instances of the concept corresponding to the table T_i with the same values in the attributes of the primary key field and, in addition, these cannot be null. This is possible by using the *"HasKey"* axiom provided by OWL2.

What is the importance of modelling some integrity constraints of the data extracted from the SDB? According to Connolly and Begg [5], the integrity constraints allow defining the way in which the database manager will automatically require the integrity of the database. These constraints define rules regarding the values allowed in the columns and constitute the standard mechanism to require integrity. The requirement of data integrity guarantees the quality of the data provided by the SDB. This requirement is key in our proposal since, if the integrity constraints were not modelled in the ontology, systems that use the generated ontology as a data source would not be able to maintain the correctness and completeness of the information.

Finally, for each individual a unique key is generated. This is formed by the prefix *"DB-"* followed by the name of the table and the primary key of the individual. This new identifier will serve to build the IRI of the individual in the generated ontology.

3.2   Automatic Inference of Spatial Relationships

Larín-Fonseca [13] refers to the diversity of ontology types that have been proposed in the literature, but he focuses on the knowledge that is not being used yet, as the one related to geospatial data. He also points out that the relations between geographic objects are as important as the objects themselves in the geospatial domain. For this reason, all the pairs of individuals that are related by means of some of the object properties defined in the preliminary ontology are automatically identified in the proposed method. For each pair of spatial objects (*object1* and *object2*), our proposal verifies the existence of the 21 object properties defined in the preliminary ontology by using the ESRI Geometry API for Java[4].

During the second phase of the proposed method spatial relationships are also inferred by using four features (reflexivity, symmetry, transitivity and inverse) that are defined in the object properties of the preliminary ontology, in a similar way to a classic reasoner. For example, if *object1* is related to *object2* through the relation *"contains"* and *object2* is related to *object3* through the relation *"contains"* as well, then a new relationship is automatically added to the ontology between *object1* and *object3* due to the transitivity of the *"contains"* relationship. Similarly, the spatial relationship *"inside"* is defined as the inverse of the relationship *"contains"*, so if *object1* is related to *object2* by the spatial relationship *"inside"*, then it is automatically inferred and added to the ontology that *object2* is also related to *object1* by the spatial relationship *"contains"*.

---

[4] http://github.com/Esri/geometry-api-java.

3.3 Managing the Generated Ontology from External Memory: Ontology-Based Database (OBDB)

To support the transformation of a large SDB into a geographic ontology and generate new assertions of object properties, some data from the OWL file were extracted and stored in external memory. On the one hand, the axioms of assertions of data properties and assertions of object properties from the ABOX data were extracted and stored in external memory while, on the other hand, the TBOX data were fully managed by internal memory with the aim of using the reasoners for some specific tasks such as the inference processes. Thus, we ensured to maintain the reasoning capacity on the ontology in internal memory always. The OWL API[5] was used to manage the generated ontology through its associated OWL file. Figure 5 illustrates the distribution of responsibilities between the OWL API framework and the SDB when the components of the ontology are managed.

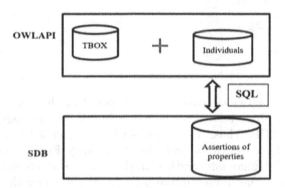

Fig. 5. Distribution of responsibilities between the OWL API framework and the SDB

4 Experimental Evaluation Results

Firstly, in order to assess the effectiveness of the proposed method, a Spatial Database (SDB) was manually generated from the spatial information provided by Geocuba[6], which is an association of Cuban state companies responsible for elaborating and commercializing information, technologies, products and services in areas such as Geodesy, Photogrammetry, Remote Sensing, Hydrography, Marine Studies, Cartography, Environmental Studies, Graphic Arts and Aid for Maritime Navigation. Some examples of spatial data included in the SDB were: streets, coasts, capitals, provinces, offices, rivers, lagoons or country towns, all of them belonging to Cuba. Table 2 shows the structure of the SDB generated for the experiments[7].

---

[5] http://owlcs.github.io/owlapi.

[6] https://www.geocuba.cu.

[7] A backup of the SDB generated is available at http://sinai.ujaen.es/bde-geocuba.

Table 2. Structure of the SDB generated for the experiments

Tables	Primary key	Foreign key
streetpoints_polyline (gid, elementype, geom)	gid	-
capital (gid, blank, geom)	gid	-
cayos (gid, blank, geom)	gid	-
costs (gid, blank, geom)	gid	-
costscuba_polyline (gid, elementype, field2, geom)	gid	-
GeocubaOffices (PKGeocubaOffices, Name office, quantity projects, FKgeocubaProvince, FKworkers)	PKGeocubaOffices	FKgeocubaProvince and FKworkers
GeocubaProvinces (PKGeoCubaProvinces, NameProvince, QuantityEmployees)	PKGeoCubaProvinces	-
hydro (gid, blank, geom)	gid	-
lagoons (gid, blank, geom)	gid	-
blockscuba_region (gid, elementype, geom)	gid	-
sea_cuba_region (gid, elementype, geom)	gid	-
country_towns (gid, blank, geom)	gid	-
rivers (gid, blank, geom)	gid	-
embankment_cuba_polyline (gid, elementype, width, geom)	gid	-
Workers (PKWorkers,NameSurname,Age)	PKWorkers	-

Secondly, the automatic part of the proposed method comes into play by running the first phase related to the extension of the ontology from the data provided by the SDB. Thus, the rules described in Sect. 3.1 were automatically performed in order to enrich the preliminary ontology. Figure 3 shows the results without and with human intervention. In this sense, the concepts of the preliminary ontology were not reused in the process. Finally, once the first phase was concluded, the automatic generation of spatial relationships was carried out, as described in Sect. 3.2.

Table 3 compares the main characteristics of the preliminary ontology versus the extended ontology generated by applying the proposed method. From these results, a significant enrichment of the information provided by the extended ontology is observed. For instance, the number of concepts was increased from 15 to 30, 49 new data properties were added or 82 new taxonomic relations were inferred. During the experiments, new four object properties of type "*mereological*" were generated, two of the subtype "*isPartOf*" and two of the subtype "*isWholeOf*", as shown in Fig. 6. This type of object properties models one-to-many and many-to-many relationships between the tables of a relational database.

Regarding the assertions of object properties, 16 of them were generated from the relational model of the SDB, and 697,500 of them were generated from the spatial properties of the data. The latter were stored in a database instead of the OWL file in order to take advantage of the capabilities of the RDBM system and overcome the limitations of the OWL API framework. Both, the extended

Table 3. Comparison of the main characteristics of the preliminary ontology versus the generated ontology

	Original components	Primary key	Foreign key
TBOX	Concepts	15	30
	Data properties	44	93
	Object properties	21	25
	Taxonomic relations	14	96
ABOX	Individuals	0	432
	Assertions of object properties	0	16 + 697,500
	Assertions of data properties	0	$1,788^*$

* They are stored in the SDB and not in the OWL file

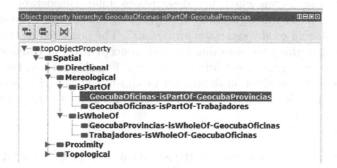

Fig. 6. New object properties of type *mereological* generated by the proposed method

ontology and the backup of the database that stores the assertions of object properties have been made available to the scientific community[8].

Comparing the solution proposed in this work with those analysed in Table 1, the following remarks should be pointed out:

- The proposed solution satisfies the eight variables used. In the case of the variable *"Spatial Data supported"*, our proposal follows the same approach presented in [2].
- Regarding the three basic types of spatial data, our proposal follows the approach described in [6]: *"The points are represented through the spatial location, the lines are defined through points and the polygons are defined through lines"*. Only in [2] the geometric field is modelled with a data property: the WKT string. Modelling spatial data as data properties is an advantage compared to modelling through object properties, since access to property is more efficient if it is modelled as a single data property and not as a combination of object properties. This variant increases the computational cost because the assertions object properties should be identified, which is further aggravated when large ontologies are managed, as in our case, where the assertions of

---

[8] http://sinai.ujaen.es/ontogeocuba.

properties are of the order of the millions and are stored in external memory. It is also important to point out that the WKT string constitutes a standard of the OGC[9].

The generated ontology was assessed with the OOPS tool [14]. According to the author, it is the most complete tool for evaluating ontologies due to the number of errors that it is able to detect regarding the complexity of an ontology. The errors are classified in three levels: *critical, important* and *minor*. As shown in Table 4, from the errors detected during the evaluation of the generated ontology, only one (P30) was classified as *important*. In this sense, OOPS requires that concepts that have the same meaning should be defined as equivalent. However, the identification of synonyms in OOPS is carried out through WordNet queries without considering the context. For example, *Store* and *Store-house* are considered synonyms when their descriptions differ considerably: *Store* is *"a building where goods and/or services are offered for sale"*, while *Store-house* is *"a building for storing goods, especially provisions"*. The proposed method includes annotations describing the meaning for each concept without considering if the names can be synonyms according to WorNed. For this reason, the error P30 detected during the evaluation should not be considered as such one because the *Countries* and *Area* classes are not equivalent according to the context of the generated ontology.

Table 4. Evaluation results of the generated ontology by using OOPS

Category	Evaluation results	Error level
Functional dimension	No errors detected	
Consistency	No errors detected	
Completeness	No errors detected	
Conscience	No errors detected	
Structural dimension	Error **P30**: equivalent classes not explicitly declared: *Countries* and *Area*	Important
Usability-profiling dimension	Error **P22**: Using different naming conventions in the ontology. Error **P08**: missing annotations	Minor

5 Conclusions

This work presents an automatic method to extend geographic ontologies from the data provided by a Spatial Database (SDB) that should be in First Normal Form at least. The proposed method allows enriching a preliminary ontology by generating automatically new concepts, data and object properties, taxonomic relations or even new spatial relationships between the geographic objects of the SDB. The novelty of our proposal lies in that it is able to model two main aspects of a SDB: (1) the three main types of spatial data (point, line and polygon)

---

[9] http://www.opengeospatial.org.

are modelled as a data property and not as an object property. (2) Four data integrity constraints: First Normal Form, Not Null, Unique and Primary Key.

Another relevant contribution is related to the support for generating large ontologies, an aspect that is not provided by other traditional tools of ontological engineering such as Protégé or OWL API. This was achieved by applying an Ontology-Based Database (OBDB) approach. Finally, the following conclusions can be drawn:

- The fact of modelling the three types of spatial data by using data properties and not object properties guarantees a greater efficiency in the management of the spatial information.
- By modelling the integrity of the data extracted from the SDB, the quality of the spatial information is guaranteed in the generated ontology.
- The large number of new assertions of data properties and object properties inferred by the proposed method increases the possibilities of using the extended ontology by GIR systems or similar tools.
- The ontology generated by using the proposed method can be considered correct according to the OOPS tool, since only two minor errors related to the *Usability-Profiling* dimension were detected.

Acknowledgments. This work has been partially supported by FEDER and the State Research Agency (AEI) of the Spanish Ministry of Economy and Competition under grant MERINET: TIN2016-76843-C4-2-R (AEI/FEDER, UE).

References

1. An, J., Park, Y.B.: Methodology for automatic ontology generation using database schema information. Mob. Inf. Syst. **2018**, 1–13 (2018). https://doi.org/10.1155/2018/1359174
2. Athanasiou, S., Bezati, L., Giannopoulos, G., Patroumpas, K., Skoutas, D., Stadler, C.: Proyecto GeoKnow. Deliverable 2.2.1 Integration of External Geospatial Databases (2013). http://svn.aksw.org/projects/GeoKnow/Public/D2.2.1_Integration_of_Geospatial_Databases.pdf
3. Baglioni, M., Giovannetti, E., Masserotti, M.V., Renso, C., Spinsanti, L.: Ontology-supported querying of geographical databases. Transact. GIS **12**(s1), 31–44 (2008). https://doi.org/10.1111/j.1467-9671.2008.01136.x
4. Baglioni, M., Masserotti, M.V., Renso, C., Spinsanti, L.: Building geospatial ontologies from geographical databases. In: Fonseca, F., Rodríguez, M.A., Levashkin, S. (eds.) GeoS 2007. LNCS, vol. 4853, pp. 195–209. Springer, Heidelberg (2007). https://doi.org/10.1007/978-3-540-76876-0_13
5. Connolly, T., Begg, C.: Database Systems: A Practical Approach to Design, Implementation, and Management, 6th edn. Pearson, Harlow (2015)
6. Lima, D., Mendonça, A., Salgado, A.C., Souza, D.: Building geospatial ontologies from geographic database schemas in peer data management systems. In: Proceedings XII GEOINFO, pp. 1–12 (2011)
7. Garea Llano, E.: Estado actual de la interpretación semántica de datos espaciales. Blue Series. Pattern Recognition. CENATAV (2007). http://www.cenatav.co.cu/doc/RTecnicos/RT%20SerieAzul_001web.pdf

8. Gruber, T.R.: Toward principles for the design of ontologies used for knowledge sharing. Int. J. Hum.-Comput. Stud. **43**(5–6), 907–928 (1995). https://doi.org/10.1006/ijhc.1995.1081

9. Hess, G.: Towards effective geographic ontology semantic similarity assessment. Ph.D. thesis, Universidade Federal do Rio Grande do Sulinstituto de Informática, Porto Alegre (2008). https://www.lume.ufrgs.br/bitstream/handle/10183/14973/000674854.pdf?sequence=1

10. Hess, G.N., Iochpe, C., Ferrara, A., Castano, S.: Towards effective geographic ontology matching. In: Fonseca, F., Rodríguez, M.A., Levashkin, S. (eds.) GeoS 2007. LNCS, vol. 4853, pp. 51–65. Springer, Heidelberg (2007). https://doi.org/10.1007/978-3-540-76876-0_4

11. Jain, V., Prasad, A.V.: Mapping between RDBMS and ontology: a review. Int. J. Sci. Technol. Res. **3**(11), 307–313 (2014). http://www.ijstr.org/final-print/nov2014/Mapping-Between-Rdbms-And-Ontology-A-Review.pdf

12. Jiménez-Ruiz, E., et al.: BootOX: Practical mapping of RDBs to OWL 2. In: Arenas, M., et al. (eds.) ISWC 2015. LNCS, vol. 9367, pp. 113–132. Springer, Cham (2015). https://doi.org/10.1007/978-3-319-25010-6_7

13. Larín-Fonseca, R.: Nuevo tipo de ontología para la representación semántica de objetos geoespaciales. Ph.D. thesis, Instituto Técnico Militar "José Martí", La Habana (2012)

14. Poveda Villalón, M.: Ontology Evaluation: a pitfall-based approach to ontology diagnosis. Tesis doctoral, Universidad Politécnica de Madrid, Escuela Técnica Superior de Ingenieros Informáticos. España (2016). http://oa.upm.es/39448/1/MARIA_POVEDA_VILLALON.pdf

15. Pasha, M., Sattar, A.: Building domain ontologies from relational database using mapping rules. Int. J. Intell. Eng. Syst. **5**(1), 20–27 (2012)

16. Mogotlane, K.D., Dombeu, J.V.F.: Automatic conversion of relational databases into ontologies: a comparative analysis of protégé plug-ins performances. Int. J. Web Semant. Technol., 7(3/4) (2016). https://doi.org/10.5121/ijwest.2016.7403

17. Pillai, M., Karabatis, G.: Enhancing spatial query results using semantics and multiplex networks. In: Spatial Query Results using Semantics and Multiplex Networks HETERONAM, p. 8, (2018). https://doi.org/10.13016/M2W37KX5Z

18. Purves, R.S., Clough, P., Jones, C.B., Hall, M.H., Murdock, V.: Geographic information retrieval: progress and challenges in spatial search of text. Found. Trends Inf. Retrieval **12**(2–3), 164–318 (2018). https://doi.org/10.1561/1500000034

19. Ramathilagam, C., Valarmathi, M.L.: Mapping of relational databases to ontology a survey. Data Min. Knowl. Eng., 4(9) (2012). http://www.ciitresearch.org/dl/index.php/dmke/article/view/DMKE082012005

20. Riboni, D., Bettini, C.: OWL 2 modeling and reasoning with complex human activities. Pervasive Mob. Comput. **7**(3), 379–395 (2011). https://doi.org/10.1016/j.pmcj.2011.02.001

21. Stanimirović, A., Bogdanović, M., Stoimenov, L.: Methodology and intermediate layer for the automatic creation of ontology instances stored in relational databases. Softw. Pract. Exp. **43**(2), 129–152 (2013). https://doi.org/10.1002/spe.2103

22. Tolaba, A.C., Caliusco, M.L., Galli, M.R.: Representación del Conocimientode la Información Geográfica siguiendo un Enfoque basado enOntologías. Revista Ibérica de Sistemas y Tecnologías de la Información **14**, 101–106 (2014). https://doi.org/10.17013/risti.14.101-116

23. Vega Ramírez, A., Grangel González, I., Sáez Mosquera, I., García Castro, R.: Procedimiento para la obtención de un modelo ontológico para representar la información contenida en bases de datos. In: CEUR Workshop Proceedings of Actas del 1er Taller Cubano de Web Semántica, TCWS 2014, pp. 46–59 (2014). http://oa.upm.es/cgi/export/36716/

24. Vera Voronisky, F., Garea Llano, E.: Alineamiento de Ontologías en el Dominio Geoespacial. Reporte Técnico. Reconocimiento de Patrones, CENATAV (2009)

25. Vilches-Blázquez, L.M., Saavedra, J.: A framework for connecting two interoperability universes: OGC web feature services and linked data. Transact. GIS **23**(1), 22–47 (2019). https://doi.org/10.1111/tgis.12496

26. Yeh, J., Yang, N.: Ontology construction based on latent topic extraction in a digital library. In: Buchanan, G., Masoodian, M., Cunningham, S.J. (eds.) ICADL 2008. LNCS, vol. 5362, pp. 93–103. Springer, Heidelberg (2008). https://doi.org/10.1007/978-3-540-89533-6_10

27. Tou, J.T.: Information systems. In: von Brauer, W. (ed.) GI 1973. LNCS, vol. 1, pp. 489–507. Springer, Heidelberg (1973). https://doi.org/10.1007/3-540-06473-7_52

28. Zhang, L., Li, J.: Automatic generation of ontology based on database. J. Comput. Inf. Syst. **7**(4), 1148–1154 (2011)

Towards the Semantic Enrichment of Existing Online 3D Building Geometry to Publish Linked Building Data

Maarten Bassier[(✉)], Mathias Bonduel, Jens Derdaele, and Maarten Vergauwen

Department of Civil Engineering, TC Construction, KU Leuven, Ghent, Belgium
{maarten.bassier,mathias.bonduel,jens.derdaele,
maarten.vergauwen}@kuleuven.be
https://iiw.kuleuven.be/onderzoek/geomatics

Abstract. Currently, existing online 3D databases each have their own structure according to their own needs. Additionally, the majority of online content only has limited semantics. With the advent of Semantic Web technologies, the opportunity arises to semantically enrich the information in these databases and make it widely accessible and queryable. The goal is to investigate whether online 3D content from different repositories can be processed by a single algorithm to produce the desired semantics. The emphasis of this work is on extracting building components from generic 3D building geometry and publish it as Linked Building Data.

An interpretation framework is proposed that takes as input any building mesh and outputs its components. More specifically, we use pretrained Support Vector Machines to classify the separate meshes derived from each 3D model. As a preliminary test case, realistic examples from several repositories are processed. The test results depict that, even though the building content originates from different sources and was not modeled according to any standards, it can be processed by a single machine learning application. As a result, building geometry in online repositories can be semantically enriched with component information according to classes from Linked Data ontologies such as BOT and PRODUCT. This is an important step towards making the implicit content of geometric models queryable and linkable over the Web.

Keywords: Existing data · 3D geometry · Linked building data · Classification

1 Introduction

The number of online digital models is rapidly increasing. Every day, thousands of new 3D models are flooding the Web originating from varying sources including 3D printing hobbyists, CAD designers and remote sensing specialists. Aside from documentation, these models are used to create games, virtual tours,

B. Villazón-Terrazas and Y. Hidalgo-Delgado (Eds.): KGSWC 2019, CCIS 1029, pp. 134–148, 2019.
https://doi.org/10.1007/978-3-030-21395-4_10

building designs and so on [8,13,17]. In order to organize this vast amount of inputs, databases are created with a certain data structure and a set of semantics. Currently, most of these data structures are unique and field specific. Also, the depth of the semantics involved is typically limited to describing the geometry model as a whole e.g. a car, building or 3D printable model. As databases are expanding and becoming increasingly widespread, their data structures also have to expand. However, their lack of standardized ontologies is halting this procedure. Additionally, the provided content is typically classified manually by contributors or moderators which is labor intensive and error prone. As a result, online repositories suffer from data heterogeneity and unstructured data. This severely limits the accessibility and usefulness of the information since there is no uniform data access method and detailed queries cannot be run on the data for analysis and management purposes [7].

In this work, we discuss the opportunities of extracting semantics from existing 3D content in such a way that the output can become queryable and linkable. We specifically target 3D data that has limited semantics in order to enrich them. Basic semantics are used defined in public ontologies related to the building domain, such as the Building Topology Ontology (BOT) [14] and PRODUCT Building Elements ontology [15]. Both ontologies are designed within the Linked Building Data Community Group of the World Wide Web consortium (W3C-LBD-CG) and are prepared for standardization. By publishing the identified building components of each 3D model as Linked Data using the above public ontologies, they can be linked to content of other Linked Data databases and analyzed in a standardized manner.

While Linked Data is applicable to all types of content, we specifically investigate the enrichment of unstructured building-related geometry. In recent years, the amount of building information has skyrocketed. Numerous sources are currently available for this type of information (Fig. 1). For instance, there is the Architectural, Engineering and Construction (AEC) industry that now have the majority of their assets designed in 3D. This includes both as-design models as well as-built datasets. Also, there are the building models created by heritage experts based on prior documents. These structures are digital representations of built heritage throughout history. Additionally, structures are also digitally represented in databases such as Google maps, Google Earth and national GIS databases based on remote sensing technologies. Last but not least there are numerous repositories of virtual content originating from hobbyists and the gaming industry. Overall, it is stated that a formidable amount of fictional and non-fictional building data is digitally represented many times over with varying degrees of detailing, data structures and from different time periods. It is our hypothesis that since each of these entities are in fact buildings, that there is the common denominator of building logic shared across all of these datasets. Furthermore, we consider each building as an aggregate of its components including the walls, floors, ceilings, roofs and other entities that have definitions within existing standards. The definition of a building itself also serves as a powerful semantic to discriminate buildings from other objects. In general, this is

Fig. 1. Overview varying unstructured model representations of the Konzerthaus, Berlin in different databases. Google maps 3D representation based on landsat imagery, 2018 (a), 3DCityDB LOD2 GIS database representation 2012 (b), automated point-cloud reconstruction from photogrammetry (c), textured mesh generated from point-cloud (d) and manually modeled gaming object by nurogames based on photogramme-try output (e).

already present in online repositories and it is our hypothesis that these custom repository classes do in fact discriminate regular building content. Given these assumptions, the emphasis of this work is on the investigation of the opportunities of extracting more detailed semantics from building geometries found in online repositories that currently do not have data related to their building components.

The remainder of this work is structured as follows. The background and related work are presented in Sect. 2. In Sect. 3, a methodology is presented to extract the semantics from building geometry. In Sect. 4, the methodology is tested on 3D models from several online repositories. Finally, the conclusions are presented in Sect. 5 along with the future work.

2   Background and Related Work

While the extraction of semantics from structureless online 3D geometry repositories is still a gap in the current literature, the subject of classifying a set of observations is a widely discussed topic. The extraction of semantics from a set of inputs is a data association paradigm that is subject of ongoing research. In the case of assigning class labels to a number of observations, it is considered an instance of supervised pattern recognition. Several researchers have proposed methods to extract object classes from building geometry. For instance, Armeni et al. [2] and Nikoohemat et al. [11] compute labels of building components in a variety of scenes. In addition to heuristic methods, machine learning procedures are proposed to deal with the wide variety of object parameters, classes and observations. Xiong et al. [19,20] extract features from preprocessed meshes and classify them using stacked learning. Markov Random Fields (MRF) and Conditional Random Fields (CRF) are also proposed for the classification of indoor scenes [1,10,18]. In general, these methods are designed to process sensor data such as Light detection and ranging (Lidar) data or photogrammetric point clouds [9]. However, within the context of processing generic online 3D models, there are few algorithms capable of dealing with the multiple data representations and formats. It is within the scope of this work to test if machine learning methods can be expanded to process building geometries from different sources and successfully extract component information from the geometric models.

The uptake of Linked Data in the building domain is mainly related to the need for reliable data exchange between stakeholders and their applications [13]. From the perspective of BIM, the use of Linked Data offers extra functionality such as fine grained linking between datasets, the use of a standardized query language SPARQL and the power of generic reasoning engines. For the building domain, several Linked Data ontologies or data schemas have been proposed over the years to facilitate the sharing of structured data over the web. Notably, there are the IfcOWL ontologies from the BuildingSMART Linked Data Working Group and the new modular Linked Building Data (LBD) ontologies from the W3C-LBD Community Group [12]. The IfcOWL ontologies are a Linked Data mirror of the large and complicated original IFC schemas in the EXPRESS language. In contrast, the LBD ontologies are lightweight and modular, making them better suited for usage in a Semantic Web context [16]. In the presented paper, the LBD ontologies BOT[1] and PRODUCT[2], together with the File Ontology for Geometry formats (FOG)[3], are preferred over IfcOWL for these reasons. The Building Topology Ontology (BOT) was designed as a minimal, central building ontology containing core concepts of a building (e.g. Site, Building, Storey, Space, Element, etc.), possible relations between instances of these classes (e.g. hasBuilding, adjacentElement, etc.) and how these classes and properties are related to each other [16]. The PRODUCT ontology on the other hand, describes classes of building components (e.g. Wall, Beam, Roof, etc.) in a taxonomy and is loosely based on the IFC product definitions. Currently, it contains a small core part and three subdivisions for respectively (general) Building Elements, MEP and Furniture. This ontology can easily be extended with additional, more specific classes of building components if necessary. For this research, we propose to use classes from the PRODUCT Building Elements module to label building components extracted from online 3D models. Finally, FOG can be used as a flexible ontology with specific properties to connect building objects to geometry descriptions, based on the used geometry format (e.g.

---

[1] https://w3id.org/bot#.
[2] https://github.com/w3c-lbd-cg/product.
[3] https://w3id.org/fog#.

STL, OBJ, PLY, etc.). The current state of the art focuses on publishing LOD from data that already posses semantics. The paper suggests an alternative approach for the creation of Linked Building Data graphs. Instead of converting traditional BIM data e.g. via the IFCtoLBD converter [5] as a downstream process, it is also possible to extract a LBD graph from a pure geometrical 3D model using our approach.

3   Methodology

In this paper, we look to bridge the gap between unstructured building geometry stored in online repositories and Linked Data. The first step in this procedure is the evaluation of the input data and the retrieval of a generic geometry representation for building components that is shared among online repositories. Next, a previously developed framework [3] is presented to extract the target semantics. The presented approach is solely data driven as the source geometry does not yet contain any semantics. To construct a proper basis, we look to extract basic semantics such as walls, ceilings, floors, roofs and beams conform existing ontologies. A clutter class is also defined for observations that do not correspond to one of the predefined classes. No semantics are derived for this class and operators are encouraged to employ different information sources aside from the geometry to retrieve the proper semantics. Finally, the building is represented as an aggregate of buildings components which are labeled using classes from the BOT and PRODUCT ontologies. In the following paragraphs, the method is discussed in detail.

3.1   Inputs

In order to properly process any geometry with a single algorithm, some restrictions are applied to the input data. A first aspect is the compatibility of the information, which should be made available in a common geometry representation such as NURBS, meshes or point clouds. In this work, we operate on any mesh geometry in a common data format such as .obj, .ply and .stl since it allows highly detailed geometry representations. A second aspect is the type of structure that we process. As previously discussed, the target semantics comprise of building components such as walls, ceilings and so on. We therefore state that the input geometry, whether fictional or non-fictional, should in fact be buildings which can be represented as an aggregate of said building components. These are mostly planar structures which are ordered according to common buildings logic.

3.2   Feature Extraction

In order to classify a set of observations, a number of characteristics or features is computed for every observation and its context. As previously stated, the hypothesis is that common building logic apply to the input data. For instance, this indicates that walls are generally near vertical structures that enclose floors and support ceilings and roofs. While there certainly is significant variance between models from different sources, we state that the inputs can be described sufficiently discriminative to be recognized as one of the above classes. In this work, both local and contextual information is exploited for the various features [3]. The former encodes the object's geometric information such as the size and orientation while the latter encodes both associative and non-associative information in relation to other meshes e.g. coplanarity, parallelity, proximity and so on. In our approach, the contextual information is computed for nearby meshes as well as for specific reference groups. For instance, the coplanarity of a surface is tested with nearby sufficiently large reference surfaces as they yield more information on the class of the observation. The resulting feature values are stored in a feature vector which is normalized.

3.3   Classification

Given the feature vectors, one of k labels is predicted for the individual observations. In this research, Support Vector Machines [6] are proposed to classify the observed surfaces. The model choice is driven by the sparsity and specificity of the training data. A major advantage of SVM's is the use of support vectors instead of the bulk of the training data to establish the decision function. This allows for a proper model creation with smaller but more distinct training data sets which is the case in this experiment. SVM's are non-probabilistic functions that separate the feature space in two by defining a hyperplane given the feature values. They typically represent linear models of the form

$$y(X) = \boldsymbol{w}^T \emptyset(X_i) + b \tag{1}$$

where $\emptyset(X_i)$ denotes a fixed feature-space transformation (kernel function) with the dimensionality equal to the dimensionality of the input feature vectors X, b the bias and $\boldsymbol{w} = \{w_1, \ldots, w_f\}$ is the weight of the features [4]. Given the hyperplane, new observations are labeled by computing on which side of the boundary their feature vector is located. The feature space distance of an observation's feature vector X_i to the hyperplane is given by

$$\frac{y(\boldsymbol{w}^T \emptyset(X_i) + b)}{\|\boldsymbol{w}\|} \tag{2}$$

New observations are classified by evaluating the signed distance function $y(X, \boldsymbol{w}, b)$ from the hyperplane to the corresponding feature vector. As Support Vector Machines are fundamentally two-class classifiers, we employ multiple SVM's in a one-versus-one configuration. $k(k-1)/2$ different two-class functions are computed on all possible pairs of classes. The model parameters are learned from a large set of known observations. During the training, cross-validation is employed to enhance the model performance. The data is partitioned into K-folds. Each partition is consecutively withheld as the other partitions are used for training. The final optimized maximum-margin hyperplane is given by the

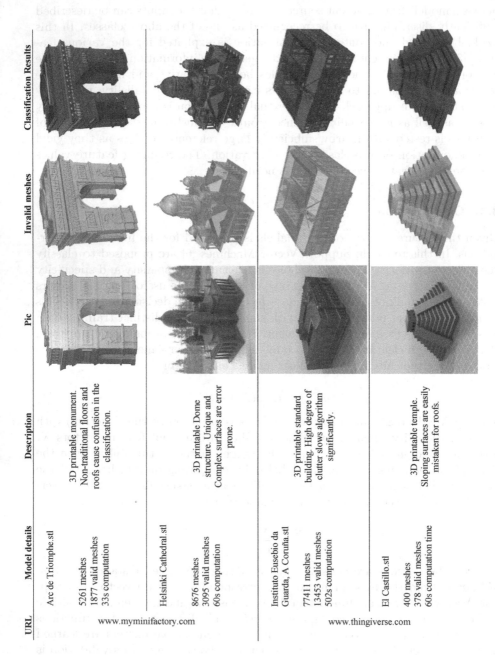

Fig. 2. Overview classification results of varying databases.

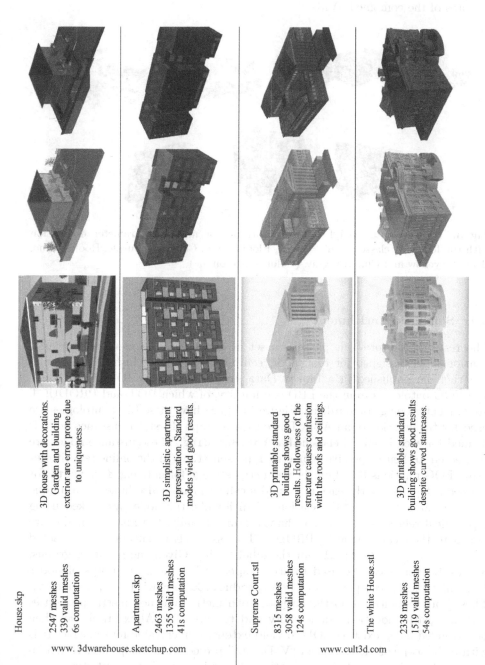

House.skp

2547 meshes
339 valid meshes
6s computation

3D house with decorations. Garden and building exterior are error prone due to uniqueness.

www. 3dwarehouse.sketchup.com

Apartment.skp

2463 meshes
1355 valid meshes
41s computation

3D simplistic apartment representation. Standard models yield good results.

Supreme Court.stl

8315 meshes
3058 valid meshes
124s computation

3D printable standard building shows good results. Hollowness of the structure causes confusion with the roofs and ceilings.

www.cult3d.com

The white House.stl

2338 meshes
1519 valid meshes
54s computation

3D printable standard building shows good results despite curved staircases.

Fig. 2. (*continued*)

averaged model parameters. New surfaces are labeled according to the number of votes of the combined SVMs.

Fig. 3. Training data used for the support vector machine parameter estimation with the following classes: Walls = green, Floors = red, Ceilings = purple, Roofs = blue, Beams = yellow and Clutter = gray. (Color figure online)

3.4   Semantic Enrichment

The result of the previous phase is a set of geometrical segments with classification labels assigned for roof, floor, ceiling, beam, wall, clutter. The results can then be published in a Linked Data graph, using the BOT, PRODUCT and FOG ontologies from the LBD community, of which BOT and PRODUCT are currently being standardized. Figure 4 depicts how these LBD ontologies are used for the creation of an ABox Linked Data graph. First, an instance node is defined for each building, classified as `bot:Building`. These instance nodes are connected to their respective geometric representations in the online repositories using FOG relations based on the geometry storage format (e.g. `fog:asStl` for .stl geometry). Similarly, each extracted mesh segment is also linked to a unique instance node using a FOG relation. Additionally, the nodes are linked using topological relations such as `bot:hasElement`. Finally, the instance nodes are linked to their corresponding PRODUCT class labels to encode the extracted semantics (e.g. `product:Wall` for the label 'wall'). Given the resulting graphs, SPARQL queries can be used to access specific instances or groups of nodes (e.g. all building components of type `product:Column` with their geometry). These core semantics form the basis of both metric and non-metric properties such as relative location, connectivity and texture. The Abox graph can then be extended using existing LOD to yield extensive query-able information. It is within the scope of the European "V4Design" project do develop these technologies of which the presented classification of existing data is the first step.

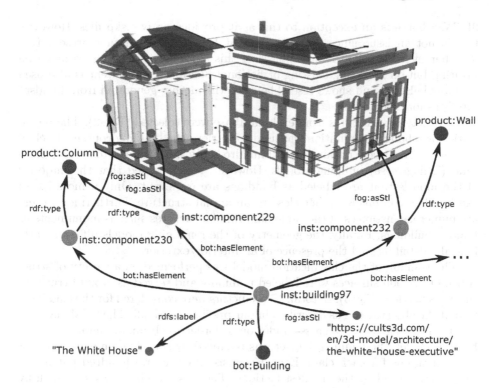

Fig. 4. Conceptual architecture of a linked data ABox graph that can be created on top of the extracted data, using the BOT, PRODUCT and FOG ontologies

4 Experiments

In this section, a realistic test case is presented to evaluate the limitations of our proposed general approach to process data from a multitude of online databases. The hypothesis is that, in order to publish LOD, a proper semantic enrichment is mandatory. Therefore, this preliminary test focuses on the compatibility of the input data from different sources and the label extraction of the building components.

The opportunities to classify existing data is investigated as follows. A number of sample buildings is selected from online repositories without regards for their origin, size, creation process or purpose. Four major geometry databases are considered. MyMiniFactory is a 3D printing database with over 50.000 models ranging from gadgets to the Eifeltower. A small section of building objects is also present. It mostly comprises of popular monuments and famous buildings (Fig. 2). The same can be said of the other databases. Thingiverse and Cult3d are similar databases but on a much larger scale (1.1 million models). However, MyMiniFactory guarantees printability, indicating better quality models with limited non-manifold meshes. Since all these databases are for 3D printing, the widely used .stl file format is provided. The fourth database, Trimble Sketchup's

3D Warehouse is an exception to this as it provides native .skp files. However, this is not an issue since its mesh content has the same data representation as other mesh formats. The emphasis of this database is also not so much on printing but on modeling existing or fictional buildings. Its content is also used for Google Earth and shows resemblance to the meshes generated from Landsat satellites for Google Maps.

A variety of structures from each database were selected (Fig. 2). The repositories own building definition was used to retrieve the building content. Each of the target databases contains several hundred (MyMiniFactory) to several thousand (Thingiverse) building models. However, it is revealed that the majority of the models that are labeled as buildings are irrelevant. Only a mere 5% of the building content is in fact close to an actual structure. Furthermore, there are numerous instances of the same handful of structures such as monuments or famous buildings. Finally, the geometry of the remaining models differs greatly in scale, detailing and the presence of an interior/exterior.

The training of the classification model was performed on a variety of structures. Over 7000 surfaces were labeled manually and served as ground truth for the classification (Fig. 3). In total, 17 predictors were considered for the classification of the observations as described in our previous work [3]. The SVM classifier was trained with a $K = 5$ cross-validation. In order to obtain an unbiased classification model, the training dataset was balanced by sampling an equal number of observations for each class. Each K consisted of several hundred patches of each class limited by the smallest factions. The class variance was kept high by mixing observations from different buildings.

Several buildings are processed from each database. The results can be seen in Fig. 2 in the far right column. Prior to the classification, a segmentation is performed on the mesh geometry to separate the individual mesh components from the models. During this procedure, invalid and non-manifold meshes are removed as they would obstruct the classification process. This is performed by the built-in Rhino mesh checker. As expected, the user created models are littered with invalid meshes due to the lack of expertise and standardization. Overall, all models were able to be processed by the classification procedure. This is very promising since the input models were created by varying people using different tools. However, upon inspecting the models in detail, some errors still remain. In Fig. 2, several shortcomings are listed that inherently cause issues in the data enrichment. First of all, structures that show little resemblance to an actual building are error prone. For instance, the Arc de Triomphe and other monuments are challenging to interpret due to their uniqueness. Despite the fact that these assets are also constructed from the same classes, their configuration of objects is atypical and thus causes confusion in the interpretation. Another problem is the lack of building interiors which is common for 3D printing objects and Sketchup Warehouse models. For instance, Fig. 5 depicts the classification results of a replica of the white house for 3D printing. It is revealed that while the majority of walls are properly found, some issues occur with the classification of the roof, floor and ceiling geometry. The lack of the structure's interior introduces confusion in the classification since the identification of ceilings is intrinsically linked to the surrounding floors and walls. Other failures are also described in Figs. 2 and 4 including the presence of fictional objects such as watermarks. Despite these shortcomings, the classification algorithm shows promising results for the semantic enrichment of the input data. The inputs and outputs have been made available on https://jender.stackstorage.com/s/pHS49dCfMyP9Wvt.

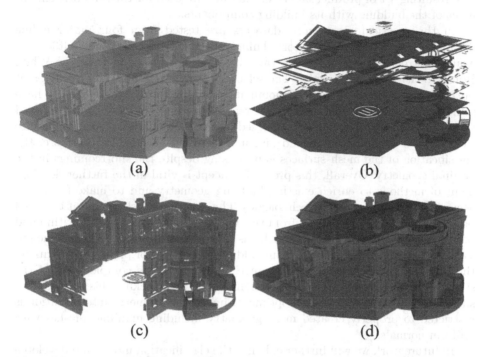

Fig. 5. Overview classification results of the "White House" dataset of the Cult3D database: Mesh model depicting hollow structure (a), identified roof, floor and ceiling geometry (b), identified wall geometry (c) and total result (d).

5   Conclusion and Future Work

In this paper, a proof of concept is discussed to semantically enrich existing geometry. More specifically, the opportunities are investigated to extract semantics of structureless geometry from various online repositories. The emphasis of this work is on the extraction of building component information conform existing Linked Building Data ontologies. It is our purpose to produce content that can be accessed and analyzed in a standardized manner by Semantic Web technologies.

The issue of introducing intelligence to structureless data is considered as a data association problem. We therefore propose the use of machine learning algorithms that are specially designed for this type of supervised pattern recognition applications. Given a set of observations, namely the individual mesh surfaces of each 3D model, and a set of characteristics, standardized product labels can be computed for these observations. In this work, we use local and global features developed in previous work along with a pretrained Support Vector Machine classifier to test whether machine learning methods can be expanded towards the processing of online buildings geometry models from different repositories. The resulting set of product labels and meshes are used for the semantic enrichment of the building with its building components.

In the practical case study, datasets are tested from four major online databases including MyMinifactory, Thingiverse, 3D Warehouse and Cult3d. The example structures comprise of a variety of buildings ranging from the White House to the Arc de Triomphe. The selected models were designed for different purposes and had no common denominator aside from the fact that they have some building resemblance and mesh representation. The test results showed that all models could indeed be processed by the classification algorithm despite the presence of numerous invalid and non-manifold meshes. Furthermore, the classification of the mesh surfaces is promising despite the shortcomings in the original geometry. Overall, this proof of concept is vital in the further development of methods to enrich existing building geometry and to make the result accessible by Semantic Web Technologies. The experiments show that it is indeed possible to process information from varying sources with a single algorithm and parameter set. However, the approach has several limitations. As it is designed to target generic building geometry, any odd structure is error prone. Furthermore, the building logic embedded in the method relies on the completeness of the structure. Consequently, the classification of structures lacking this information, such as printable models, is sub-optimal. Finally, the geometry interpretation is restricted to properly created mesh geometry including manifold meshes with uniform normals.

In future work we will further enhance the classification model and develop a procedure to represent the computed semantics in a Linked Data graph. Further research will also focus on selecting the best-suited method to relate 3D geometries to a Linked Data context. Also, an evaluation tool will be developed that filters the non-suitable data from the inputs.

Acknowledgment. This project has received funding from the European Research Council (ERC) under the European Union's Horizon 2020 research and innovation programme (grant agreement 779962), the Research Foundation Flanders (FWO) in the form of a personal Strategic Basic research grant and the Geomatics research group of the Department of Civil Engineering, TC Construction at the KU Leuven.

References

1. Anand, A., Koppula, H.S., Joachims, T., Saxena, A.: Contextually guided semantic labeling and search for 3D point clouds. Int. J. Robot. Res. **32**(1), 19–34 (2012). https://doi.org/10.1177/0278364912461538
2. Armeni, I., et al.: Joint 2D–3D-Semantic Data for Indoor Scene Understanding. arXiv:1702.01105 [cs.CV] (2017), http://arxiv.org/abs/1702.01105
3. Bassier, M., Van Genechten, B., Vergauwen, M., Genechten, B.V., Vergauwen, M.: Classification of sensor independent point cloud data of buildingobjects using random forests. J. Build. Eng. **21**, 1–10 (2018). https://doi.org/10.1016/j.jobe.2018.04.027
4. Bishop, C.M.: Pattern Recognition and Machine Learning. Springer, Berlin (2006)
5. Bonduel, M., Oraskari, J., Pauwels, P., Vergauwen, M., Klein, R.: The IFC to linked building data converter - current status. In: 6th Linked Data in Architecture and Construction Workshop, London (2018)
6. Criminisi, A., Shotton, J.: Decision Forests for Computer Vision and Medical Image Analysis. Springer, Heidelberg (2013). https://doi.org/10.1007/978-1-4471-4929-3
7. Hohmann, B., Havemann, S., Krispel, U., Fellner, D.: A GML shape grammar for semantically enriched 3D building models. Comput. Graph. **34**, 322–334 (2010). https://doi.org/10.1016/j.cag.2010.05.007
8. Lu, W., Qin, Y., Liu, X., Huang, M., Zhou, L., Jiang, X.: Computer-aided design enriching the semantics of variational geometric constraint data withontology. Comput. Aided Des. **63**, 72–85 (2015). https://doi.org/10.1016/j.cad.2014.12.008
9. Maxwell, A.E., Warner, T.A., Fang, F.: Implementation of machine-learning classification in remote sensing: an applied review. Int. J. Remote Sens. **39**(9), 2784–2817 (2018). https://doi.org/10.1080/01431161.2018.1433343
10. Niemeyer, J., Rottensteiner, F., Soergel, U.: Contextual classification of lidar data and building object detection in urban areas. ISPRS J. Photogramm. Remote Sens. **87**, 152–165 (2014). https://doi.org/10.1016/j.isprsjprs.2013.11.001. http://linkinghub.elsevier.com/retrieve/pii/S0924271613002359
11. Nikoohemat, S., Peter, M., Oude Elberink, S., Vosselman, G.: Exploiting indoor mobile laser scanner trajectories for semantic interpretation of point clouds. ISPRS Ann. Photogramm. Remote Sens. Spat. Inf. Sci. **IV–2/W4v**, 355–362 (2017). https://doi.org/10.5194/isprs-annals-IV-2-W4-355-2017. https://www.isprs-ann-photogramm-remote-sens-spatial-inf-sci.net/IV-2-W4/355/2017/
12. Pauwels, P., Terkaj, W.: Express to OWL for construction industry: towards are commendable and usable ifcOWL ontology. Autom. Constr. **63**, 100–133 (2016). https://doi.org/10.1016/j.autcon.2015.12.003
13. Pauwels, P., Zhang, S., Lee, Y.C.: Semantic web technologies in AEC industry: a literature overview. Autom. Constr. **73**, 145–165 (2017). https://doi.org/10.1016/j.autcon.2016.10.003
14. Rasmussen, M.H., Pauwels, P., Lefrançois, M., Schneider, G.F., Hviid, C.A., Karshøj, J.: Recent changes in the building topology ontology. In: 5th Linked Data in Architecture and Construction (LDAC2017) Workshop (2017)
15. Terkaj, W., Schneider, G.F., Pauwels, P.: Reusing domain ontologies in linked building data: the case of building automation and control. In: CEUR Workshop Proceedings **2050** (2017)
16. Terkaj, W., Šojić, A.: Ontology-based representation of IFC EXPRESS rules: an enhancement of the ifcOWL ontology. Autom. Constr. **57**, 188–201 (2015). https://doi.org/10.1016/j.autcon.2015.04.010

17. Törmä, S.: Semantic linking of building information models. In: Proceedings - 2013 IEEE 7th International Conference on Semantic Computing, ICSC 2013, pp. 412–419 (2013). https://doi.org/10.1109/ICSC.2013.80
18. Wolf, D., Prankl, J., Vincze, M.: Fast semantic segmentation of 3D point clouds using a dense CRF with learned parameters. In: IEEE International Conference on Robotics and Automation (ICRA) (2015)
19. Xiong, X., Adan, A., Akinci, B., Huber, D.: Automatic creation of semantically rich 3D building models from laser scanner data. Autom. Constr. **31**, 325–337 (2013). https://doi.org/10.1016/j.autcon.2012.10.006. http://linkinghub.elsevier.com/retrieve/pii/S0926580512001732
20. Xiong, X., Huber, D.: Using context to create semantic 3D models of indoor environments. In: Procedings of the British Machine Vision Conference 2010, pp. 45.1–45.11 (2010). https://doi.org/10.5244/C.24.45, http://www.bmva.org/bmvc/2010/conference/paper45/index.html

A Method for Automatically Generating Schema Diagrams for OWL Ontologies

Cogan Shimizu[1]([✉]), Aaron Eberhart[1], Nazifa Karima[1], Quinn Hirt[1],
Adila Krisnadhi[2], and Pascal Hitzler[1]

[1] Data Semantics Laboratory, Wright State University, Dayton, OH, USA
shimizu.5@wright.edu
[2] Faculty of Computer Science, Universitas Indonesia, Depok, Indonesia

Abstract. Interest in Semantic Web technologies, including knowledge graphs and ontologies, is increasing rapidly in industry and academics. In order to support ontology engineers and domain experts, it is necessary to provide them with robust tools that facilitate the ontology engineering process. Often, the schema diagram of an ontology is the most important tool for quickly conveying the overall purpose of an ontology. In this paper, we present a method for programmatically generating a schema diagram from an OWL file. We evaluate its ability to generate schema diagrams similar to manually drawn schema diagrams and show that it outperforms VOWL and OWLGrEd. In addition, we provide a prototype implementation of this tool.

1 Introduction

Engineering an ontology is a complex and time-consuming process [15]. Providing a broad and sophisticated set of tools and methodologies to support ontology engineers can help mitigate these factors. This method is part of an overall thrust at improving the ontology engineering process. Specifically, we focus on so-called Modular Ontology Modelling.

In this paper we describe an algorithm that generates a schema diagram from an OWL file and evaluate a corresponding prototype implementation. The evaluation shows that our approach is superior to the related visualization tools WebVOWL[1] [14] and OWLGrEd[2] [2] specifically for the type of schema diagrams that we have found to be most useful. Our prototype tool, SDOnt, is publicly available online.[3]

A schema diagram is a commonly used and invaluable tool for both understanding and developing ontologies. A survey we conducted shows that it ranks among the most important components in the documentation of an ontology [11]. Schema diagrams provide a view, albeit limited, of the structure of the relationships between concepts in an ontology. Frequently, a schema diagram is

---

[1] http://vowl.visualdataweb.org/.
[2] http://owlgred.lumii.lv/.
[3] http://dase.cs.wright.edu/content/sdont.

© Springer Nature Switzerland AG 2019
B. Villazón-Terrazas and Y. Hidalgo-Delgado (Eds.): KGSWC 2019, CCIS 1029, pp. 149–161, 2019.
https://doi.org/10.1007/978-3-030-21395-4_11

generated manually during the design phase of the engineering process. At that time the diagram is a conceptual, mutable document. After the schema diagram has been created, an OWL file is created to model the diagram with OWL axioms which precisely capture its semantics. We call this a *diagram-informed OWL file*. As we discuss in Sect. 5, this method may lead to unforeseen problems, e.g. whether an OWL file faithfully represents its diagram. A tool that generates a schema diagram programmatically allows for ontology engineers to create an *OWL-informed diagram*. Additionally, it would provide a mechanism by which schema diagrams may be easily updated in the case of a newer versioned OWL file.

In this paper, we describe our method for generating schema diagrams from OWL files. The programmatically generated schema diagrams visualize the same information as those that are manually generated following a specific visualization paradigm which we found to be most effective in practice. We evaluate its effectiveness by comparing it to two existing OWL visualization tools, VOWL and OWLGrEd. We would like to note that for now we are ignoring layout questions; we consider only the question of what *content* should be in a graph. We intend to explore layout issues in follow-up work.

The rest of the paper is organized as follows. Section 2 describes existing visualization tools and how they differ from our method and tool. Section 3 describes the process of schema diagram generation. Section 4 gives a very brief description of our implementation and our method. Section 5 evaluates our method, details possible points of improvement, and discusses the results. Finally, in Sect. 6 we conclude and outline our next steps and future work.

2   Related Work

Visualization is critical to understanding the purpose and content of an ontology [4,5,11]. There are many tools that provide visualization capabilities. We are interested in how meaningfully they construct a visualization, rather than the details of their implementations. For instance, many of these tools offer some sort of interactivity, such as drag and drop construction and manipulation or folding for dynamic exploration. This differs from our intent to provide a method for constructing a diagram that portrays the *relationships* between concepts. Our approach also does not provide specific support for visualizing an ABox; our emphasis is on supporting the creation and use of schema diagrams.

Below, we have selected for comparison a few tools that are representative in their functionality. For a more complete survey see [6]. VOWL and OWLGrEd were chosen for comparison to our method. They are described in Sect. 5.

NavigOWL[4] is a plugin for the popular tool Protégé[5]. NavigOWL provides a graph representation of the loaded ontology such that the representation follows a power-law distribution, which is a type of force-directed graph representation. It also provides a mechanism for filtering out different relational edges while

---

[4] http://home.deib.polimi.it/hussain/navigowl/.
[5] https://protege.stanford.edu/.

exploring an ontology [1]. This tool is not supported in the current version of Protégé.[6] It is particularly well suited to visualizing the ABox, which is outside the scope of our intent and method.

OWLviz is also a Protégé plugin. It generates an IS-A hierarchy for the loaded ontology rooted with the concept owl:Thing. OWLviz displays *only* subclass relations between concepts and does not extract properties from those axioms. Hovering over the nodes in the graph representation provides axioms related to the class represented by that node. This plugin is not supported by the current version of Protégé. The lack of relational specificity per edge is non-ideal for our purposes. Furthermore, information accessible only through interaction is not desired in a reference diagram.

TopBraid Composer is a standalone tool similar in functionality to Protégé with OWLviz; it is developed, maintained, and sold by TopQuadrant, Inc.[7] There is no free version for academic purposes.

OntoTrack is a standalone tool for visualizing the subsumption hierarchy of an ontology rooted at owl:Thing. Properties are not extracted from axioms and used to label edges. The tool only supports ontologies in the deprecated OWL-Lite⁻ and automatically augments the visualization with subsumptions found with the reasoner RACER[8] [13]. Between the limitations on OWL and the interactivity, this tool is not strictly suitable for creating schema diagrams.

MEMO GRAPH was developed to be a memory prosthesis for users suffering from dementia [6]. As such, it is particularly focused on representing the relations between family members. It is not currently available for public use.

RDF Gravity is a standalone tool that provides a visualization for an ontology via graph metrics. The tool generates a force-directed graph representation of the underlying ontology. We could not find any data on how it handles blank nodes, represents class disjointness, and other non-graph metrics, as, at time of this writing, the tool is unavailable, no publication on its method can be found, and it seems to be survived only by screenshots. We include this entry for the sake of completeness.

OntoGraf[9] is a plugin for Protégé that supports interative navigation through OWL ontologies. In particular, it allows the user to navigate and filter relationships and nodes based on certain criteria (e.g. subclass, individuals, domain/range object properties, and equivalence). OntoGraf is not supported on newer versions of Protégé (5.0+).

In all, we note that there are many tools for visualizing ontologies, however many of them older and no longer supported or provide only limited support past graph-metric data, which in our experience is insufficient for conveying the purpose of an ontology. It also seems that out of this general line or research, VOWL and its associated tools (e.g., WebVOWL) emerged as the prominent paradigm - yet a paradigm that addresses different use cases than those of concern for us.

---

[6] https://protegewiki.stanford.edu/wiki/NavigOWL.
[7] https://www.topquadrant.com/products/.
[8] https://www.ifis.uni-luebeck.de/index.php?id=385.
[9] https://protegewiki.stanford.edu/wiki/OntoGraf.

3   Method

A schema diagram does not necessarily aim to represent all information encoded in an ontology. As mentioned in Sect. 2, there are several tools that attempt to do so, in particular, VOWL and OWLGrEd. However our experiences with ontology modeling with domain experts from many different fields shows us that it is necessary to strike a good balance between complexity and understandability. In fact, in these collaborations we gravitate towards diagrams that merely capture classes and the relationships between them. This omits most semantic aspects such as whether a relationship between classes does or does not indicate domain or range restrictions or even more complex logical axioms. We find that the exact semantics are better conveyed using either natural language sentences or logical axioms (preferably in the form of rules [17]) in conjunction with a very simplified diagram.

Typically, we create ontologies by first drawing schema diagrams with domain experts and then capturing the exact logical axioms that constitute the ontology. In this paper we reverse the process: start with the logical axioms and automatically derive the schema diagrams.[10] We do this to help us to deal with ontologies constructed by others for which no suitable schema diagrams are provided. As we will see later in Sect. 5, our visualization approach can also be helpful in finding errors in OWL files or in manually drawn schema diagrams.

To maximize information and minimize clutter we define some guidelines:

- All classes inherit from owl:Thing, so it is unhelpful to clutter a diagram with subclass edges from concepts to owl:Thing.
- We do not represent any logical connectives (e.g. disjunction) or complex axioms (e.g. a domain restriction that contains an intersection) since, in our experience, this type of information is better conveyed non-visually.
- Disjointness of classes does not need explicit graphical representation. In most cases, disjointness is immediately clear for a human with some knowledge about the domain.
- Inverse relations are not represented, as they are syntactic sugar for any relation.
- The ABox [9] is disregarded; instances of classes are not represented.

With these assumptions in mind, we detail our method using the rules below:

Steps 3 and 4 may be omitted if there are no direct domain or range restrictions given. However, because there are multiple ways of expressing the same information in OWL, domain and range may appear in the declarations of the Object or the Datatype Properties.

---

[10] At this time, we do not consider owl:Imports as the tool is completely offline. Additionally, we wish to only generate a schema diagram for those axioms directly in the OWL file of interest.

1. Create a node for each class in the ontology's signature.
2. Create a node for each datatype in the ontology's signature.
3. Generate a directed edge for each Object Property based on its domain and range restrictions, if such are given. The source of the edge is the Property's domain and the target of the edge is the Property's range.
4. Generate a directed edge for each Datatype Property, in the same manner as for an Object Property, if domain and range restrictions are present.
5. For each other axiom in the TBox:
   Case 1: if the subclass and superclass are atomic, generate a subclass edge between them.
   Case 2: if the axiom is of the forms presented in (1) and (2) below, generate the associated directed edge.
   Case 3: apply rules (3) to (6), as listed below, recursively until the resulting axiom sets can be handled by Cases 1 and 2.
6. Display.

Fig. 1. The algorithm for generating a schema diagram.

In Step 5 it is important to note the differences between logical and schematic equivalence. *Schematic equivalence* between two ontologies means they share the same graphical representation. Consider, for example, the definitions for scoped domain and range restrictions (Fig. 1):

$$\exists R.B \sqsubseteq A \tag{1}$$

$$A \sqsubseteq \forall R.B \tag{2}$$

Logically, (1) and (2) convey two different meanings. Schematically, though, they may be represented by the same artifact in a graph: $A \xrightarrow{R} B$. Thus we consider them schematically equivalent. We may also break down more complex axioms using the rules defined in (3) through (6). These rules hold for both intersection ($\sqcap$) and union ($\sqcup$). We list only the union versions. Note that not all of these are logically equivalent transformations.

$$A \sqsubseteq \forall R.(B \sqcup C \sqcup \cdots) \Rightarrow \begin{cases} A \sqsubseteq \forall R.B \\ A \sqsubseteq \forall R.C \\ \vdots \end{cases} \tag{3}$$

and

$$\exists R.(B \sqcup C \sqcup \cdots) \sqsubseteq A \Rightarrow \begin{cases} \exists R.B \sqsubseteq A \\ \exists R.C \sqsubseteq A \\ \vdots \end{cases} \tag{4}$$

(5) and (6) are used only in the union case as shown here. (5) is not a logically equivalent transformation.

$$B \sqcup C \sqcup \cdots \sqsubseteq A \Rightarrow \begin{cases} B \sqsubseteq A \\ C \sqsubseteq A \\ \vdots \end{cases} \tag{5}$$

$$A \sqsubseteq B \sqcup C \sqcup \cdots \Rightarrow \begin{cases} A \sqsubseteq B \\ A \sqsubseteq C \\ \vdots \end{cases} \tag{6}$$

We may recursively apply (3) through (6) for non-atomic concepts $A, B, \cdots$ until we have reached axioms of the form (1) and (2) or atomic subclass relationships.

The time complexity for this process is minimal. If c is the maximum number of concepts and datatypes in any axiom in the ontology then there are at most $\binom{c}{2}$ so-called "simple" axioms that together are schematically equivalent to the "complex axiom." Thus, there are at most $\binom{c}{2} \cdot n$ edges to parse per ontology, where n is the number of axioms in the TBox, giving our method a time complexity of $O(n)$. This calculation ignores algorithms for the graph layout.

The goal of our approach is to generate a static schema diagram for a particular OWL file. However, there are practical limitations. For sufficiently large number of classes and properties (and connectivity, thereof), nearly any graph visualization will become essentially unreadable. Indeed, our approach is primarily meant for smaller (i.e. limited number of classes and properties) OWL files, such as ontology design patterns [7] or ontology modules [12]. For use with this approach, ontologies of the former variety (many classes, properties, etc.) should be organized into modules and the tool applied to each module in order to create a collection of interrelated schema diagrams. In fact, this would likely result in a better engineered ontology [10].

4   Implementation

Our prototype implementation, SDOnt, is a pipeline consisting of three parts: a GUI, a parser module, and a rendering module. SDOnt is developed in Java and provided as an executable JAR file. Ontology manipulations are done using the OWLAPI. Online we provide the source code, test set, evaluation results, and a tutorial for the tool's use.[11]

The GUI is implemented using Java Swing and serves as an interface for navigating and loading ontologies into the program. The Ontology Parser is an implementation of our algorithm as described in Sect. 3. The parser provides a set of nodes to the rendering module that represent the classes and datatypes in the ontology's signature and the node-edge-node artifacts that represent their properties, domains, and ranges for the visualization.

---

[11] http://dase.cs.wright.edu/content/sdont.

The rendering module takes those node-edge-node artifacts and the node set and combines them to create the visualization and render it to the screen. The rendering module utilizes the library JGraphX[12] for generating, laying out, and displaying the schema diagram. JGraphX is an open source library written in Java for displaying and manipulating graphs. However, the SDOnt code-base has been written in such a way that any visualization library may be used. That is, the algorithm is implemented in a modular fashion; an external developer may code against the SDOnt code-base with no changes necessary to the method.

5   Evaluation

In this evaluation we describe the closest alternatives to SDOnt and their methods in Sect. 5.1, the method by which we conduct our evaluation in Sect. 5.2, our choice of test set in Sect. 5.3, and discuss the results of our evaluation in Sect. 5.4.

5.1   Compared Tools

We evaluate SDOnt by comparison with author supplied visualizations, Web-VOWL, and OWLGrEd.

Each of the ontologies in our test set, which is outlined in Sect. 5.3, has a general visualization provided by the authors. We use these diagrams as a baseline against which the tools can be judged and assume that these represent the authors' best attempt to generalize the semantics of the ontology. However, there may be some irregularities in the methodologies different authors use to produce these visualizations. Indeed, some of the methodologies are very distinct–some are very minimal; others take inspiration from UML. Some of the diagrams appear to be created automatically from Protégé or some other automated tool, while others are manually draw using a variety of graphing utilities. The variations in these sources may be partially responsible for suboptimal results, especially as none of the three compared tools use a UML-style visualization.

VOWL is a graphical notation tool for OWL. The specification can be viewed in detail in [14]. VOWL represents ontologies using detailed force-directed graphs. We use the web implementation WebVOWL[13] to generate visualizations of our ontologies. The website application has a high degree of potential customization. In the settings, we choose to filter out only class disjointness axioms and set the degree of collapsing to 0 since we use smaller ontologies.

WebVOWL is able to quickly produce a visualization for every valid OWL file that we analyze. Usually the output animation clearly represents the intent of the ontology. Occasionally, however, the result contains incomplete or missing information. In our experience WebVOWL is often ambiguous when it tries to display complex statements, which could be the cause of this.

---

[12] https://github.com/jgraph/jgraphx.
[13] http://www.visualdataweb.de/webvowl/.

OWLGrEd is a Graphical Ontology Editor that allows for interactive, drag-and-drop creation of ontologies [2]. It utilizes UML-like visualizations for displaying axioms associated to a class. In addition, it provides Manchester Syntax translations of axioms. OWLGrEd displays *all* axioms, sometimes as additional nodes. The visualization is hierarchical, so there is a subClass edge between an owl:Thing node and every un-subsumed concept in the ontology's signature.

Figure 2 shows examples of what each tool outputs in comparison to a manually created schema diagram.[14]

5.2   Comparison Scheme

The method for constructing schema diagrams for ontology patterns and modules, as introduced in the previous section, results in a diagram similar to published reference diagrams which follow the visualization paradigm that we found most useful in interactive modeling sessions with domain experts. In order to provide a meaningful evaluation, we use as gold-standard reference the manually drawn diagrams that have been published in papers or on websites by the ontologies' authors. These diagrams have been designed with human understandability in mind and their creation pre-dates our automated diagram generation method.

We compare the diagrams generated by SDOnt, WebVOWL and OWLGrEd with the gold-standard diagrams taken from the respective publications or.

To define some terminology, we say a *node* represents a class or concept. An *edge* represents a relationship or role, where the source of the edge is the relationship's domain and the head of the edge represents the relationship's codomain – domain and codomain are not meant to be formal technical terms in the sense of OWL restrictions or RDFS domain/range declarations, but rather intuitive notions that are ambiguous like a schema diagram. An edge from class A to class B in the diagram indicates that A is in the domain of the relation and B is in the codomain of the relation. There may also be an edge with the same role label between two different classes C and D elsewhere in the diagram, without making the classes A and C (or B and D) identical, as would happen if these were formal domain or range declarations.

All three visualization tools generate directed edges. To conduct this comparison, we evaluate the following criterion for node-edge-node artifacts:

For every node-edge-node artifact in the generated diagram, does it appear in the reference diagram, and vice-versa?

However, there are a few different cases, as we outline below. By using this vocabulary it becomes natural to calculate an F_1–measure for each diagram. We report the average F_1–measure for each tool in Table 1.

---

[14] For this diagram, SDOnt utilized an "orthagonal layout" that is pre-defined in the associated visualization library. Our method for generating a schema diagram, at this time, makes no assertions about the placement of nodes in the graph.

- True Positive: the artifact appears in both generated and reference diagrams
- False Positive: the artifact appears in the generated diagram, but not the reference diagram.
- False Negative: the artifact does not appear in the generated diagram, but does appear in the reference diagram.

Of course, we cannot calculate True Negatives as there are an infinite number of items that do not occur in the generated diagram nor in the reference diagram.

5.3 Test Set

In order to test our process, we constructed a test set of ontology design patterns. Our process for selecting the patterns was simply searching the main publishing outlets and ontologydesignpatterns.org and choosing those patterns that had published diagrams, as well as unbroken links to their OWL files. All test data and the complete set of ontologies we used for our evaluation can be found on our tool's website.[15]

In some cases, it was necessary to make minor changes to the OWL files during this evaluation. Both OWLGrEd and WebVOWL produced errors on importing certain external resources.[16] Whenever removing an import allowed us to continue with the analysis we did so, using the new OWL file for both tools, even if the file worked for the others tools initially. However, there were still some patterns that failed to work for any tool. Our results report only on those OWL files that could be successfully processed by each of the compared tools. After these criteria were met, our test set contains 63 ontology design patterns. These 63 patterns are also available in the SDOnt portal.

5.4 Results and Discussion

The results of our evaluation are summarized in Tables 1 and 2. The node-edge-node triple sets are determined manually. During this process we take care to use a consistent naming format. This allows us to conduct our comparison programmatically. The code utilized for this comparison, with some documentation for its use, is also available in the online portal.

We see that in Table 1, the F_1–measures are very low. SDOnt has an F_1–measure of 0.465, OWLGrEd has an F_1–measure of 0.269, and WebVOWL has an F_1–measure of 0.163. However, we also note that there are many stylistic differences in the generation of diagrams. Many of the reference diagrams are presented in UML-esque manner. Comparing these to a force directed graph, such as those produced by WebVOWL would, of course, perform very poorly.

---

[15] http://www.dase.cs.wright.edu/content/sdont.

[16] We note that there has been an update to both of these web application since we conducted our evaluation. However, due to time constraints, we were unable to go back and re-run the evaluation. Fortunately, we do not punish any tool for being unable to render a document; we only compare performance against the subset of patterns that *every* tool successfully processed.

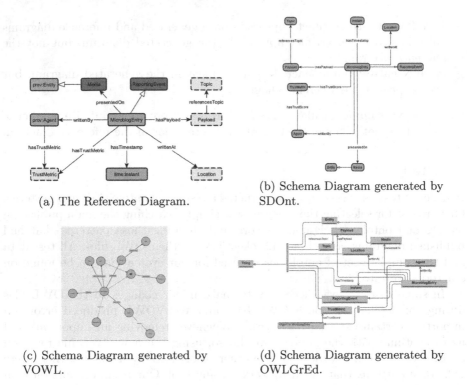

(a) The Reference Diagram.

(b) Schema Diagram generated by SDOnt.

(c) Schema Diagram generated by VOWL.

(d) Schema Diagram generated by OWLGrEd.

Fig. 2. The manually curated reference diagram (a) followed by the generated schema diagrams by SDOnt, VOWL, and OWLGrEd, for the MicroblogEntry ontology design pattern.

In this evaluation we do not encounter any false positives that are a misrepresentation of an axiom. Instead, false positives are strictly caused by the OWL file containing more information than expected. The exact reasons for this seem to vary from case to case. We speculate that in some cases the reason may be that the diagram may look more elegant or the name of a concept may imply its natural superclass. For example, in the Hazardous Event pattern [3], HazardousEvent is a subclass to Event, but this is not indicated in the reference diagram, leading to a false positive. In other cases, the OWL file could be malformed.

To formally compare the performances we run three Wilcoxon signed rank tests, with null hypothesis that there are no difference in performance. Our tests show that SDOnt performs significantly better than OWLGrEd ($p < 0.001$), and WebVOWL ($p < 0.001$). As well as that OWLGrEd performs significantly better than WebVOWL ($0.05 < p < 0.01$).

There are also motivating cases for using schema diagrams as error checkers during ontology development. The tools do poorly on many of the diagrams simply because the respective OWL files do not actually contain the information

Table 1. F_1–Measure for each of the tool's performance.

	F_1–Measure
SDOnt	0.465
OWLGrEd	0.269
WebVOWL	0.163

Table 2. Significance of Pairwise comparison of the tools using the Wilcoxon signed rank test.

SDOnt vs OWLGrEd	SDOnt vs WebVOWL	OWLGrEd vs WebVOWL
$p < 0.001$	$p < 0.001$	$0.05 < p < 0.01$

the diagram implies. This may be that they contain *more* information (e.g. alignments to different patterns) or lack information (e.g. errors).

VOWL and OWLGrEd consistently performed worse than SDOnt for two reasons. First, VOWL had many duplicated edges for different functional properties, even after adjusting settings in an attempt to prevent them. Secondly, both OWLGrEd and VOWL had trouble extracting properties from complex axioms. For OWLGrEd these axioms were represented as anonymous nodes, leading to false positive artifacts. Set operation nodes in WebVOWL also lead to additional false positive artifacts.

6   Conclusions

Our results are promising even if they do not present as such. A lack of a consistent visual notation for diagrams in our test set and poor quality control in the OWL files definitely contribute to a poor, raw showing. However, we note that even given our low F_1–measures the results are consistent. And we see that SDOnt performs significantly better than both OWLGrEd and WebVOWL for generating schema diagrams that are most similar to the reference diagrams.

To be fair, the test set against which we evaluated contained many UML-esque diagrams, to which none of the evaluated tools are well-suited. VOWL and OWLGrEd were used for comparison simply because they are the current state-of-the-art for generalized ontology visualization and they are the tools which produced the most similar diagrams to the desired ones. Our results do not invalidate VOWL or OWLGrEd: they simply serve other purposes.

There are still many ways to improve our method and its implementation. First, we see in many diagrams that namespaces are frequently color coded, as well as providing different node styles for external patterns. As ontology engineering practices mature, we expect to see these distinctions to be formally encoded in the ontology, e.g., according to the Ontology Design Pattern Representation Language (OPLa) as described in [8]. As such, once the necessary tooling support for OPLa has been realized, SDOnt will be able to leverage the annotations and inform style and placement of nodes for increased clarity in the schema diagram. We will also explore different styles of incorporating UML-like visualizations for datatypes. The manually created reference diagrams are fallible or simply unclear from the perspective of the OWL file which information is necessary to convey. We believe incorporating OPLa and augmenting SDOnt to account for these annotations will also help in this regard.

Secondly, we intend to investigate the most effective ways of creating a good layout beyond force-directed graphs and will explore the option of providing our work as an additional rendering capability for the OWLAPI.

Finally, we will integrate SDOnt with other existing Protégé plugins developed in our lab, including ROWL,[17] OWLax,[18] and OWL2DL[19] [16–18], in order to work towards a well-rounded ontology engineering suite which supports the Modular Ontology Modeling paradigm.

Acknowledgement. Cogan Shimizu acknowledges support by the Dayton Area Graduate Studies Institute (DAGSI). This work was partially supported by the Air Force Office of Scientific Research under award number FA9550-18-1-0386.

References

1. Hussain, A., Latif, K., Rextin, A.T., Hayat, A., Alam, M.: Scalable visualization of semantic nets using power-law graphs. Appl. Math. **8**, 355–367 (2014)
2. Barzdins, J., Barzdins, G., Cerans, K., Liepins, R., Sprogis, A.: UML style graphical notation and editor for OWL 2. In: Forbrig, P., Günther, H. (eds.) BIR 2010. LNBIP, vol. 64, pp. 102–114. Springer, Heidelberg (2010). https://doi.org/10.1007/978-3-642-16101-8_9
3. Cheatham, M., Ferguson, H., Charles Vardeman, I., Shimizu, C.: A modification to the hazardous situation ODP to support risk assessment and mitigation. In: Proceedings of WOP, vol. 16 (2016)
4. Dadzie, A.-S., Rowe, M.: Approaches to visualising linked data: a survey. Semant. Web **2**(2), 89–124 (2011)
5. Geroimenko, V., Chen, C.: Visualizing the Semantic Web: XML-Based Internet and Information Visualization. Springer, New York (2005). https://doi.org/10.1007/1-84628-290-X
6. Ghorbel, F., Ellouze, N., Mtais, E., Hamdi, F., Gargouri, F., Herradi, N.: MEMO GRAPH: an ontology visualization tool for everyone. Proc. Comput. Sci. **96**(Supplement C), 265–274 (2016)
7. Hitzler, P., Gangemi, A., Janowicz, K., Krisnadhi, A., Presutti, V. (eds.): Ontology Engineering with Ontology Design Patterns - Foundations and Applications. Studies on the Semantic Web, vol. 25. IOS Press (2016)
8. Hitzler, P., Gangemi, A., Janowicz, K., Krisnadhi, A.A., Presutti, V.: Towards a simple but useful ontology design pattern representation language. In: Proceedings WOP 2017, October 2017 (2017, to appear)

---

[17] http://dase.cs.wright.edu/content/modeling-owl-rules.
[18] http://dase.cs.wright.edu/content/ontology-axiomatization-support.
[19] http://dase.cs.wright.edu/content/owl2dl-rendering.

9. Hitzler, P., Krötzsch, M., Rudolph, S.: Foundations of Semantic Web Technologies. Chapman and Hall/CRC Press, Boca Raton (2010)
10. Hitzler, P., Shimizu, C.: Modular ontologies as a bridge between human conceptualization and data. In: Chapman, P., Endres, D., Pernelle, N. (eds.) ICCS 2018. LNCS (LNAI), vol. 10872, pp. 3–6. Springer, Cham (2018). https://doi.org/10.1007/978-3-319-91379-7_1
11. Karima, N., Hammar, K., Hitzler, P.: How to document ontology design patterns. In: Hammar, K., Hitzler, P., Lawrynowicz, A., Krisnadhi, A., Nuzzolese, A., Solanki, M. (eds.) Advances in Ontology Design and Patterns. Studies on the Semantic Web, vol. 32, pp. 15–28. IOS Press, Amsterdam (2017)
12. Krisnadhi, A., Hitzler, P.: Modeling with ontology design patterns: chess games as a worked example. In: Hitzler, P., Gangemi, A., Janowicz, K., Krisnadhi, A., Presutti, V. (eds.) Ontology Engineering with Ontology Design Patterns - Foundations and Applications. Studies on the Semantic Web, vol. 25, pp. 3–21. IOS Press (2016)
13. Liebig, T., Noppens, O.: ONTOTRACK: combining browsing and editing with reasoning and explaining for OWL lite ontologies. In: McIlraith, S.A., Plexousakis, D., van Harmelen, F. (eds.) ISWC 2004. LNCS, vol. 3298, pp. 244–258. Springer, Heidelberg (2004). https://doi.org/10.1007/978-3-540-30475-3_18
14. Lohmann, S., Negru, S., Haag, F., Ertl, T.: Visualizing ontologies with VOWL. Semant. Web 7(4), 399–419 (2016)
15. Nicola, A.D., Missikoff, M., Navigli, R.: A software engineering approach to ontology building. Inf. Syst. 34(2), 258–275 (2009)
16. Sarker, M.K., Krisnadhi, A., Carral, D., Hitzler, P.: Rule-based OWL modeling with ROWLTab Protégé plugin. In: Blomqvist, E., Maynard, D., Gangemi, A., Hoekstra, R., Hitzler, P., Hartig, O. (eds.) ESWC 2017. LNCS, vol. 10249, pp. 419–433. Springer, Cham (2017). https://doi.org/10.1007/978-3-319-58068-5_26
17. Sarker, M.K., Krisnadhi, A., Hitzler, P.: OWLAx: a Protégé plugin to support ontology axiomatization through diagramming. In: Kawamura, T., Paulheim, H. (eds.) Proceedings of the ISWC 2016 Posters & Demonstrations Track Co-located with 15th International Semantic Web Conference (ISWC 2016), 19 October 2016, Kobe, Japan, vol. 1690. CEUR Workshop Proceedings. CEUR-WS.org (2016)
18. Shimizu, C., Hitzler, P., Horridge, M.: Rendering OWL in description logic syntax. In: Blomqvist, E., Hose, K., Paulheim, H., Lawrynowicz, A., Ciravegna, F., Hartig, O. (eds.) ESWC 2017. LNCS, vol. 10577, pp. 109–113. Springer, Cham (2017). https://doi.org/10.1007/978-3-319-70407-4_21

Conformance Test Cases for the RDF Mapping Language (RML)

Pieter Heyvaert[1]([✉]) [iD], David Chaves-Fraga[2] [iD], Freddy Priyatna[2] [iD],
Oscar Corcho[2] [iD], Erik Mannens[1] [iD], Ruben Verborgh[1] [iD],
and Anastasia Dimou[1] [iD]

[1] IDLab, Department of Electronics and Information Systems,
Ghent University – imec, Ghent, Belgium
pheyvaer.heyvaert@ugent.be
[2] Ontology Engineering Group, Universidad Politécnica de Madrid,
Madrid, Spain

Abstract. Knowledge graphs are often generated using rules that apply
semantic annotations to data sources. Software tools then execute these
rules and generate or virtualize the corresponding RDF-based knowledge graph. RML is an extension of the W3C-recommended R2RML
language, extending support from relational databases to other data
sources, such as data in CSV, XML, and JSON format. As part of the
R2RML standardization process, a set of test cases was created to assess
tool conformance the specification. In this work, we generated an initial
set of reusable test cases to assess RML conformance. These test cases
are based on R2RML test cases and can be used by any tool, regard-
less of the programming language. We tested the conformance of two
RML processors: the RMLMapper and CARML. The results show that
the RMLMapper passes all CSV, XML, and JSON test cases, and most
test cases for relational databases. CARML passes most CSV, XML,
and JSON test cases regarding. Developers can determine the degree of
conformance of their tools, and users determine based on conformance
results to determine the most suitable tool for their use cases.

Keywords: RML · R2RML · Test case

1 Introduction

Knowledge graphs are often generated based on rules that apply semantic annotations to raw or semi-structured data. For example, the DBpedia knowledge
graph is generated by applying classes and predicates of the DBpedia ontology
to Wikipedia [1]. Software tools execute these rules and generate corresponding
RDF triples and quads [2], which materialize knowledge graphs. In the past,
custom scripts prevailed, but lately, rule-driven tools emerged. Such tools distinguish the *rules* that define how RDF terms and triples are generated from

© Springer Nature Switzerland AG 2019
B. Villazón-Terrazas and Y. Hidalgo-Delgado (Eds.): KGSWC 2019, CCIS 1029, pp. 162–173, 2019.
https://doi.org/10.1007/978-3-030-21395-4_12

the *tool* that executes those rules. R2RML [3] is the W3C-recommended language to define such rules for generating knowledge graphs from data in relational databases (RDBs). An R2RML processor is a tool that, given a set of R2RML rules and a relational database, generates an RDF dataset. Examples of R2RML processors include Ultrawrap [4], Morph-RDB [5], Ontop [6], and XSPARQL [7]. A subset of them was included in the RDB2RDF Implementation Report [8] which lists their *conformance* to the R2RML specification. Conformance is assessed based on whether the correct knowledge graph is generated for a set of rules and certain relational database.

Given that R2RML is focused on relational databases only, extensions and adaptations were applied to account for other types of data sources. These include RML [9], XSPARQL [7], and xR2RML [10]. RML provides an extension of R2RML to support heterogeneous data sources, including different *formats* such as CSV, XML, JSON, and *access interfaces*, such as files and Web APIs. Various RML processors emerged, such as the RMLMapper[1], CARML[2], GeoTriples [11], and Ontario[3]. Unlike R2RML, there are no test cases available to determine the conformance to the RML specification. As a result, processors are either not tested or only tested with custom test cases, which do not necessarily assess every aspect of the specification. Consequently, no implementation report is available that allows comparing the different processors that generate knowledge graphs from heterogeneous data sources based on the conformance to the specification. This way, it is hard to determine the most suitable processor for a certain use case.

In this work, we introduce an initial set of RML test cases, which contains 297 test cases based on the 62 existing R2RML test cases. Instead of only considering relational databases as data sources, we also consider data in CSV, XML, and JSON format. Furthermore, we tested the conformance of the RMLMapper and CARML: every test case was executed by both processors and we noted whether the generated knowledge graph matches the expected one. The corresponding implementation report is available at http://rml.io/implementation-report. This helps determining which processor is the most suitable for a certain use case. For example, do users want a processor that supports the complete specification, or do they prefer a processor that does not support certain aspects of the specification, but executes the rules faster?

The test cases results shows that the RMLMapper (v4.3.2) passes all test cases regarding CSV, XML, and JSON format, and most test cases for RDBs, but fails the test cases for automatic datatyping of literals. CARML (v0.2.3) passes most test cases regarding CSV, XML, and JSON format, except of the test cases that deal, for example, with multiple RDF terms generation. Users can now determine how conformant the different processors are to the RML specification and use this conformance to determine the most suitable processor for their use cases.

---

[1] RMLMapper, https://github.com/RMLio/rmlmapper-java.
[2] CARML, https://github.com/carml/carml.
[3] Ontario, https://github.com/WDAqua/Ontario.

The remainder of the paper is structured as follows. In Sect. 2, we discuss related work. In Sect. 3, we discuss the test cases. In Sect. 4, we elaborate on the test cases execution and results. In Sect. 5, we conclude the paper.

2   Related Work

In this section, we describe the related work that is relevant to the paper. First, we explain the most important knowledge graph generation language specifications, including R2RML and RML, and processors that execute those rules. Second, we discuss the differences between R2RML and RML. Finally, we describe the R2RML test cases, how they are defined and implemented and their corresponding implementation report with results of a few processors.

2.1   Knowledge Graph Generation Languages and Tools

R2RML [3] is the W3C recommended language for describing rules to generate RDF from data in RDBs. Currently, many tools support this specification. These tools follow either an Extract-Transform-Load (ETL) process, where a knowledge graph is materialized, e.g., DB2Triples[4] and R2RMLParser[5], or they provide virtual RDF views, focusing more on formalizing the translation from SPARQL to SQL and optimizing the resulted SQL query, e.g., Morph-RDB[6] and Ontop[7].

We describe in more details pioneering tools for executing R2RML rules: DB2Triples is a tool for extracting data from relational databases, semantically annotating the data extracts according to R2RML rules and generating Linked Data. The R2RMLParser [12] deals in principle with incremental Linked Data generation. Each time a knowledge graph is generated, not all data is used, but only the one that changed (so-called incremental transformation). Morph-RDB [5] and Ontop [6] adapt the algorithm defined by Chebotko, Lu, and Fotouhi [13] on SPARQL-to-SQL translation, using the information provided by the R2RML rules. Both apply several semantic optimizations (e.g., self join elimination) that generate efficient SQL queries to speed up the evaluation time.

RML [9] is defined as an extension of R2RML to specify rules for generating knowledge graphs from data in different formats, such as CSV, JSON, XML, and different access interfaces, e.g., open data connectivity and Web APIs [14]. Different other languages build upon RML for generating knowledge graphs from heterogeneous data sources, e.g., xR2RML [10] or RMLC [15].

A set of processors that support the RML specification are proposed. The RMLMapper is a Java library and command line interface that executes RML rules to generate RDF. Following the same approach, CARML executes RML rules, but also includes its own extensions, such as MultiTermMap (to deal with arrays) and XML namespace (to improve XPath expressions). GeoTriples [11]

---

[4] DB2triples, https://github.com/antidot/db2triples.
[5] R2RMLParser, https://github.com/nkons/r2rml-parser.
[6] Morph-RDB, https://github.com/oeg-upm/morph-rdb.
[7] Ontop, https://github.com/ontop/ontop.

Table 1. Summary of the main differences between R2RML and RML

	R2RML	RML
Input reference	Logical Table	Logical Source
Data source language	SQL (implicit)	Reference Formulation (explicit)
Value reference	Column	Logical reference (valid expression following Reference Formulation)
Iteration	Per row (implicit)	Per record (explicit – valid expression following Reference Formulation)

is a processor that generates and executes RML rules for generating RDF from geospatial data from different sources. The processor supports data stored in raw files (shapefiles, CSV, KML, GML, and so on), but also geospatial RDBs such as PostGIS[8] and MonetDB[9]. The generated RDF is based on well-known geospatial vocabularies, such as GeoSPARQL [16] and stSPARQL [17]. Ontario [18] is a federated query processor that uses RML rules to transform heterogeneous data sources during the query processing. Basically, the processor performs the generation using RML during the query processing step and executes federated SPARQL queries over the resulted RDF graphs. These processors are evaluated using ad-hoc examples or feasibility approaches, but a thorough representation of their capabilities is not provided. For that reason, we notice that RML test cases are needed to assess the capabilities of the different processors.

2.2   R2RML and RML Differences

RML is an extension of R2RML and, thus, follows the core concepts of R2RML's specification, such as Triples Maps, Term Maps, Subject Maps, and so on. However, there is a difference on the reference to the data to support heterogeneous data sources with respect to their format, e.g. CSV, XML, JSON, and access interface, e,g. files or Web APIs (see Table 1).

Logical Source. A Logical Source extends R2RML's Logical Table and describes the input data source used to generate the RDF. The Logical Table is only able to describe relational databases, whereas the Logical Source defines different heterogeneous data sources, including relational databases.

Reference Formulation. As RML is designed to support heterogeneous data sources, data sources in different formats needs to be supported. One refers to data in a specific format according to the grammar of a certain formulation, which might be path and query languages or custom grammars. For example, one can refer to data in an XML file via XPath and in a relational database via SQL. To this end, the *Reference Formulation* was introduced indicating the formulation used to refer to data in a certain data source.

---

[8] PostGIS, https://postgis.net/.
[9] MonetDB, https://www.monetdb.org/.

Iterator. In R2RML it is specified that processors iterate over each row to generate RDF. However, as RML is designed to support heterogeneous data sources,
the iteration pattern cannot always be implicitly assumed. For example, iterating
over a specific set of objects is done by selecting them via a JSONPath expression. To this end, the *Iterator* was introduced which determines the iteration
pattern over the data source and specifies the extract of data used to generate
RDF during each iteration. The iterator is not required to be specified if there
is no need to iterate over the input data.

Logical Reference. When referring to values in a table or view of a relational
database, R2RML relies on column names. However, as RML is designed to
support heterogeneous data sources, rules may also refer to elements and objects,
such as in the case of XML and JSON. Consequently, references to values should
be valid with respect to the used reference formulation. For example, a reference
to an attribute of a JSON object should be a valid JSONPath expression. To
this end, (i) the `rml:reference` is introduced to replace `rr:column`, (ii) when a
template is used, via `rr:template`, the values between the curly brackets should
have an expression that is valid with respect to the used reference formulation,
and (iii) `rr:parent` and `rr:child` of a Join Condition should also have an
expression that is valid with respect to the used reference formulation.

2.3 W3C Recommendations and Their Test Cases

In the context of Semantic Web, several specifications were recommended by
W3C, such as SPARQL [19], RDF [2], SHACL [20], Direct Mapping of relational
data to RDF (DM) [21], and R2RML [3]. Each of these specifications has several related tools that support them. A set of test cases was defined for each
one of them (SPARQL test cases[10], RDF 1.1 test cases[11], SHACL test cases[12],
and R2RML and Direct Mapping test cases[13], respectively) that provides useful
information to choose the tool that fits better to certain needs. It is also a relevant step in the standardisation process of an technology or specification. We
describe the R2RML in more details as it is related to the scope of this paper.

Determining the conformance of tools executing R2RML rules in the process
of RDF generation is a step to provide objective information about the features
of each tool. For this reason, the R2RML test cases [22] were proposed. It provides a set of 63 test cases. Each test case is identified by a set of features, such as
the SQL statements to load the database, title, purpose, specification reference,
review status, expected result, and corresponding R2RML rules. All the test
cases are semantically described using the RDB2RDF-test[14] and Test Metadata
Vocabulary[15]. Several R2RML processors were assessed for their conformance

---

[10] https://www.w3.org/2001/sw/DataAccess/tests/r2.
[11] http://www.w3.org/TR/rdf11-testcases/.
[12] http://w3c.github.io/data-shapes/data-shapes-test-suite/.
[13] https://www.w3.org/TR/2012/NOTE-rdb2rdf-test-cases-20120814/.
[14] http://purl.org/NET/rdb2rdf-test#.
[15] https://www.w3.org/TR/2005/NOTE-test-metadata-20050914/.

with the R2RML specification running the test-cases. The results are available in the R2RML implementation-report [8]. The results are also annotated semantically using the Evaluation and Report Language (EARL) 1.0 Schema[16].

3   RML Test Cases

In this section, we propose test cases to determine the conformance of RML processors to the RML specification. The proposed test cases are based on the R2RML test cases, but they take into account different heterogeneous data sources and the corresponding differences in RML (see Sect. 2.2). Our preliminary set of test cases includes (i) adjusted R2RML test cases for relational databases (including MySQL[17], PostgreSQL[18], and SQL Server[19]) and (ii) new test cases for files in the CSV, XML (with XPath as the reference formulation), and JSON format (with JSONPath as the reference formulation). The test cases are described at http://rml.io/test-cases/ and the corresponding files are available at https://github.com/rmlio/rml-test-cases. In Sect. 3.1, we describe the data model that is used to represent the test cases. In Sect. 3.2, we elaborate on the different files making up a test case. In Sect. 3.3, we discuss the differences between the R2RML and RML test cases.

3.1   Data Model

We describe the test cases semantically to increase their reusability and sharability. To this end, we created a semantic data model[20], with as main entity the test case (see Fig. 1). For each test case, the following details are described: unique identifier, title, description, relevant aspect of the RML specification, data sources (optional), expected knowledge graph or error, and RML rules.

To provide the corresponding semantic descriptions, the model uses mostly the Evaluation and Report Language (EARL) 1.0 Schema[21], the Test case manifest vocabulary[22], the Test Metadata vocabulary[23], and the Data Catalog Vocabulary[24]. A test case is annotated with the classes `earl:TestCase`, `test:TestCase`, and `mf:ManifestEntry`. The identifier, title, description, and the specific aspect of the RML specification that is being tested are added as datatype properties. The files that are provided as input to the tools are linked to the test cases via `test:informationResourceInput` and `dcterms:hasPart`. The file with the RML rules is also linked via `rml-tc:rules`[25]. The objects

---

[16] https://www.w3.org/TR/EARL10/.
[17] https://www.mysql.com/.
[18] https://www.postgresql.org/.
[19] https://www.microsoft.com/en-us/sql-server/.
[20] http://rml.io/test-cases/#datamodel.
[21] https://www.w3.org/TR/EARL10/, with prefix `earl`.
[22] http://www.w3.org/2001/sw/DataAccess/tests/test-manifest#, with prefix `mf`.
[23] https://www.w3.org/2006/03/test-description#, with prefix `test`.
[24] https://www.w3.org/TR/vocab-dcat/, with prefix `dcat`.
[25] http://rml.io/ns/test-cases, with prefix `rml-tc`.

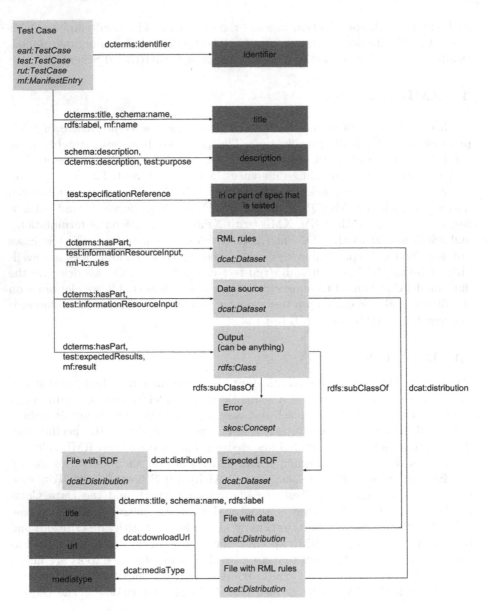

Fig. 1. Data model of the RML test cases

of these properties are of the class `dcat:Dataset`, which in turn link to a `dcat:Distribution` that includes a link to a file. The expected output, whether that is a knowledge graph or an error, is linked via `test:expectedResults`, `mf:result`, and `dcterms:hasPart`. In the case of a knowledge graph, the object of these properties is a `dcat:Dataset`, linked to a `dcat:Distribution`, to describe the file containing the graph. In the case of an error, we link to the expected error.

3.2 Test Case Files

Each test case consists of a set of files that contain the input data sources, the RML rules, and the expected RDF output. In practice, the files are organized as follows: all files for a single test case are contained in a single folder.

There are three types of files for each test case:

- 0 or more **data source files** for CSV (with extension .csv), XML (with extension .xml), and JSON (with extension .json), or 1 file with SQL statements to create the necessary tables for relational databases (called `resource.sql`);
- 1 **file with the RML rules** (in Turtle format, called `mapping.ttl`); and
- 0 or 1 **file with the expected RDF** (in N-Quads format, called `output.nq`).

Distinct test cases assess different behaviours of the processors. Certain test cases assess the behaviour of the tools when (i) the required data sources are not available, and others when (ii) an error occurs and no output is generated. In the former, no data sources files or SQL statements are provided. In the latter, no file with the expected RDF is provided. The test cases are independent of how the processors materialize the knowledge graph: a data dump, as done by the RMLMapper, or on the fly, as done by Ontario [23].

3.3 Differences with R2RML Test Cases

For most R2RML test cases, we created an RML variant for CSV, XML, JSON, MySQL, PostgreSQL, and SQL Server, leading to 6 RML test cases per R2RML test case. For R2RML test cases that focus on specific features of SQL queries, we only created 3 RML test cases, i.e., for MySQL, PostgreSQL, and SQL Server.

For test cases with CSV, XML, and JSON files as data sources, we created the corresponding files with the data based on the tables of the relational databases. For CSV, we used the table created by the SQL statements of the R2RML test case and stored it as a CSV file. For XML, the name of the table was used for the root of the XML document and every row of the table was used to create an XML element. Within this element, elements were created for each column and their values are the values of the corresponding columns in the table. For JSON, we followed a similar approach as XML. The file contains a JSON object at the root with the name of the table as the only attribute. This attribute has as value an array, where each element of the array corresponds with a row in the table. For each row, attributes were created for each column and their values are the values of the corresponding columns in the table.

Data Errors. 2 of the R2RML test cases expect a data error to happen, e.g., when the subject IRI of an entity cannot be generated. In this case, an error is thrown and no knowledge graph is generated. With RML for entities where no subject IRI can be generated there is also no output generated, but, in contrast to R2RML, for the other entities the corresponding output is still generated. Therefore, for the corresponding RML test cases the processors can still throw an error, but the generation of the knowledge graph must not be halted.

Inverse Expressions. 3 of the R2RML test cases are designed to test the use of inverse expressions[26]. However, inverse expressions are only used to optimize the knowledge graph generation and no differences are observed in the generated knowledge graph. Thus, whether inverse expressions are used by a processor or not cannot be verified by such test cases. Thus, we do not include them for RML.

SQL-Specific Features. 18 of the R2RML test cases focus on specific features of SQL queries, e.g., a duplicate column name in a SELECT query. As there are no corresponding RML test cases for CSV files, XML files with XPath, and JSON files with JSONPath, we only provide 54 corresponding test cases for MySQL, PostgreSQL, and SQL Server.

Null Values. 1 of the R2RML test cases tests null values in the rows. However, a corresponding RML test case cannot be provided for the CSV and XML format, because both formats do not support null values.

Spaces in Columns. 1 of the R2RML test cases is designed to test the behaviour when dealing with spaces in the columns of the SQL tables. However, a corresponding RML test case cannot be provided for the XML format, because it does not allow spaces in names.

In total, we have 297 test cases: 39 for CSV, 38 for XML, 40 for JSON, and 180 for relational databases. Of these 297, 255 test cases expect an knowledge graph to be generated, while 36 expect an error that halts the generation.

4   Test Case Execution and Results

In this section, we describe the execution of the test cases and their results for two RML processors: the RMLMapper (v4.3.2) and CARML (v0.2.3). The implementation report can be found at http://rml.io/implentation-report.

We ran the RML test cases over the RML processors and annotated the obtained results using the EARL Schema. Three types of results are possible per test case: "passed", "failed", and "inapplicable". **Passed** (`earl:passed`) is used either when the actual output matches the expected output when no error is expected, or when the tool throws an error when an error is expected. **Failed** (`earl:failed`) is used either when the actual output does not match the expected output if no error is expected, the processor returns an error trying to execute a test or the tool does not throw error if an error is expected. **Inapplicable** (`earl:inapplicable`) is used when the tool clearly states that specific features are not supported.

---

[26] https://www.w3.org/TR/r2rml/#inverse.

Table 2. The RMLMapper (v4.3.2) passes the majority of test cases, with the exception of 20 cases for relational databases.

	CSV	XML	JSON	MySQL	Postgres	SQL Server	Total
Passed	39	38	40	53	54	53	**277**
Failed	0	0	0	7	6	7	**20**
Inapplicable	0	0	0	0	0	0	**0**

Table 3. CARML (v0.2.3) passes almost 3 out of 4 test cases, but does not support relational databases.

	CSV	XML	JSON	MySQL	Postgres	SQL Server	Total
Passed	29	28	27	0	0	0	**84**
Failed	10	10	13	0	0	0	**33**
Inapplicable	0	0	0	60	60	60	**180**

In Table 2 we show the results for the RMLMapper processor. It passes all CSV, JSON and XML test cases, but fails in 20 test cases for the RDBs. The failures are related to the automatic datatyping of literal for RDBs specified by R2RML[27]. RMLMapper should pass the failed test cases in next versions of the processor.

In Table 3 we show the results for the CARML processor. It partially passes the CSV, JSON and XML test cases, but it does not provide support for any of the RDBs test cases. The failures are related to the unsupported for multiple Subject Maps, multiple Predicate Maps, and Named Graphs. The developers of the tool declare that CARML will support these features in next versions of the processor. However, at the moment of writing, we do not have any information about whether CARML will provide support for RDBs.

Finally, we can declare that testing a RML processor with the defined cases and analysing the obtained results offers a general view of the current status of it. These results also give useful information to the tool developers on knowing where they should put their effort to improve the conformance of the processor.

5   Conclusion

With the introduction of an initial set of RML test cases (i) developers can determine how conformant their RML processors are to the RML specification, and (ii) users can use the test cases results to select the most appropriate processor for a specific use case. Before, users were only able to rely on the custom test cases, if any, which not necessarily assess every aspect of the specification. Now, users can rely on well-defined set of test cases that (a) clearly define what the

---

[27] https://www.w3.org/TR/r2rml/#dfn-natural-rdf-literal.

input and expected output is, and (b) are reusable across different processors written in different programming languages.

The results of the test cases execution with the RMLMapper and CARML show that the CSV, XML, and JSON formats are almost fully supported, but RDBs cause difficulties or are not supported at all. The RMLMapper passes more test cases than CARML and therefore, the former is better when considering the conformance to the RML specification.

Our set of test cases is based on the R2RML test cases, and therefore, it covers a big part of the RML specification, as it is based on R2RML. However, as the R2RML test cases focus on relational databases, they do not take into account the specifics of hierarchical data formats, such as nested structures in JSON and XML files, which can be used with RML. Therefore, further research should be directed towards creating new test cases that tackle these specifics taking into account the differences between the different hierarchical formats and their corresponding reference formulations.

Acknowledgements. The described research activities were funded by Ghent University, imec, Flanders Innovation & Entrepreneurship (AIO), the Research Foundation – Flanders (FWO), and the European Union. The work presented in this paper is partially supported by the Spanish Ministerio de Economía, Industria y Competitividad and EU FEDER funds under the DATOS 4.0: RETOS Y SOLUCIONES - UPM Spanish national project (TIN2016-78011-C4-4-R) and by an FPI grant (BES-2017-082511).

References

1. Lehmann, J., et al.: DBpedia - a large-scale, multilingual knowledge base extracted from Wikipedia. Semant. Web **6**, 167–195 (2015)
2. Cyganiak, R., Wood, D., Lanthaler, M.: RDF 1.1 Concepts and Abstract Syntax. Recommendation. World Wide Web Consortium (W3C), February 2014. http://www.w3.org/TR/rdf11-concepts/
3. Das, S., Sundara, S., Cyganiak, R.: R2RML: RDB to RDF Mapping Language. W3C Recommendation. W3C (2012). http://www.w3.org/TR/r2rml/
4. Sequeda, J.F., Miranker, D.P.: Ultrawrap: SPARQL execution on relational data. In: Web Semantics: Science, Services and Agents on the WWW (2013). ISSN 1570-8268. https://doi.org/10.1016/j.websem.2013.08.002. http://www.sciencedirect.com/science/article/pii/S1570826813000383
5. Priyatna, F., Corcho, O., Sequeda, J.: Formalisation and experiences of R2RML-based SPARQL to SQL query translation using morph. In: 23rd International Conference on WWW (2014). ISBN 978-1-4503-2744-2
6. Calvanese, D., et al.: Ontop: answering SPARQL queries over relational databases. Semant. Web J. **8**, 471–487 (2017)
7. Bischof, S., et al.: Mapping between RDF and XML with XSPARQL. J. Data Semant. (2012). ISSN 1861-2040. https://doi.org/10.1007/s13740-012-0008-7
8. Villazón-Terrazas, B., Hausenblas, M.: RDB2RDF Implementation Report. W3C Note. W3C (2012). https://www.w3.org/TR/rdb2rdf-implementations/
9. Dimou, A., et al.: RML: a generic language for integrated RDF mappings of heterogeneous data. In: LDOW (2014)

10. Michel, F., et al.: Translation of relational and non-relational databases into RDF with xR2RML. In: WEBIST (2015)
11. Kyzirakos, K., et al.: GeoTriples: transforming geospatial data into RDF graphs using R2RML and RML mappings. J. Web Semant. **52**, 16–32 (2018)
12. Konstantinou, N., et al.: Exposing scholarly information as Linked Open Data: RDFizing DSpace contents. Electron. Libr. **32**(6), 834–851 (2014). https://doi.org/10.1108/EL-12-2012-0156
13. Chebotko, A., Lu, S., Fotouhi, F.: Semantics preserving SPARQL-to-SQL translation. Data Knowl. Eng. **68**(10), 973–1000 (2009)
14. Dimou, A., et al.: Machine-interpretable dataset and service descriptions for heterogeneous data access and retrieval. In: Proceedings of the 11th International Conference on Semantic Systems, SEMANTICS 2015. ACM (2015). ISBN 978-1-4503-3462-4. https://doi.org/10.1145/2814864.2814873
15. Chaves-Fraga, D., et al.: Virtual statistics knowledge graph generation from CSV files. In: Emerging Topics in Semantic Technologies: ISWC 8 Satellite Events. Studies on the Semantic Web, vol. 36, pp. 235–244. IOS Press (2018)
16. Battle, R., Kolas, D.: GeoSPARQL: enabling a geospatial semantic web. Semant. Web J. **3**(4), 355–370 (2011)
17. Koubarakis, M., Kyzirakos, K.: Modeling and querying metadata in the semantic sensor web: the model stRDF and the query language stSPARQL. In: Aroyo, L., et al. (eds.) ESWC 2010. LNCS, vol. 6088, pp. 425–439. Springer, Heidelberg (2010). https://doi.org/10.1007/978-3-642-13486-9_29
18. Vidal, M.-E., Endris, K.M., Jozashoori, S., Karim, F., Palma, G.: Semantic data integration of big biomedical data for supporting personalised medicine. In: Alor-Hernández, G., Sánchez-Cervantes, J.L., Rodríguez-González, A., Valencia-García, R. (eds.) Current Trends in Semantic Web Technologies: Theory and Practice. SCI, vol. 815, pp. 25–56. Springer, Cham (2019). https://doi.org/10.1007/978-3-030-06149-4_2
19. Harris, S., Seaborne, A.: SPARQL 1.1 Query Language. Recommendation. World Wide Web Consortium (W3C), March 2013. https://www.w3.org/TR/sparql11-query/
20. Knublauch, H., Kontokostas, D.: Shapes Constraint Language (SHACL). Recommendation. World Wide Web Consortium (W3C) (2017). https://www.w3.org/TR/shacl/
21. Arenas, M., et al.: A Direct Mapping of Relational Data to RDF. W3C Recommendation. W3C, September 2012. https://www.w3.org/TR/rdb-direct-mapping/
22. Villazón-Terrazas, B., Hausenblas, M.: R2RML and Direct Mapping Test Cases. W3C Note. W3C (2012). http://www.w3.org/TR/rdb2rdf-test-cases/
23. Dimou, A., et al.: What factors influence the design of a linked data generation algorithm? In: Berners-Lee, T., et al. (eds.) Proceedings of the 11th Workshop on Linked Data on the Web, April 2018. http://events.linkeddata.org/ldow2018/papers/LDOW2018_paper_12.pdf

Expressive Context Modeling
with Description Logics

Rolando Ramírez-Rueda[1]([✉]), Everardo Bárcenas[2], Carmen Mezura-Godoy[1],
and Guillermo Molero-Castillo[2]

[1] Universidad Veracruzana, Xalapa-Enríquez, Mexico
zs17000714@estudiantes.uv.mx, cmezura@uv.mx
[2] Universidad Nacional Autónoma de México, Mexico City, Mexico
ebarcenas@unam.mx, gmoleroca@fi-b.unam.mx

Abstract. Modeling and verification of context-aware systems have
been proven to be a challenging task mainly because expressive modeling implies, in most cases, expensive verification algorithms. On the
other side, description logics have been successfully applied as a modeling and verification framework in many settings, such as in the semantic
Web and bioinformatics, just to mention some. The main factor for this
success is the delicate balance between expressiveness and computational
cost of the corresponding algorithms in description logics. In the current
work, we propose the use of an expressive description logics to model
the consistency of context-aware systems. We show this expressive modeling language is capable to succinctly express complex properties, such
as temporal ones.

Keywords: Context-aware systems · Semantic reasoning ·
Description logic

1 Introduction

The semantic Web comprises a set of technological World Wide Web Consortium (W3C) standards of data formats and exchange protocols on the Web. The
Web Ontology Language (OWL), the resource description framework (RDF),
and the RDF query language SPARQL are among the most distinctive of these
standards. As its name suggests, OWL is a family of knowledge representation
languages used to describe ontologies, which can be seen as a formal and hierarchical representation of knowledge on the Web domain. Mainly due to its formal
foundations and practical relevance, OWL has been successfully applied in several other domains, such as bioinformatics, just to mention one. OWL formal
foundations are built upon Description Logics (DL). DL is a family of knowledge representation logics. Standards DL are known to be an efficiently decidable
fragment of classical First-Order Logic.

One of the domains, where description logics have been recently studied as a
modeling and reasoning framework, is in context-aware systems [3,9]. With the

© Springer Nature Switzerland AG 2019
B. Villazón-Terrazas and Y. Hidalgo-Delgado (Eds.): KGSWC 2019, CCIS 1029, pp. 174–185, 2019.
https://doi.org/10.1007/978-3-030-21395-4_13

relatively recent ubiquity of computer systems, complex contexts, composed by a conglomerate of variables and the corresponding intricate relations, challenge these systems to quickly adapt and correspondingly react. Traditional modeling and reasoning methods have resulted limited in the context-aware domain mostly by two factors: expressiveness and efficiency [7]. Modern contexts demand powerful modeling languages capable of expressing complex properties. However, in most cases, the most expressive the modeling language, corresponds to the most expensive reasoning algorithms. The delicate balance between expressive power and reasoning efficiency of description logics, positions them as a promising modeling and reasoning framework in the context-aware setting. In the current paper, we propose the use of an expressive description logic [2], to model the consistency of context-aware systems.

1.1 Related Works and Motivations

Initial modeling approaches in the context-aware setting include the context modeling language (CML) [5]. Limitations when modeling hierarchies prevent CML to properly express several well-known context properties, such as the ones involving time and location, that is, temporal and spatial properties. Regarding spatial modeling languages, many specially purposed approaches have been designed [4]. However, the representation of temporal context properties becomes an issue in these domain-specific languages.

There are some known approaches to model complex context properties using description logics [3,9]. In particular, it is reported in an extensive survey on reasoning and modeling methods for context-aware system in [3]. Also, it proposed OWL as a specification language for temporal properties. More complex properties, required to model human activities in smart environments, are studied in [9]. An extension of OWL, named OWL 2, is proposed as modeling language. In our proposal, we study an expressive description logic with arithmetic operators [2]. These operators allow to express more complex quantity properties that OWL 2 cannot express.

Most related work to our proposal is reported in [7]. In this paper, authors model consistency in context-aware systems in terms of the μ-calculus and expressive modal logic. Temporal properties are succinctly expressed as μ-calculus formulas. Moreover, several experiments are also reported in order to test practical efficiency. However, in this paper, it is not shown whether or not properties about quantities can be modeled. In the description logics approach of our proposal, arithmetic operators are shown to be useful for modeling quantity properties. In order to illustrate our approach, we model the consistency of a context-aware communication system in terms of knowledge base reasoning.

1.2 Outline

In Sect. 3, we describe an expressive description logic for trees [2]. We also present the notion of knowledge base reasoning in terms of the consistency of terminological axioms (TBoxes) and assertion axioms (ABoxes). We define the notion of consistency of context-aware systems in Sect. 2. This notion is defined in terms of a tree-shaped consistency model as in [2]. In Sect. 4, we show how to test consistency in terms of knowledge base reasoning. In order to illustrate the approach, we test the consistency of a context-aware communication system. Finally, in Sect. 5, we give a summary of this paper, together with a brief discussion of further research directions.

2   Context-Aware Consistency

In this Section, we give a precise description of the notion of consistency of context-aware systems. For this aim, we first introduce a context-aware communication system inspired from [5] and [7]. The system has the following context variables.

- A set of communication channels Cc, which can be either asynchronous or synchronous, that is, $Cc = Ac \cup Sc$ and $As \cap Sc = \emptyset$. For instance, a mobile phone signal is a synchronous communication channel, whilst email is an asynchronous one.
- A set of user communication preference Up composed by pairs (u, c), where u is a user and c is a communication channel. For example, user u_1 may not be able to use a computer, and hence, cannot use email as a communication channel, whilst u_1 does have a mobile phone.
- A set of communication constraints for locations Lc composed by pairs (l, c), where l is a location and c is a communication channel. That is, in each location there some particular communication channels available. For instance, in some physics labs, no mobile signals are allowed.
- A time schedule Sch is a set composed by triples (u, t, l), where u is a user, t is a time and l is a location. A triple means user location at a particular time. The schedule contains location of each user of the communication system for some time length, which may be as short or long as a particular application of the system requires. For instance, in a school, this time length may be as long as a semester. In contrast, in a hospital, the time length may be more useful by day.

We now illustrate the notion of a context-aware communication system (Fig. 1).

Example 1. Consider a system with 3 different time periods, 2 locations, 3 communication channels, and 2 users.

- The set of communication channels are:
  $Cc = \{c_1, c_2, c_3\}$.
- The set of user preferences are:
  $Up = \{(u_1, c_1), (u_1, c_2), (u_2, c_1), (u_2, c_2), (u_2, c_3)\}$.
- The set of location constraints are:
  $Lc = \{(l_1, c_1), (l_1, c_2), (l_2, c_1), (l_2, c_2), (l_2, c_3)\}$.
- The schedule is the following set:
  $Sch = \{(u_1, t_1, l_1), (u_1, t_2, l_1), (u_1, t_3, l_1), (u_2, t_2, l_2), (u_2, t_3, l_2)\}$.

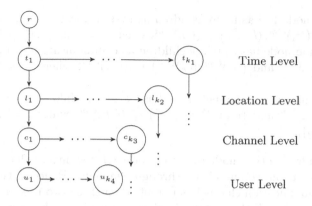

Fig. 1. Graphical representation of a consistency model.

Intuitively, we say a communication system is not consistent when two users cannot communicate by any means at any time. In Example 1, it is easy to see that user u_1 can communicate with u_2 at any time with the t_1. This means the system is not consistent with respect to synchronous communication. However, if the setting is asynchronous communication, the two users can always communicate because they have always available all communication channels, in particular the asynchronous channels. Another scenario is if location l_2 would not have communication channels c_1 and c_3 available, then users would not be able to communicate at all. In such a case, the system would not be consistent both synchronously and asynchronously.

Before giving a precise definition of context-aware consistency, we need to introduce the notion of a consistency model. For this aim, we first define tree interpretations. A tree interpretation $\mathcal{I}$ is defined as a pair $(\Delta^{\mathcal{I}}, \cdot^{\mathcal{I}})$, where $\Delta^{\mathcal{I}}$ a finite non-empty set of nodes called domain, and $\cdot^{\mathcal{I}}$ is an interpretation function, mapping a set of nodes in the domain to each concept name, that is $(A)^{\mathcal{I}} \subseteq \Delta^{\mathcal{I}}$, a set of pairs of nodes to each role name, that is $(R)^{\mathcal{I}} \subseteq \Delta^{\mathcal{I}} \times \Delta^{\mathcal{I}}$, such that the interpretation of roles forms a tree structure. More precisely, the interpretation of each role is the following: $(Ch)^{\mathcal{I}}$ denotes the child relation, $(Rsib)^{\mathcal{I}}$ the right siblings, $(Par)^{\mathcal{I}}$ is the converse of Ch, and the converse of $Rsib$ is $(Lsib)^{\mathcal{I}}$.

Given a context-aware communication system, described by its context variables (Ch, Up, Lc, Sch), the intuition behind the notion of a consistency model is a tree interpretation, with 4 children layers below the root, one for system times, one for locations, one for communication channels, and last one for users. See Fig. 2, for a graphical representation of a consistency model. We now give a precise definition of a consistency model Cm as a tree interpretation, such that:

– the root node is labeled by r, $(r)^{Cm} \subseteq \Delta^{Cm}$;
– the root node has many children as system times, that is, $(t_i)^{Cm} \subset \Delta^{Cm}$ and $((r)^{Cm}, (t_i)^{Cm}) \subseteq (Ch)^{Cm}$, where $i = 1, 2, \ldots, |\{t \mid (u, t, l) \in Sch\}|$;

- each time node has as many children as system locations, that is, $(l_j)^{Cm} \subset \Delta^{Cm}$ and $((t_i)^{Cm}, (l_j)^{Cm}) \subseteq (Ch)^{Cm}$, where $j = 1, 2, \ldots, |\{l \mid (l, c) \in Lc\}|$;
- each location node has as many children as communication channels, that is, $(c_k)^{Cm} \subset \Delta^{Cm}$ and $((l_j)^{Cm}, (c_k)^{Cm}) \subseteq (Ch)^{Cm}$, where $k = 1, 2, \ldots, |Cc|$; and
- each communication channel node has as many children as users, that is, $(u_l)^{Cm} \subset \Delta^{Cm}$ and $((c_k)^{Cm}, (u_l)^{Cm}) \subseteq (Ch)^{Cm}$, where $l = 1, 2, \ldots, |\{u \mid (u, c) \in Up\}|$.

Each path from a time node to a user node, t, l, c, u, means that at time t and location l, user u can communicate through channel c. Hence, if two users have the same communication channel as parent, then these two users can communicate with each other. If the communication channel is synchronous and the user nodes are descendants of the same time node, then the user can communicate synchronously. When the communication channel is asynchronous and the user nodes are descendants of different time nodes, then the user whose position is on the left can communicate asynchronously with the user on the right. These time constraints distinguish our work from the one in [5], where the communication system is modeled with CML but time constraints are not supported.

We say a communication system is not consistent when two users are not able to communicate by any mean at any time, either synchronously or asynchronously. This notion of consistency is defined in terms of a consistency model. Before giving this definition, we need some notation. Given a tree interpretation $\mathcal{I} = (\Delta^{\mathcal{I}}, \cdot^{\mathcal{I}})$, we say a node $n_k \in \Delta^{\mathcal{I}}$ is descendant of a node $n_0 \in \Delta^{\mathcal{I}}$, written $(n_0, n_k) \in (Ds)^{\mathcal{I}}$, if and only if, there is a non-empty sequence $(n_i, n_{i+1}) \in (Ch)^{\mathcal{I}}$, where $i = 0, 1, \ldots, k - 1$. In the same setting, we also say n_k is a following sibling of n_0, written $(n_0, n_k) \in (Ds)^{\mathcal{I}}$, if and only if, there is a non-empty sequence $(n_i, n_{i+1}) \in (Rsib)^{\mathcal{I}}$.

Definition 1 (System Consistency). *Given a context-aware communication system (Cc, Up, Lc, Sch), and the corresponding consistency model Cm we say it is consistent, if and only if, for any two users u_1 and u_2,*

- *(synchronously) there are channel and time nodes $n_{c_i}, n_t \in \Delta^{Cm}$, such that $(n_{c_i}, n_{u_i}) \in (Ch)^{Cm}$ and $(n_t, n_{u_i}) \in (Ds)^{Cm}$, where $i = 1, 2$, $(u_i)^{Cm} = n_{u_i}$, $(c)^{Cm} = n_{c_i}$, $(t)^{Cm} = n_t$, c is a synchronous communication channel, and t is a time in the schedule of the system;*
- *(asynchronously) there are channel and time nodes $n_{c_i}, n_{t_i} \in \Delta^{Cm}$, such that $(n_{c_i}, n_{u_i}) \in (Ch)^{Cm}$, $(n_{t_i}, n_{u_i}) \in (Ds)^{Cm}$, $(n_{t_1}, n_{t_2}) \in (Fs)^{Cm}$, where $i = 1, 2$, $(u_i)^{Cm} = n_{u_i}$, $(c)^{Cm} = n_{c_i}$, $(t_i)^{Cm} = n_{t_i}$, c is a asynchronous communication channel, and t_i are times in the schedule of the system.*

3 An Expressive Description Logic

In this Section, we present an expressive description logic for trees with fixed-points, inverse roles, nominals and counting constraints [2].

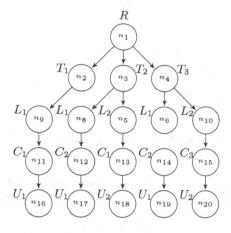

Fig. 2. The consistency model of Example 1.

Consider a countable sets of concept names and variables, and the following set of role names $\{Ch, Rsib, Par, Lsib\}$.

Concept descriptions are defined by the following grammar.

$$C := a \mid \neg C \mid C \sqcup C \mid \exists R.C \mid C - C > k \mid \mu x.C$$

where a is a concept name, x a variable, and R a role name.

The existence of fixed-points requires variables occur bounded and under an odd number of negations. Also, consider the following notation: $C_1 \sqcap C_2 := \neg(\neg C_1 \sqcup \neg C_2)$, $\top := C \sqcap \neg C$, $\bot := \neg\top$, $\forall R.C := \neg\exists R.\neg C$, and $\nu x..C := \mu x.\neg C[\neg x/x]$.

Before given a precise semantics for concept descriptions, consider a valuation function ρ for variables, that is, $\rho(x) \subseteq \Delta^{\mathcal{I}}$, for a given tree interpretation $\mathcal{I}$.

Given a tree interpretation $\mathcal{I} = (\Delta^{\mathcal{I}}, \cdot^{\mathcal{I}})$ and a valuation ρ, concept descriptions are interpreted as follows:

$$(x)^{\mathcal{I}}_{\rho} = \rho(x) \subseteq \Delta^{\mathcal{I}}$$

$$(a)^{\mathcal{I}}_{\rho} = (a)^{\mathcal{I}} \subseteq \Delta^{\mathcal{I}}$$

$$(\neg C)^{\mathcal{I}}_{\rho} = \Delta^{\mathcal{I}} \backslash (C)^{\mathcal{I}}_{\rho}$$

$$(C_1 \sqcup C_2)^{\mathcal{I}}_{\rho} = (C_1)^{\mathcal{I}}_{\rho} \cup (C_2)^{\mathcal{I}}_{\rho}$$

$$(\exists R.C)^{\mathcal{I}}_{\rho} = \{s \in \Delta^{\mathcal{I}} \mid (s,s') \in (R)^{\mathcal{I}}, s' \in (C)^{\mathcal{I}}_{\rho}\}$$

$$(C_1 - C_2 > k)^{\mathcal{I}}_{\rho} = \{s \in \Delta^{\mathcal{I}} \mid \mid \{s' \mid (s,s') \in (Ch)^{\mathcal{I}}, s' \in (C_1)^{\mathcal{I}}_{\rho}\} \mid -$$
$$\mid \{s'' \mid (s,s'') \in (Ch)^{\mathcal{I}}, s'' \in (C_2)^{\mathcal{I}}_{\rho}\} \mid > k\}$$

$$(\mu x.C)^{\mathcal{I}}_{\rho} = \bigcap \{\varepsilon \subseteq \Delta^{\mathcal{I}} \mid (C)^{\mathcal{I}}_{\rho[x/\varepsilon]} \subseteq \varepsilon\}$$

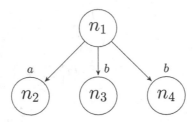

Fig. 3. A model for $(b - a) > 0$.

If $(C)_\rho^\mathcal{I} \neq \emptyset$ for any ρ, we say the tree interpretation I satisfies the concept C, we also say I is a model of C. As an example, consider the following concept.

$$(B - A) > 0$$

This concept holds at nodes with more b children than a ones. In Fig. 3 it is depicted a graphical representation of a corresponding model, where the concept holds at n_1.

In order to illustrate concept semantics, consider the following example:

$$\mu x.C \sqcup \exists Ch.x$$

This concept is interpreted as nodes named C or with a C descendant. A model for this concept is depicted in Fig. 4. In this model, the concept holds in n_1, n_2, n_4, n_5 and n_6.

A knowledge base is composed by: a finite set of terminology axioms, called a TBox $\mathcal{T}$; and a finite set of assertion axioms, called an ABox $\mathcal{A}$.

A terminology axiom is an expression of the form $C_1 \sqsubseteq C_2$, where C_1 and C_2 are concept descriptions. When both $C_1 \sqsubseteq C_2$ and $C_2 \sqsubseteq C_1$ occur in a TBox $\mathcal{T}$, it is instead often written $C_1 \equiv C_2$. We say a tree interpretation $\mathcal{I}$ is a model of $C_1 \sqsubseteq C_2$ if $(C_1)_\rho^\mathcal{I} \subseteq (C_2)_\rho^\mathcal{I}$ for any ρ. A tree interpretation is a model of a TBox $\mathcal{T}$ when it is a model of each of its terminology axioms.

There are two kind of assertion axioms: role assertions $R(a, b)$, where R is a role name, and a and b are individual names; and concept assertions $C(a)$, where C is a concept description and a is an individual name. Individual names are interpreted as individuals in the domain, that is, for any individual name a, $|a^\mathcal{I}| = 1$. Additionally, for any two individual names a and b, $a \neq b$ implies $a^\mathcal{I} \neq b^\mathcal{I}$. A tree interpretation $\mathcal{I}$ satisfies a role assertion $R(a, b)$ whenever $(a^\mathcal{I}, b^\mathcal{I}) \in R^\mathcal{I}$. Analogously, $\mathcal{I}$ satisfies $C(a)$ when $a^I \in (C)_\rho^I$ for any ρ. A tree interpretation $\mathcal{I}$ is a model of a ABox if it satisfies each of its assertions. We say an ABox $\mathcal{A}$ is consistent with respect to a TBox $\mathcal{T}$ if there is a common model for both $\mathcal{A}$ and $\mathcal{T}$ [1].

We conclude this section by remembering the consistency complexity of this description logic.

Theorem 1 (Consistency complexity [2]**).** *Deciding whether or not an ABox is consistent with respect to a TBox is in EXPTIME.*

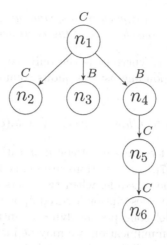

Fig. 4. A model for $\mu x.C \sqcup \exists Ch.x$.

4   Consistency Testing

Consistency of a context-aware communication system is tested in terms of an ABox consistency with respect to a TBox. The ABox represents the corresponding consistency model, whilst the TBox represents the type of communication.

Definition 2 (Synchronous communication). *Given a context-aware communication system (Cc, Up, Lc, Sch), and two users u_1, u_2 of this system, we define a synchronous communication TBox $\mathcal{T}_s$ as follows:*

$$\bigsqcup_{j=1}^{k_2}\left(t_j \sqcap \exists Ch.\exists Ch. \bigsqcup_{i=1}^{k_1} c_i\right) \sqsubseteq \bigsqcup_{i=1}^{k_1} \exists Ch.\exists Ch.(c_i \sqcap \exists Ch.u_1) \sqcap \exists Ch.\exists Ch.(c_i \sqcap \exists Ch.u_2)$$

where $k_1 > 0$ is the number of synchronous communication channels and $k_2 > 0$ is the number of times.

Recall Example 1. Suppose channels c_1 and c_2 are synchronous. Then the corresponding synchronous communication TBox $\mathcal{T}_s$ is defined as follows:

$$(t_1 \sqcap \exists Ch.\exists Ch.(c_1 \sqcup c_2)) \sqcup (t_2 \sqcap \exists Ch.\exists Ch.(c_1 \sqcup c_2)) \sqcup (t_3 \sqcap \exists Ch.\exists Ch.(c_1 \sqcup c_2))$$
$$\sqsubseteq$$
$$((\exists Ch.\exists Ch.(c_1 \wedge \exists Ch.u_1)) \sqcap (\exists Ch.\exists Ch.(c_1 \wedge \exists Ch.u_2)))$$
$$\sqcup ((\exists Ch.\exists Ch.(c_2 \wedge \exists Ch.u_1)) \sqcap (\exists Ch.\exists Ch.(c_2 \wedge \exists Ch.u_2)))$$

Definition 3 (Asynchronous communication). *Given a context-aware communication system (Cc, Up, Lc, Sch), and two users u_1, u_2 of this system, we define an asynchronous communication TBox $\mathcal{T}_a$ as follows:*

$$r \sqsubseteq \bigsqcup_{i=1}^{k} \exists Ch.(\exists Ch.\exists Ch.(c_i \sqcap \exists Ch.u_1) \sqcap \mu x.\exists Ch.\exists Ch.(c_i \sqcap \exists Ch.u_2) \sqcup \exists Rsib.x)$$

where $k > 0$ is the number of asynchronous communication channels and r is a special concept name denoting the root of the corresponding consistency model.

Consider again Example 1, where c_3 is the only asynchronous communication channel. Then the corresponding asynchronous communication TBox T_a is the following:

$$r \sqsubseteq \exists Ch.(\exists Ch.\exists Ch.(c_3 \wedge \exists Ch.u_1) \sqcap \mu x.\exists Ch.\exists Ch.(c_3 \sqcap \exists Ch.u_2) \sqcup \exists Rsib.x)$$

We have just defined two notions of communications, one synchronous and one asynchronous, as in [7]. These notions are defined in terms of the existence of at least one time in the schedule, when two users are able to communicate. Nevertheless, our expressive description logic equipped with arithmetic operators can also help us to model concepts involving quantities. For instance, in the setting of synchronous communication, we may be interested that two users can communicate at least twice. This can be modeled as follows:

$$\left(\bigsqcup_{j=1}^{k_2} \left(t_j \sqcap \exists Ch.\exists Ch. \bigsqcup_{i=1}^{k_1} c_i \right) \right) > 1$$

$$\sqsubseteq$$

$$\left(\bigsqcup_{i=1}^{k_1} \exists Ch.\exists Ch.(c_i \sqcap \exists Ch.u_1) \sqcap \exists Ch.\exists Ch.(c_i \sqcap \exists Ch.u_2) \right) > 1$$

where k_1 is the number of synchronous communication channels and k_2 is the number of times.

We now define an ABox in order to characterize the consistency model. Intuitively, there is an individual for the root and each variable of the corresponding communication system. These individuals are characterized by concept assertions. The topology of the consistency model is characterized by role assertions. A precise definition of this consistency ABox is given as follows.

Definition 4 (Consistency ABox). *Given a context-aware communication system (Cc, Up, Lc, Sch), such that*

$$\begin{aligned} Cc &= \{c_i \mid i = 1, \ldots, k_1\} \\ Up &= \{(u_i, c_j) \mid i = 1, \ldots, k_1; j = 1, \ldots, k_2\} \\ Lc &= \{(l_i, c_j) \mid i = 1, \ldots, k_3; j = 1, \ldots, k_2\} \\ Sch &= \{(u_i, t_j, l_r) \mid i = 1, \ldots, k_2; j = 1, \ldots, k_4; r = 1, \ldots, k_3\} \end{aligned}$$

we define a consistency ABox A_c as follows.

 – *Concept assertions:*

$$(\neg \exists Lsib.\top)(r') \qquad r(r') \qquad (\neg \exists Rsib.\top)(r') \qquad (\neg \exists Par.\top)(r')$$

$$(\neg\exists Lsib.\top)(t'_1) \qquad t_i(t'_i) \qquad\qquad (\neg\exists Rsib.\top)(t'_{k_4}) \qquad i = 1, \ldots, k_4$$

$$(\neg\exists Lsib.\top)(l'_{1,i}) \qquad l_j(l'_{j,i}) \qquad\qquad (\neg\exists Rsib.\top)(l'_{k_3,i}) \qquad j = 1, \ldots, k_3$$

$$(\neg\exists Lsib.\top)(c'_{1,j,i}) \qquad c_s(c'_{s,j,i}) \qquad\qquad (\neg\exists Rsib.\top)(c'_{k_1,j,i}) \qquad s = 1, \ldots, k_1$$

$$(\neg\exists Lsib.\top)(u'_{1,s,j,i}) \quad (u_z \wedge \neg\exists Ch.\top)(u'_{z,s,j,i}) \qquad (\neg\exists Rsib.\top)(u'_{k_2,s,j,i})$$
$$z = 1, \ldots, k_2$$

– *Role assertions:*

$$Ch(r', t'_1) \qquad\qquad Rsib(t'_i, t'_{i+1}) \qquad\qquad i = 1, \ldots, k_4$$

$$Ch(t'_i, l'_{1,i}) \qquad\qquad Rsib(l'_{j,i}, l'_{j+1,i}) \qquad\qquad j = 1, \ldots, k_3$$

$$Ch(l'_{j,i}, c'_{1,j,i}) \qquad\qquad Rsib(c'_{s,j,i}, c'_{s+1,j,i}) \qquad\qquad s = 1, \ldots, k_1$$

$$Ch(c'_{s,j,i}, u'_{1,s,j,i}) \qquad\qquad Rsib(u'_{z,s,j,i}, u'_{z+1,s,j,i}) \qquad\qquad z = 1, \ldots, k_2$$

In order to illustrate the consistency ABox notion, consider now the corresponding consistency ABox $\mathcal{A}_c$ of Example 1.

– Concept assertions:

$$(\neg\exists Lsib.\top)(r') \qquad r(r') \qquad\qquad (\neg\exists Rsib.\top)(r') \qquad (\neg\exists Par.\top)(r')$$

$$(\neg\exists Lsib.\top)(t'_1) \quad t_1(t'_1) \qquad t_2(t'_2) \qquad t_2(t'_2) \qquad t_3(t'_3) \qquad (\neg\exists Rsib.\top)(t'_3)$$

$$(\neg\exists Lsib.\top)(l'_{1,1}) \qquad l_1(l'_{1,1}) \qquad l_1(l'_{1,2}) \qquad l_1(l'_{1,3})$$
$$l_2(l'_{2,1}) \qquad\qquad l_2(l'_{2,2}) \qquad l_2(l'_{1,3}) \qquad (\neg\exists Rsib.\top)(l'_{2,3})$$

$$(\neg\exists Lsib.\top)(c'_{1,1,1}) \qquad c_1(c'_{1,1,1}) \qquad c_2(c'_{2,1,1}) \qquad (\neg\exists Rsib.\top)(c'_{2,1,1})$$
$$(\neg\exists Lsib.\top)(c'_{1,2,1}) \qquad c_1(c'_{1,2,1}) \qquad c_2(c'_{2,2,1}) \qquad c_2(c'_{3,2,1})$$
$$(\neg\exists Rsib.\top)(c'_{3,2,1})$$
$$(\neg\exists Lsib.\top)(c'_{1,1,2}) \qquad c_1(c'_{1,1,2}) \qquad c_2(c'_{2,1,2}) \qquad (\neg\exists Rsib.\top)(c'_{2,1,2})$$
$$(\neg\exists Lsib.\top)(c'_{1,2,2}) \qquad c_1(c'_{1,2,2}) \qquad c_2(c'_{2,2,2}) \qquad c_2(c'_{3,2,2})$$
$$(\neg\exists Rsib.\top)(c'_{3,2,2})$$
$$(\neg\exists Lsib.\top)(c'_{1,1,3}) \qquad c_1(c'_{1,1,3}) \qquad c_2(c'_{2,1,3}) \qquad (\neg\exists Rsib.\top)(c'_{2,1,3})$$
$$(\neg\exists Lsib.\top)(c'_{1,2,3}) \qquad c_1(c'_{1,2,3}) \qquad c_2(c'_{2,2,3}) \qquad c_2(c'_{3,2,3})$$
$$(\neg\exists Rsib.\top)(c'_{3,2,3})$$

$(\neg\exists Lsib.\top)(u'_{1,1,1,1})$ $(u_1 \wedge \neg\exists Ch.\top)(u'_{1,1,1,1})$ $(\neg\exists Rsib.\top)(u'_{1,1,1,1})$

$(\neg\exists Lsib.\top)(u'_{1,2,1,1})$ $(u_1 \wedge \neg\exists Ch.\top)(u'_{1,2,1,1})$ $(\neg\exists Rsib.\top)(u'_{1,2,1,1})$

$(\neg\exists Lsib.\top)(u'_{1,1,1,2})$ $(u_1 \wedge \neg\exists Ch.\top)(u'_{1,1,1,2})$ $(\neg\exists Rsib.\top)(u'_{1,1,1,2})$

$(\neg\exists Lsib.\top)(u'_{1,2,1,2})$ $(u_1 \wedge \neg\exists Ch.\top)(u'_{1,2,1,2})$ $(\neg\exists Rsib.\top)(u'_{1,2,1,2})$

$(\neg\exists Lsib.\top)(u'_{2,1,2,2})$ $(u_2 \wedge \neg\exists Ch.\top)(u'_{2,1,2,2})$ $(\neg\exists Rsib.\top)(u'_{2,1,2,2})$

$(\neg\exists Lsib.\top)(u'_{2,2,2,2})$ $(u_2 \wedge \neg\exists Ch.\top)(u'_{2,2,2,2})$ $(\neg\exists Rsib.\top)(u'_{2,2,2,2})$

$(\neg\exists Lsib.\top)(u'_{2,3,2,2})$ $(u_2 \wedge \neg\exists Ch.\top)(u'_{2,3,2,2})$ $(\neg\exists Rsib.\top)(u'_{2,3,2,2})$

$(\neg\exists Lsib.\top)(u'_{1,1,1,3})$ $(u_1 \wedge \neg\exists Ch.\top)(u'_{1,1,1,3})$ $(\neg\exists Rsib.\top)(u'_{1,1,1,3})$

$(\neg\exists Lsib.\top)(u'_{1,2,1,3})$ $(u_1 \wedge \neg\exists Ch.\top)(u'_{1,2,1,3})$ $(\neg\exists Rsib.\top)(u'_{1,2,1,3})$

$(\neg\exists Lsib.\top)(u'_{2,1,2,3})$ $(u_2 \wedge \neg\exists Ch.\top)(u'_{2,1,2,3})$ $(\neg\exists Rsib.\top)(u'_{2,1,2,3})$

$(\neg\exists Lsib.\top)(u'_{2,2,2,3})$ $(u_2 \wedge \neg\exists Ch.\top)(u'_{2,2,2,3})$ $(\neg\exists Rsib.\top)(u'_{2,2,2,3})$

$(\neg\exists Lsib.\top)(u'_{2,3,2,3})$ $(u_2 \wedge \neg\exists Ch.\top)(u'_{2,3,2,3})$ $(\neg\exists Rsib.\top)(u'_{2,3,2,3})$

- Role assertions:

$Ch(r', t'_1)$ $Rsib(t'_1, t'_2)$ $Rsib(t'_2, t'_3)$

$Ch(t'_1, l'_{1,1})$ $Rsib(l'_{1,1}, l'_{2,1})$

$Ch(t_2, l'_{2,1})$ $Rsib(l'_{2,1}, l'_{2,2})$

$Ch(t'_3, l'_{1,3})$ $Ch(l'_{1,3}, l'_{2,3})$

$Ch(l'_{1,1}, c'_{1,1,1})$ $Rsib(c'_{1,1}, c'_{2,1,1})$

$Ch(l'_{2,1}, c'_{1,2,1})$ $Rsib(c'_{1,2,1}, c'_{2,2,1})$ $Rsib(c'_{2,2,1}, c'_{3,2,1})$

$Ch(l'_{1,2}, c'_{1,1,2})$ $Rsib(c'_{1,1,2}, c'_{2,1,2})$

$Ch(l'_{2,2}, c'_{1,2,2})$ $Rsib(c'_{1,2,2}, c'_{2,2,2})$ $Rsib(c'_{2,2,2}, c'_{3,2,2})$

$Ch(l'_{1,3}, c'_{1,1,3})$ $Rsib(c'_{1,1,3}, c'_{2,1,3})$

$Ch(l'_{2,3}, c'_{1,2,3})$ $Rsib(c'_{1,2,3}, c'_{2,2,3})$ $Rsib(c'_{2,2,3}, c'_{3,2,3})$

$Ch(c'_{1,1,1}, u'_{1,1,1,1})$ $Ch(c'_{2,1,1}, u'_{1,2,1,1})$

$Ch(c'_{1,1,2}, u'_{1,1,1,2})$ $Ch(c'_{2,1,2}, u'_{1,2,1,2})$

$Ch(c'_{1,2,2}, u'_{2,1,2,2})$ $Ch(c'_{2,2,2}, u'_{2,2,2,2})$ $Ch(c'_{3,2,2}, u'_{2,3,2,3})$

$Ch(c'_{1,1,3}, u'_{1,1,1,3})$ $Ch(c'_{2,1,3}, u'_{1,2,1,3})$

$Ch(c'_{1,2,3}, u'_{2,1,2,3})$ $Ch(c'_{2,2,3}, u'_{2,2,2,3})$ $Ch(c'_{3,2,3}, u'_{2,3,2,3})$

From Theorem 1, we then conclude the main result of this paper.

Theorem 2 (Context-aware consistency). *A context-aware communication system* (Cc, Up, Lc, Sch) *is consistent, if and only if, the ABox $\mathcal{A}_c$ is consistent with respect to each of the TBoxes $\mathcal{T}_c$ and $\mathcal{T}_a$, for any pair of users.*

5   Conclusions

In this paper, we proposed a description logic based method to test the consistency of context-aware systems. Modeling complex context properties usually imply expensive reasoning algorithms. We showed that the delicate balance between expressive power and efficiency reasoning in descriptions logics positions this logic based approach as an expressive modeling and efficient reasoning framework.

As a further research direction, we plan to implement the corresponding reasoning algorithm of the modeling approach proposed in this paper. It is already known a non-trivial correspondence between the description logic proposed in the current paper as a modeling language, and the μ-calculus [2]. Efficient satisfiability algorithms for the μ-calculus [8] can thus be helpful in the construction of a description logic-based reasoning framework for context-aware systems.

We are also interested in context-aware modeling and reasoning in other smart environment settings. In particular, smart learning environments [6] is one of our research perspectives.

Acknowledgment. This work was partially developed under the support of the National Council of Science and Technology (CONACYT).

References

1. Baader, F., Calvanese, D., McGuinness, D.L., Nardi, D., Patel-Schneider, P.F.: The Description Logic Handbook: Theory Implementation and Applications, 2nd edn. Cambridge University Press, New York (2010)
2. Bárcenas, E., Molero, G., Sánchez, G., Benítez-Guerrero, E., Mezura-Godoy, C.: Reasoning on expressive description logics with arithmetic constraints. In: 2016 International Conference on Electronics, Communications and Computers (CONIELECOMP), pp. 180–185. IEEE (2016)
3. Bettini, C., et al.: A survey of context modelling and reasoning techniques. Pervasive Mob. Comput. **6**(2), 161–180 (2010)
4. Dey, A.K.: Understanding and using context. Pers. Ubiquit. Comput. **5**(1), 4–7 (2001)
5. Henricksen, K., Indulska, J.: Developing context-aware pervasive computing applications: models and approach. Pervasive Mob. Comput. **2**(1), 37–64 (2006)
6. Hernández-Calderón, J., Benítez-Guerrero, E., Rojano, R.: Towards an intelligent desk matching behaviors and performance of learners. In: Proceedings of the XVIII International Conference on Human Computer Interaction, Interacción, pp. 29:1–29:6 (2017)
7. Limón, Y., Bárcenas, E.: On the consistency of context-aware systems. J. Intell. Fuzzy Syst. **34**, 3373–3383 (2018)
8. Limón, Y., Bárcenas, E., Benítez-Guerrero, E., Medina, M.: Depth-first reasoning on trees. Computación y Sistemas **22**(1), 1–7 (2018). https://dblp.org/rec/bibtex/journals/cys/LimonPBN18
9. Riboni, D., Bettini, C.: OWL 2 modeling and reasoning with complex human activities. Pervasive Mob. Comput. **7**(3), 379–395 (2011)

Dimensions Affecting Representation Styles in Ontologies

Pablo Rubén Fillottrani[1,2] and C. Maria Keet[3(✉)]

[1] Departamento de Ciencias e Ingeniería de la Computación,
Universidad Nacional del Sur, Bahía Blanca, Argentina
prf@cs.uns.edu.ar
[2] Comisión de Investigaciones Científicas,
La Plata, Provincia de Buenos Aires, Argentina
[3] Department of Computer Science,
University of Cape Town, Cape Town, South Africa
mkeet@cs.uct.ac.za

Abstract. There are different ways to formalise roughly the same knowledge, which negatively affects ontology reuse and alignment and other tasks such as formalising competency questions automatically. We aim to shed light on, and make more precise, the intuitive notion of such 'representation styles' through characterising their inherent features and the dimensions by which a style may differ. This has led to a total of 28 different traits that are partitioned over 10 dimensions. The operational-isability was assessed through an evaluation of 30 ontologies on those dimensions and applicable values. It showed that it is feasible to use the dimensions and values and resulting in three easily recognisable types of ontologies. Most ontologies had clearly one or the other trait, whereas some were inherently mixed due to inclusion of different and conflicting design decisions.

1 Introduction

Ontology developers and logic-savvy domain experts are familiar with the question "how to formalise it?", which has been asked for many years [2], observing the problems of alternative ways of representing the same piece of information or knowledge. For instance, whether to represent the entity Marriage as a class or as relationship, say, married to and whether to represent Spouse as a subclass of Person or as a role that a person plays. Some ontologies may exhibit more than one alternative modelling options, which may result in conflicting decisions in the modelling stage, such as with the Organisation ontology [18] that is being standardised and updated with the W3C, which has both Membership as a class and memberOf as an object property. When the same modelling decision is chosen throughout an ontology, including, e.g., process-as-class, this gives rise to the notion of a 'representation style'.

Besides the philosophical questions whether one way of representing a piece of knowledge is truly better than another, having such alternative ways of representing it in an ontology poses a range of engineering issues. A notion of an

© Springer Nature Switzerland AG 2019
B. Villazón-Terrazas and Y. Hidalgo-Delgado (Eds.): KGSWC 2019, CCIS 1029, pp. 186–200, 2019.
https://doi.org/10.1007/978-3-030-21395-4_14

"ontology building style" was already observed with several bio-ontologies [20], as was style due to representation language [21], identification of "regularities" in ontology metrics [12] and "emerging design patterns" based on axiom patterns in ontologies [10], and alternate "ontology patterns" that roughly fit a 'foundational' and 'applied' style [4], but what the 'styles' are precisely, is not clear. On top of its lack of clarity, representation incompatibilities between ontologies hamper easy reuse; e.g., when the two ontologies have represented the domain at different levels of detail or other choices, such as class vs object property like aforementioned Marriage vs married to [4]. Knowing the style upfront could be a parameter for decision as to which ontology to reuse. Even before reuse, the issue can present itself, however. Wiśniewski et al. [23] manually converted competency question into SPARQL-OWL queries, observing that one competency question (CQ) pattern (a sentence without the ontology's vocabulary) can map onto multiple SPARQL-OWL signatures, i.e., the same information request can be realised in different ways. Knowing the style would thus be helpful for automating converting CQs into SPARQL-OWL queries as well as into axioms [3,8]. This remains a laborious manual process for as long as there is no clear insight into which ways this can be done systematically.

In this paper, we aim to shed light on the fuzzy notion of 'representation style' by aiming to characterise its inherent features and the dimensions by which a style may differ. Some values of dimensions combine well together, some do not. This is subsequently evaluated with 30 ontologies to determine its potential for operationalisation so that one could classify an ontology to be of one or another style or a mix thereof and whether perhaps a dimension was missed. The first round of testing revealed the need for, especially, more precise descriptions to evaluate an ontology on that dimension, which have been added. The second round of evaluation showed high inter-annotator agreement and revealed preliminary trends among the test ontologies, especially in the values between the theory-oriented ontologies versus applied ontologies. Knowing an ontology's representation style or choosing one for an ontology that is yet to be developed is expected to streamline and support further automation of the use and evaluation of CQs, ontology alignment, and the option to automatically change one's style, and improve the quality of one's own ontology though adhering to the same modelling decision.

The remainder of the paper is structured as follows. Section 2 presents the main theoretical contribution of the attempt to clarify what a representation style is (and is not) and elucidates its dimensions. Section 3 presents the evaluation of classifying a set of different types of ontologies. We discuss in Sect. 4 and conclude in Sect. 5.

2   Representation Styles

We first aim to characterise the fuzzy notion of 'representation style', why some artefacts that sound relevant are not styles, and discuss related work. Section 2.2 lists and justifies the dimensions for determining a style.

2.1   Core Features of a Representation Style

The first main question one should ask is: *what is a representation style?* We identified the following set of characteristics features toward a specification:

- It is a way of representing some piece of knowledge or information in a particular way;
- It may be formalised differently in different logics, and differently even in the same logic, depending on the constructors at one's disposal, which indicates it is a sort of 'conceptual thing' where there is informally meaningful sameness, but possibly no axiomatic equivalence;
- It is independent of the subject domain;
- A style is a possible/common/well-known way of representing some piece of knowledge. This does not mean that way of representing it is an unqualified 'good' way of doing things, and some style may be bad for some purpose;
- They are knowledge engineering/representation decisions (not ontological) a modeller takes about the conceptual thing.

These aspects considered, we arrive at the following short-hand description.

Definition 1 (Representation style, first version). *A* representation style *is a way of representing a particular piece of conceptualisation or (understanding of) reality, for which there are alternative ways to represent it formally that are generally considered to be meaningfully equivalent (though not necessarily logically).*

The list above and the shorthand definition are still very generic, in that it would include artefacts of which one can state they are not representation styles. To clarify this further, let us look at related works that allude to styles and similar notions, but are excluded from 'style' for various reasons, i.e.: what is *not* a style, but sounds closely related nonetheless?

- A content Ontology Design Pattern (ODP) [5]. At best, a content ODP is an *instantiation of* a style, adhering to the principles of a particular style. An ODP, if not formalised by specification, may be formalised in different ways. This may make it look like a style, but the content ODP is for that ontology with that subject domain specifically. What might be the case is that when one analyses multiple informal content ODPs, an (instantiation of) a style might emerge.
- Anti-patterns (e.g., [19]). They are at least sub-optimal, if not outright bad, modelling decisions, which is largely due to inexperience of the modellers. Conversely, general guidelines are then also not styles by definition.
- One or more related axioms. Such a set, or mini-module or micro-theory, may respect or not violate a representation style. This thus also means one will not be able find a representation style bottom-up through mining a large or small set of ontologies, alike the pattern/style/regularities finding in [10,12,13]. This also suggests that recurring collections of axioms/mini-modules (say, 'axiom signature') do not make a representation style, because it can be

formalised in different ways. A simple example of different formalisations would be using inverse readings or not (e.g., has part and part of vs. has part and Inv(has part)).
- Workarounds for language limitations, because by its definition a workaround is not a style. A well-known workaround is an approximation of reification due to the lack of n-aries in OWL [16].

The notion of "ontology building style" featured in [20] when they compared several bio-ontologies, which included the following parameters: application scenario, modularisation, domain/task/generic, instances or not, level of detail, and representation language. An application scenario of itself is not a style, but one may *choose a style* so that it fits with one or more desired application scenarios. Modularisation or not and instances or not certainly would indicate a representation style: the former on how one structures the knowledge and the latter on whether the artefact is intended as a database or knowledge base or as an ontology in the 'purist' sense (TBox only or ABox only). A particular representation language does not constitute a style or a dimension thereof, however, but may *enforce a style*. For instance, some designers may have decided that one is allowed to use only a few relations (say, BT, NT, RT, USE/UF in thesauri), which is then hard-coded in the representation language (e.g., SKOS [14]). Then SKOS is not the style, but the decision of few relations is a (component or value of a) style. The same decision was taken for, e.g., OBO, which percolates through to the OWL-ised OBO ontologies [7]. Finally, the 'level of detail', or granularity in representation, is a design decision to take, but possible values for such dimension are difficult to set and evaluate consistently.

The same group also proposed automatically computed "ontology design styles" [13], using 20 OWL metrics applied to the Tones repository and clustered them into five groups. Numbers of elements do no say anything about what has been represented, however; e.g., a 'two classes, two object properties, and two class expressions' does not reveal whether the modelling choice has been made to represent processes as classes or as object properties. As noted above, and also in Mikroyannidi et al.'s follow-up works on this approach [12]: a particular axiom pattern or "regularity" may only exemplify a particular realisation of a style.

Wisniewski et al. use the term "modelling style" [23] to refer to what is dubbed here 'representation style', and is thus not to be confused with a different use of "modelling style" as in, e.g., [17], that refers to the process of creating the model, like in which possible sequences of steps the information or knowledge is added to the ontology with as aim to discover editing styles [22].

Two threads reappear in these related topics, which are (1) the alternate possible formalisations of some piece of domain knowledge so that axioms or a logic alone cannot be a style but at best exhibit one, and now also (2) excluding 'negatives' such as common mistakes and workarounds, being declarations in the ontology that no one would want as a conscious choice from among known alternatives and in the ideal case. Definition 1 can thus be refined into:

Definition 2 (Representation style, refined version). *A* representation style *is set of features used for representing a particular piece of conceptualisation or (understanding of) reality, for which there may be different (meaningfully equivalent, but not necessarily logically equivalent) ways to represent it in a logic that supports the style. The representation style is a justification-based positive design decision in at least one scenario.*

2.2   Dimensions for Determining a Style

The dimensions are separated into two main categories or 'levels': one is predominantly theoretical and concerns the type of artefact one aims to create irrespective of the practical considerations, whereas the other set of dimensions amount to engineering decisions.

1. Level 1: how 'ontological' the ontology is or should be.
   (a) *Degree of adherence to ontological principles in representing the knowledge.* The two extremes on the scale are the "foundational ontology way", i.e., predominantly theory-focussed, and the "applied way" where the ontology is, arguably, a logic-based conceptual data model. The style differences fall in place because of this decision; e.g., using qualities and qualia to represent attributions, such as a class Colour, versus data properties, such as hasColour:String. The values can be set as follows:

   Theoretical: predominantly or entirely with ontological principles, such as qualities, reification of processes, inherence of roles, no data properties.

   Applied: predominantly or entirely with decisions for applications, such as attributes/data properties and processes as relations.

   Mixed: the ontology contains both such decisions.

   (b) *Granularity of relations.* The two extremes on the scale are parsimony and abundance. With the former, one chooses to limit oneself to a few core relations, such as parthood, participation, causality, and membership; with the latter, one declares relations for every subtle distinction, such as a structural parthood relation between physical objects as subtype of the generic part-of and, e.g., a celebrates relation that refines a participates in. The values can be set as follows:

   Parsimony: when there are no refinements of the basic relations.

   Abundance: when there are refinements on the basic relations or when there are domain-specific relations, or both.

   (c) *Classes or instances.* From an ontological viewpoint, an ontology is about classes or about instances, but would not combine the two into what is historically called a knowledge base. The values can be set as follows:

   Class-level only: the ontology does not contain individuals (i.e., for an OWL file, the ABox is empty), or only very few such that it is intended as an illustrative example or attempted workaround.

   KB-like: the ontology has many individuals in the 'ABox' in addition to the class-level knowledge ('TBox').

2. <u>Level 2:</u> engineering, or consequences of praxis

  (a) Tooling/user interface effects:

      i. *Hierarchy, flat, or meshed* structure of the knowledge represented; e.g., a specific TBox tab with the hierarchy or a hierarchical layout graphically (OBO-Edit, Protégé) versus other graphical interfaces that are inspired by, say, UML or ER notation (Icom). The values can be set as follows:

        `Hierarchy, bare`: there is a hierarchy with one or more branches of substantial (≥ 4) depth[1], but barely or no class expressions have been declared on the classes.

        `Hierarchy, mesh`: there is a hierarchy with one or more branches of substantial (≥ 4) depth, and many class expressions have been declared on the classes, likely to classes residing in other branches of the hierarchy.

        `Flat`: there is no substantial hierarchy (typically a depth of ≤ 3), but still properties are declared among the classes.

     ii. *Modular vs monolithic*; some tools have module management incorporated in the tool (e.g., Icom, Ontohub), facilitating dividing the subject domain into modules, versus not having that option by default (e.g., Protégé, Moki). The values can be set as follows:

        `Monolithic`: there is one file, with no imports or mergers.

        `Modular, external`: at least one ontology is imported or merged such that the import has maintained its IRI; hence, it is associated with the process of ontology reuse.

        `Modular, internal`: at least one ontology is imported, such that it is associated with the process of decomposition of a domain.

     iii. *General Concept Inclusions (GCIs) vs only named entities* on the left-hand side of the inclusion; e.g., Protégé's interface for declaring GCIs is hidden and text-based only, therewith discouraging its use. The values can be set as follows:

        `Explicitly declared GCIs`: they have been declared by the modeller, such as Property $\sqcap \exists$propertyOf.Presential $\sqsubseteq$ Presential in gfo-basic.

        `Hidden GCIs`: they have not been declared by the modeller explicitly, but they are there indirectly through other axioms: there is a pair $A \equiv C$ and $A \sqsubseteq D$ and C and D are complex class expressions[2].

        `No GCIs`: they have not been declared explicitly or implicitly.

     iv. *A separate RBox manager* interface that facilitates reuse of relations (notably: Protégé), compared to adding new ones each time one uses essentially the same relation (most conceptual modelling tools and ontology editors inspired by them). The values can be set as follows:

---

[1] A cut-off at 3 layers is subjective, based mainly on the experience that a 2–3 layer mini-hierarchy is easy to declare, whereas 4 or more requires some thought to put it right, and conceptual models typically do not have more than 2–3 layers, if there is a hierarchy at all.

[2] http://protegeproject.github.io/protege/views/ontology-metrics/.

Relation reuse: object properties declared in the RBox typically appear in more than one class expression (beyond domain and range declarations).

No reuse: object properties declared in the RBox typically do not appear in a class expression (other than, possibly, domain and range axioms).

(b) Language feature effects

    i. *Hierarchy, flat, or meshed* structure of the knowledge represented; the language has more or less features to add relations, resulting in largely a 'bare' hierarchy where a class has no or very few properties vs few hierarchies but many interconnected elements; e.g., compare the restricted set of relations in OBO and SKOS vs OWL where one can freely and easily specify new relations. The values can be set as described above in Item 2(a)i.

    ii. *Modular vs monolithic*; whether the language supports axioms for handling modules, such as OWL's `import` statement, and how the modules relate: if not or with difficulty, then the ontology necessarily will be monolithic. The values can be set as described in Item 2(a)ii.

    iii. *The commitment built into the language for 'standard view' or 'positionalist'* and, within the former, whether the language has the inverse feature; e.g., whether to represent "eating" (or any other relation) with (1) a 'forward' and 'backward' reading direction as two relations, eats and eatenBy, and declare them inverses (eats ≡ eatenBy⁻), as (2) a relation with one reading direction only (eats) and the other implicitly without a vocabulary element (Inv(eats) meaning 'eaten by'), or (3) no reading direction (eating) and two roles the objects play in that relation (say, predator and prey).[3] The values can be set as follows:

        Standard view, with inverses: as described in option 1, with forward and backward readings.

        Standard view, with Inv(): as described in option 2, in one direction only.

        Standard view, both: if both option 1 and option 2 are used in the ontology.

        Positionalist: as described in option 3.

    iv. *Values/instances/classes interplay.* Representation of certain entities that may be deemed different kind of elements, depending on one's modelling viewpoint, practicalities, and which constructors are available in the language by means of (1) nominals, (2) enumerated datatypes, or (3) class and instances; e.g., the days of the week[4]. The values can be set as follows:

        Nominals: as described in option 1; i.e., Week ≡ {Sunday, ..., Saturday} where Sunday etc. are individuals.

---

[3] There are arguments from Ontology for option 1 and 2 vs option 3, but the intended choice here the corresponding commitment built into the language.

[4] The intended choice here is also the commitment built into the language, not theory (option 3) versus applied (options 1 and 2).

Enumerated: as described in option 2; i.e., the values of a data property onWeekday can be one of the values Sunday, ..., Saturday.

Class-instance: as described in option 3; i.e., they are all classes appropriately related, and a 'Sunday 6 January 2019' is an instance of Sunday etc.

Mixed: any two or three appear in the ontology.

-: not applicable.

v. *Attributes and data types* as core language feature. The inclusion of attributes (OWL data properties) and, with it, datatypes, has certain consequences from the viewpoint of ontology—theory vs applied (Item 1a) and could be considered to be subsumed by that item, as would other theory/applied decisions be. It has been added separately, as it is of a different calibre than whether, say, qualified number restrictions are supported, because it represents a certain kind of element, at the same level as class and object property. The values can be set as follows:

Attributes: the language has that feature and it is being used.

No attributes: the language may or may not have that feature, but it is not used anyway/not present.

Note that if the representation language permits more than one option, an ontology may exhibit instances of more than one modelling style, i.e., contain conflicting design decisions, and therefore the 'both' and 'mixed' have been added to the options. For instance, using both nominals (instances as classes) and class&instances for the days of the week, or both the class Colour and a data property hasColour. Further, note that representation language is a dimension, but not a particular language, such as, e.g., the OWL 2 RL profile, because the latter incorporates selected traits (values) of the dimension rather than determining traits.

For the 'level 1' dimensions and values, it is possible to construct a simple matrix of options with the four possible combinations: Theoretical & Parsimony, Theoretical & Abundance, Applied & Parsimony, and Applied & Abundance. Adding the 'level 2' dimensions with their possible values would result in a combinatorial explosion of theoretically possible styles. This would be exacerbated if it were to be for all the specific tools and languages. On purely theoretical grounds, one should be able to exclude certain combinations upfront already. For instance, Some consequences that should follow from the theory are:

a. the ontologically abhorrent nominals and enumerated data types (Item 2(b)iv) should not appear in a foundational ontology or theory-focussed ontology;

b. there will not be GCIs in applied ontologies/conceptual data models, because such models never had either explicitly declared or implicit GCIs, except for simple domain and range declarations.

c. If no tool is used in ontology development, then no option in Item 2a can be a cause.

d. If one uses a representation language that permits only few relations (e.g., .obo ontologies, SKOS), then the relation reuse (Item 2(a)iv) is built into it.
e. If one uses a representation language that permits only few relations, then the granularity of the relations is that of parsimony (or vice versa in direction of causality: one chooses parsimony, and enforces it in the language).
f. The theory option (Item 1a) ought to go with option 3 in Item 2(b)iv and, likewise, the applied option (Item 1a) ought to go with option 2 in Item 2(b)iv, which is the typical approach in conceptual data models.
g. If the language cannot handle modules well (Item 2(b)ii), then so will the corresponding tool not have good module management and result in monolithic ontologies (Item 2(a)ii), and, one would expect, vice versa.
h. Theory-oriented ontologies (Item 1a) do not use data properties/attributes as a recurring feature other than, perhaps, a hasValue xml:anyType (Item 2(b)v).
i. Given that hierarchy/mesh/flat and monolithic/modular are listed twice (as Item 2(a)i & Item 2(a)i and 2(a)ii & Item 2(b)ii), one will not be able to say with certainty which one is the core cause, if any, when trying to assess an ontology on its style.

It remains to be seen which of these expected consequences hold up in practice.

Finally, it is possible to devise multiple reasons to choose one particular style over another, which are, effectively *imposed* engineering decisions, rather than engineering decisions based on theoretical foundations (as listed under 'level 2'). These may include, among others:

– Language and tool support; e.g., at the time of writing, OWL and Protégé are the most popular among the options, therefore, the ontology is necessarily standard view.
– Other ontologies one has to link to/import adhere to that particular style.
– Need to follow corporate or consortium styles.
– Efficiency in the implementation (prospected use of the ontology-driven information system); e.g., one cannot link an ontology in the expressive OWL 2 DL language to a database for Ontology-Based Data Access and expect the same level of performance as for relational databases, simply due to inherent computational complexity limitations (and with implementation, one veers toward at least applied, and possibly also attributes, enumerated, and no GCIs).
– Parsimony in the representation, reducing cognitive load by humans who author and read the ontology or conceptual data model, lowering the barrier of uptake of the artefact, which thus may save money.

With respect to representation styles, we will not consider them, because they all already have a style implied, i.e., they do not determine, but impose already determined styles, and we are interested in what determines a style.

3   Applying Style Dimensions to Ontologies

The aim of this evaluation is to determine whether the dimensions and traits identified in the previous section can be applied to existing ontologies, whether they suffice or another one or more have to be added, and to see whether some combinations of dimensions already emerge from the data. The materials and methods are described first, and subsequently the results and discussion thereof.

3.1   Materials and Methods

The following process was followed:

1. Select different types of ontologies: foundational, core, domain, and tutorial.
2. Classify them manually, using the dimensions and their appropriate values. This is carried out by two people (the authors) independently.
3. Check for inter-annotator agreement and whether the identified dimensions suffice; if there is disagreement, either:
   (a) Harmonise and move to Step 4, below;
   (b) Resolve conflict in classification, refine either the affected dimension's value or description thereof, and return to Step 2.
4. Analyse the data on expected consequences (see previous section; e.g., foundational ontologies without nominals and data properties) and on whether any recurring combinations of dimensions emerged.

The ontologies were handled with Protégé, WebVOWL, and the OWL Classifier tools whenever the OWL code was available. The only exceptions were SNOMED CT (BioPortal browser) and DOLCE on paper.

It is factored in that two rounds of annotations may be needed: while the list of dimensions is deemed comprehensive at the start of the evaluation, the actual inspection of the ontologies may result in emerging refinements thereof. This is facilitated by the qualitative approach taken (cf. computed metrics).

The top and tutorial ontologies were collected based on cognisance by at least one of the authors; please refer to the supplementary material online for their references[5]. The relatively well-known selected top-level ontologies are BFO, DOLCE (on paper and in OWL), GFO, SUMO, and YAMATO, and the tutorial ontologies are Pizza, Wine, Family, Books, and AWO. Six core ontologies were selected based on cognisance (stuff, biotop, time), considering general topics (e.g., events, units) and checking whether there is an ontology for it, and a simple online search for "core ontologies" (services). The selection criteria for the domain ontologies were: some of our own as that would make analysis easier (ADOLENA, DMOP), the most accessed ontologies from BioPortal[6], based on their respective names that sounded like a real ontology (FMA, DIOD, EDAM, SNOMED CT), and an arbitrary selection of W3C ontologies that appeared on the main/news page scrolling down for recent activity on it (SSN, Profiles, Organization and related UNDO).

---

[5] http://www.meteck.org/files/StyleDimensionsData.xlsx.
[6] https://bioportal.bioontology.org/visits.

3.2   Results and Discussion

The first round of annotation resulted in a low inter-annotator agreement, mainly because the scope of dimensions and several values turned out to have been interpreted differently and found in need of more precision. For instance, (i), instead of making only a distinction between yes/no GCIs, it is useful to know whether a 'yes' was deliberately added explicitly by the modeller or not; (ii) instead of 'hierarchy vs flat/mesh', where the need for three values emerged to capture the variations better (see above); (iii) instead of monolithic vs modular, an ontology may be modular through either reusing one or more ontologies and dividing up one's intended subject domain to make it more manageable. This resulted in the specification of possible values with a description of each, in order to better annotate each ontology, which have been included in the previous section. Also, when examining the ontologies, it was deemed useful to record whether it uses data properties, which also has been added (Item 2(b)v in the previous section), and whether a substantial number of individuals have been declared (Item 1c).

The same selected ontologies were then categorised anew and the data compared among the annotators, resulting consensus on the traits and interpretations. Some styles were found to be non applicable to all ontologies, and the lack of a formal version of SNOMED CT (only available through browsing a web page) made some categories difficult or impossible to evaluate. The complete results are available at the URL noted in footnote 8 and a visualisation is included in Fig. 1, where the 10 clearly `Theoretical` and `Applied` ontologies were selected and the annotations coded to generate the graph (e.g., `No attributes` as 1.0 and `Attributes` as 2.0, `Class-level only` as 0, an occasional class as 1.0, and (full-fledged) `KB-like` as 2.0).

In general, some expected outcomes were confirmed. Applied ontologies exhibit more usage of nominals, instances, and data properties. Notable exceptions are DOLCE and DMOP with a few data properties and some class instances. Since DMOP links to DOLCE and was redesigned to facilitate alignment to DOLCE [9], this is an 'inherited' style. Other expected results are the facts that either explicit or hidden GCI are mostly absent from applied ontologies (only MEO has a large number of hidden GCIs); that Books can be seen more as a conceptual data model than as an ontology; and that almost all flat ontologies have no relation reuse apart from domain/range declarations.

There were also some outcomes that we did not expect. The number of theoretical ontologies with none or only hidden GCI is higher than expected, suggesting a low level of usage for advanced ontology expressions. Relatively poor support of GCIs in popular tools such a Protégé may be a cause for this. Also, this justifies the independence of the language and tooling dimensions and distinction explicit/implicit for GCIs. The categorisation of SUMO as an applied ontology was also unexpected, because it is intended as an "upper" ontology by its developers [15]. Several ontologies declare domain and range axioms for object properties, but these declarations are mostly not reflected in other class expressions. This was especially different between theoretical and applied ontologies, as

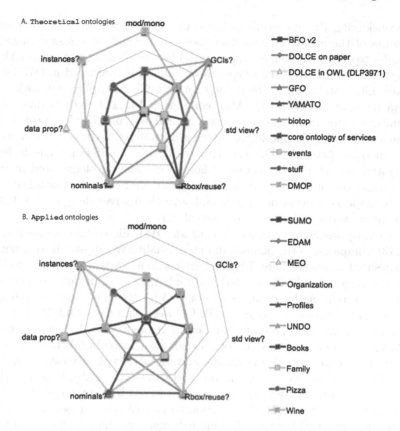

Fig. 1. Visualisation of coded annotations of ontologies that were clearly `Theoretical` and clearly `Applied` ontologies. The values of the dimensions for the evaluated ontologies have been scaled to a scale of 0–2 to produce the graph; e.g., no GCIs = 0, hidden GCIs = 1, and explicit GCIs = 2.

also shown in Fig. 1: 7 out of 10 ontologies do reuse object properties, whereas that was the case for only 3 out of the 10 applied ontologies. Yet, parsimony of relations was rarely found in any ontology (only in BFO, DOLCE on paper and MEO). As a future work, a further refinement of this dimension might be possible.

4   Discussion

The formulation of the dimensions and values that influence a representation style, while originating from theory, did show it is operationalisable. To arrive at that stage, it was crucial to have had the evaluation with independently made annotations that the annotators discussed for each disagreement. This mainly served to elucidate implicit assumptions, clarify them, and formulate them more precisely, where possible.

Reconsidering the expectations based on theory (Sect. 2.2) as compared to the results of the evaluation, most of those that could be assessed indeed did hold (refer to online supplementary material for details). Exceptions are that no ontology used enumerated data types, even though it is allowed in OWL except for OWL-Lite[7], and while there are no explicit GCIs in applied ontologies, most of them do have hidden GCIs. Also, comparing Fig. 1-A with B does show a different trend among the theoretical and applied ontologies, but it must be noted that each set has only 10 ontologies, which is a small set to draw conclusions from about emerging patterns. The positive trend toward difference merits further investigation to determine whether it holds for more ontologies and also why. For instance, one might expect `Modular, external` for applied ontologies that would be importing other ontologies and save themselves design time, but this did not occur and our data does not reveal why.

It is clearly faster to run metrics over an OWL file to find regularities, like in [10,13], compared to the manual and more qualitative approach to annotating ontologies that was taken here. The regularities do not reveal modelling decisions, however, such as granularity in relations or whether attributions are represented in a class hierarchy, and it excludes all non-OWL ontologies, such as DOLCE on paper [11] in full first-order logic, the BFO Core[8], and the COLORE repository ontologies [6] that are represented in Common Logic [1]. The list presented in Sect. 2.2 also can be applied to ontologies not formalised in OWL, for it is independent of the representation language, and, in fact, explicitly caters for it with the 'language feature effects' dimensions and values (Item 2b). It therewith also would assist in solving language issues as described by (but not systematically solved in) Uschold et al. [21], in addition to contributing to solving modelling decisions. Further, we have identified more dimensions than in [20] and also specified criteria when which value applies, which is thanks in a considerable part to the uptake of ontologies, ontology engineering research, and tooling support over the past 20 years. Finally, the ontology patterns in [4] are all examples of representing some piece of knowledge in the `Applied` way vs `Theoretical` way, hence, constitute a subset of the dimensions we propose in this paper.

Whilst trying to optimise the task of annotating the ontologies, the `No reuse` of relations typically went together with `Hierarchy, bare` or `flat`, and there were (more) data properties in `Applied` ontologies compared to `Theoretical`, which can be expected. It may be of interest to carry out the experiment with more ontologies so as to discover patterns in the values, as well as examine past ontology alignment and integration efforts on whether their ease/difficulties match with the dimensions proposed in this paper.

---

[7] https://www.w3.org/TR/owl-ref/#EnumeratedDatatype as `owl:OneOf` and in OWL 2 as `DataOneOf` (https://www.w3.org/TR/2012/REC-owl2-syntax-20121211/#Enumeration_of_Literals).

[8] http://www.acsu.buffalo.edu/~bittner3/Theories/BFO/.

5   Conclusions

The paper presented a comparatively comprehensive set of dimensions that contribute to determining representation styles in ontologies, making their intuitive notions more precise and providing a conceptual grounding step towards their formal characterisations. Each dimension is presented with a given set of possible values and their sentinel pointers to identify them in an ontology, and what other dimensions are related. We have evaluated this theory on applicability with 30 well-known published ontologies, classifying and comparing approaches and analysing the interactions and relationships between the different dimensions, laying the foundations for future research that can establish better modelling support.

Good engineering practice to develop ontologies consists of not only applying scientific techniques but also by taking modelling design choices. Such choices are taken early in the process and can have far reaching consequences. Therefore, identifying and characterising these styles—by availing of the here presented dimensions—constitute a step toward more comprehensive best practices for ontology engineering tasks such as alignment, integration, evolution, and data access. Furthermore, since style reveals basic characteristics of an ontology, it can promote the development of automated processes in tools and methods. Future work includes, therefore, among others, testing the dimensions in additional experiments both regarding more ontologies and with more ontology developers, examining the framework as a whole, analysing the interplay between styles, patterns, and quality attributes, as well as developing ontology engineering methodologies involving dimensions and styles, and ultimately studying the influence of representation style on the resulting ontology.

References

1. Common Logic (CL): A framework for a family of logic-based languages (2007). https://www.iso.org/standard/39175.html
2. Baader, F., Calvanese, D., McGuinness, D.L., Nardi, D., Patel-Schneider, P.F. (eds.): The Description Logics Handbook: Theory and Applications, 2nd edn. Cambridge University Press, Cambridge (2008)
3. Fernandez-Izquierdo, A.: Ontology testing based on requirements formalization in collaborative development environments. In: Aroyo, L., Gandon, F. (eds.) Doctoral Consortium at ISWC (ISWC-DC 2017). CEUR-WS, vol. 1962, vienna, Austria, 22 October 2017 (2017)
4. Fillottrani, P.R., Keet, C.M.: Patterns for heterogeneous TBox mappings to bridge different modelling decisions. In: Blomqvist, E., Maynard, D., Gangemi, A., Hoekstra, R., Hitzler, P., Hartig, O. (eds.) ESWC 2017. LNCS, vol. 10249, pp. 371–386. Springer, Cham (2017). https://doi.org/10.1007/978-3-319-58068-5_23
5. Gangemi, A., Presutti, V.: Ontology design patterns. In: Staab, S., Studer, R. (eds.) Handbook on Ontologies. IHIS, pp. 221–243. Springer, Heidelberg (2009). https://doi.org/10.1007/978-3-540-92673-3_10
6. Grüninger, M., Hahmann, T., Hashemi, A., Ong, D., Ozgovde, A.: Modular first-order ontologies via repositories. Appl. Ontol. **7**(2), 169–209 (2012)

7. Hoehndorf, R., Oellrich, A., Dumontier, M., Kelso, J., Rebholz-Schuhmann, D., Herre, H.: Relations as patterns: bridging the gap between OBO and OWL. BMC Bioinform. **11**(1), 441 (2010)
8. Keet, C.M., Ławrynowicz, A.: Test-driven development of ontologies. In: Sack, H., Blomqvist, E., d'Aquin, M., Ghidini, C., Ponzetto, S.P., Lange, C. (eds.) ESWC 2016. LNCS, vol. 9678, pp. 642–657. Springer, Cham (2016). https://doi.org/10.1007/978-3-319-34129-3_39
9. Keet, C.M., et al.: The data mining optimization ontology. Web Semant. Sci. Serv. Agents World Wide Web **32**, 43–53 (2015)
10. Ławrynowicz, A., Potoniec, J., Robaczyk, M., Tudorache, T.: Discovery of emerging design patterns in ontologies using tree mining. Semant. Web J. (2018, in press)
11. Masolo, C., Borgo, S., Gangemi, A., Guarino, N., Oltramari, A.: Ontology library. WonderWeb Deliverable D18 (ver. 1.0, 31-12-2003) (2003). http://wonderweb.semanticweb.org
12. Mikroyannidi, E., Iannone, L., Stevens, R., Rector, A.: Inspecting regularities in ontology design using clustering. In: Aroyo, L., et al. (eds.) ISWC 2011. LNCS, vol. 7031, pp. 438–453. Springer, Heidelberg (2011). https://doi.org/10.1007/978-3-642-25073-6_28
13. Mikroyannidi, E., Stevens, R., Rector, A.: Identifying ontology design styles with metrics. In: 7th International Workshop on Semantic Web Enabled Software Engineering (SWESE) (2011)
14. Miles, A., Bechhofer, S.: SKOS simple knowledge organization system reference. W3C recommendation, World Wide Web Consortium (W3C), 18 August 2009. http://www.w3.org/TR/skos-reference/
15. Niles, I., Pease, A.: Towards a standard upper ontology. In: Welty, C., Smith, B. (eds.) Proceedings of the 2nd International Conference on Formal Ontology in Information Systems, FOIS 2001, Ogunquit, Maine, 17–19 October 2001 (2001)
16. Noy, N., Rector, A.: Defining nary relations on the semantic web. W3C Working Group Note, 12 April 2006. https://www.w3.org/TR/swbp-n-aryRelations/
17. Pinggera, J., et al.: Styles in business process modeling: an exploration and a model. Softw. Syst. Model. **14**(3), 1055–1080 (2015)
18. Reynolds, D.: The organization ontology, January 2014. https://www.w3.org/TR/vocab-org/
19. Roussey, C., Corcho, O., Vilches-Blázquez, L.: A catalogue of OWL ontology antipatterns. In: Proceedings of K-CAP 2009, pp. 205–206 (2009)
20. Stevens, R., Goble, C.A., Bechhofer, S.: Ontology-based knowledge representation for bioinformatics. Brief. Bioinform. **1**(4), 398–414 (2000)
21. Uschold, M., Healy, M., Williamson, K., Clark, P., Woods, S.: Ontology reuse and application. In: Guarino, N. (ed.) Proceedings of the International Conference on Formal Ontology and Information Systems (FOIS 1998). IOS Press, FAIA (1998)
22. Walk, S., Singer, P., Strohmaier, M., Tudorache, T., Musen, M.A., Noy, N.F.: Discovering beaten paths in collaborative ontology-engineering projects using Markov chains. J. Biomed. Inform. **51**, 254–271 (2014)
23. Wisniewski, D., Potoniec, J., Ławrynowicz, A., Keet, C.M.: Competency questions and SPARQL-OWL queries dataset and analysis. Technical report 1811.09529, November 2018. https://arxiv.org/abs/1811.09529

Author Index

Printed in the United States
By Bookmasters